CANADA
AND THE
NUCLEAR
ARMS RACE

CANADA AND THE NUCLEAR ARMS RACE

Edited by
Ernie Regehr
and
Simon Rosenblum

James Lorimer & Company, Publishers
Toronto 1983

ISBN 0-88862-634-7 paper
      0-88862-635-5 cloth

Cover design: Don Fernley

Cover photo: Devaney Stock Photos

Illustrations page 12 and 13 used by permission of the Centre for Defense Information.

Canadian Cataloguing in Publication Data

Main entry under title:
Canada and the nuclear arms race

Includes index.

1. Canada — Military policy — Addresses, essays, lectures. 2. Atomic weapons and disarmament — Addresses, essays, lectures. 3. Atomic warfare — Addresses, essays, lectures. I. Regehr, Ernie, 1941-   II. Rosenblum, Simon.

JX1974.7.C36   355'.033071   C83-098255-8

James Lorimer & Company, Publishers
Egerton Ryerson Memorial Building
35 Britain Street
Toronto, Ontario M5A 1R7

Printed and bound in Canada

6 5 4 3 2 1   83 84 85 86 87 88

Contents

Contributors

MARK ABLEY is a Canadian journalist and broadcaster living in England.

DON G. BATES, professor in the history of medicine at McGill University, is a member of Physicians for Social Responsibility, and chairman of both the McGill Study Group for Peace and Disarmament and the task force that authored Chapter 7.

PETER BROWN is former assistant director of Operation Dismantle.

GORDON EDWARDS, founder of the Canadian Coalition for Nuclear Responsibility, teaches mathematics and science at Vanier College in Montreal.

WALTER GORDON, finance minister in the government of Lester Pearson, is chairman of the Canadian Institute for Economic Policy.

PAULINE JEWETT, MP for New Westminster-Coquitlam, is the New Democratic Party's critic for external affairs.

MARGARET LAURENCE, one of Canada's most renowned novelists, is active in Arts for Peace.

DAVID MacDONALD, a United Church minister, was secretary of state and minister of communications in the government of Joe Clark, and is currently program director and special advisor in the office of the Leader of the Opposition.

WALTER McLEAN, the Conservative MP for Waterloo, wrote the minority report on security and disarmament along with Pauline Jewett, PAUL McRAE (Liberal, Thunder Bay-Atikokan), BOB OGLE (NDP, Saskatoon East), DOUGLAS ROCHE (Conservative, Edmonton South) and TERRY SARGEANT (NDP, Selkirk-Interlake).

JOHN POLANYI, professor of chemistry at the University of Toronto, is founder of the Canadian Pugwash Conference and a member of Science for Peace.

ERNIE REGEHR is research director of Project Ploughshares, researcher
for the Institute of Peace and Conflict Studies, and author of *Making a
Killing: Canada's Arms Industry*.

SIMON ROSENBLUM, author of *The Non-Nuclear Way*, teaches labour
studies at Cambrian College in Sudbury, and is on the board of Project
Ploughshares.

T. JAMES STARK is president of Operation Dismantle.

MEL WATKINS teaches political economy and Canadian studies at
the University of Toronto, and is an editor of *This Magazine*.

Acknowledgements

During the course of preparing this volume we have become indebted to many people. In particular we wish to express our appreciation to the contributors, none of whom has accepted a fee for his or her contribution. Instead, all have agreed to sign over all of the earnings of this book to Project Ploughshares, a project of Canadian churches and development agencies for public education on disarmament and development. We owe a special thanks to Margaret Laurence for her endorsement and enthusiastic support of this project.

We are indebted to our colleagues on the board and staff of Project Ploughshares for their support and willingness to take on additional responsibilities while we devoted our attention to this project. In particular we are grateful to Dwight Burkhardt, Michael Cooke, Betty Erb, Nancy Regehr, Doug Saunders, Murray Thomson and Kathleen Wallace-Deering. As well, we thank Pamela Fawcett and Betty Erb for typing and retyping parts of the manuscript.

We wish also to express our very special thanks to our editor, Ted Mumford. His work with this project went well beyond the call of normal duty, and we acknowledge that without his help and guidance the project would not have been completed.

E.R. & S.R.

Foreword

Our lives and the lives of all generations as yet unborn are being threatened, as never before, by the increasing possibility of nuclear war. I believe that the question of disarmament is the most pressing practical, moral and spiritual issue of our times. If we value our own lives and the lives of our children and all children everywhere, if we honour both the past and the future, then we must do everything in our power to work non-violently for peace. These beliefs are not only an integral part of my social and moral stance but of my religious faith as well. Human society now possesses the terrible ability to destroy all life on earth, and our planet itself. Can anyone who has ever marvelled at the miracle of creation fail to feel concerned and indeed anguished, every single day, at this thought?

A central disagreement, of course, exists between those who think that more and yet more nuclear arms will ensure that nuclear arms will never be used, and those of us who believe that the proliferation of nuclear weapons brings us closer all the time to the actuality of nuclear war — a war that no side could possibly win; a war that would be so devastating that we cannot begin to imagine that horror. Whatever we are being told about a "limited" or a "winnable" nuclear war, the fact remains that such a war could destroy all that we, as humankind, have aspired to, all that we have achieved. It could destroy the future, not only of the world's peoples but of all creatures that share our planet with us.

As both America and the Soviet Union develop more and more nuclear arms, so the other inevitably responds in kind. Both America and the Soviet Union now possess nuclear weapons capable of wiping out all life on earth many times over. The jargon word is "overkill." Do the hawks on either side imagine that life can be "overkilled"? We die but once. Why, then, the continuing buildup of nuclear weapons? These have long since ceased to be a "deterrent," if, indeed, they were ever so, and have become by their very existence a monstrous threat. Daily, the chances are increasing for a nuclear war to break out by accident, by a failure of the intricate control and warning systems, or simply by human panic and a mutual mistrust between the superpowers.

In our own land, Canada, what can we do?

Canada could and must, I believe, have a real impact in bringing about world disarmament. We are not powerless and we are not without significance in a world sense. Yet our government has agreed to the cruise missile being tested above Alberta. The Litton plant in Ontario is producing, with the aid of millions of *our* tax dollars, guidance systems for that missile. Canada has sold nuclear reactors to such unstable and repressive regimes as Argentina, and is delivering the fuel for those reactors, despite the fact that our government is aware that nuclear weapons could soon be within Argentina's capability. These are only a few examples of Canada's complicity in the nuclear arms race.

Our prime minister, in 1978, at the United Nations Special Session on Disarmament, put forth the theory of "suffocation" of nuclear arms, and many of us took heart from that statement. Yet on 10 December 1982, in the *Globe and Mail*, a report on the cruise missile testing agreement said that "... External Affairs Minister Allan MacEachen has said growing public pressure against the tests has no bearing on the Government's thinking." I find the implications of that statement very chilling indeed. Prime Minister Trudeau, in his New Year's 1983 message to our nation, was reported as saying that although there are undoubtedly some gloomy aspects in our present situation, there are also positive signs, among them the growth of the anti-nuclear-weapons movement. I would certainly agree that the growth of disarmament and peace groups is a cause for hope. But how are we to interpret this statement, made by the very man whose government the peace and disarmament groups are seeking to communicate with? How does this statement jibe with MacEachen's earlier pronouncement on the cruise testing? These conflicting messages suggest that we must keep on pressuring our government in every possible non-violent way to make Canada's voice heard as a strong voice speaking for practical and achievable steps towards world disarmament.

I believe that our land should be declared a nuclear-weapons-free zone, with absolutely no testing of nuclear arms or production of parts for those arms allowed in our country. I believe that Canada could do a great deal to bring about a gradual and verifiable reduction of nuclear arms by both sides, monitored by neutral countries, and to bring about a freeze on the production and testing of nuclear weapons. Canada could be a powerful influence for a "no-first-use" agreement among nations, for multilateral disarmament and for world peace. To me, this goes far beyond any political party views — indeed it goes beyond any national feelings. It means, in the most profound sense, survival. It means the future. We must not give way to despair, or to what Dr. Helen Caldicott, that courageous worker in the cause of peace, calls "psychic numbing," the sense that we cannot do anything, that we are helpless. We cannot afford passivity. We must take responsibility for our lives and our world, and be prepared to make our government listen and act. To do this, we must be informed. We must not shrink from the terrible and terrifying knowledge of what could happen and what is at stake.

This collection of articles gives us much of that necessary information. It gives us a knowledge of our own land in a nuclear-weapons world. I wish that every adult Canadian could read this book. I hope that a very great many will do so, and will learn from it.

If we will not speak out for our children, and their children and their children's children, if we will not speak out for the survival of our own land and our wider home Earth, in God's name what will move us? May our hearts be touched, our minds opened, our voices raised.

Margaret Laurence
Lakefield, Ontario
1983

Introduction

As never before, relations between nations are dominated by a culture of superviolence, symbolized in our time by nuclear arsenals capable of delivering destructive power a million times greater than that visited upon the city of Hiroshima on 6 August 1945. The doctrine of nuclear deterrence is premised on the assumption that what ultimately regulates behaviour between nation-states is the threat of punitive violence. Almost forty years of peace and relative stability in Europe, despite sharp political and ideological tensions, are said to be explainable only by the presence of the promise of destruction so great that no nation or alliance has been willing to risk its unleashing by behaviour which another might find unduly provocative.

In one sense it has always been so. It is not in the present age alone that nation-states have relied upon the exercise and threat of violence for their security and national integrity. From the spear, to the crossbow, to the howitzer, and to the Pershing II and SS-20 missiles, the confidence of kings and presidents alike has always had rather a close correlation to the size of the stockpiles of whatever weapons systems represented the state-of-the-art of state violence of their particular generation.

And yet, to speak of a million "Hiroshimas" — each one recalling the incineration, in a matter of seconds, of more than fifty thousand people — is surely to acknowledge that we are in the nuclear age confronting something radically new.

While not a member of the nuclear "club," Canada *does* play a part in the perpetuation of the arms race, and *could* play an important part in reversing it. This book seeks to present a Canadian perspective on the effects of the arms race, on the ever-rising risk of nuclear war, and on the measures that could lead to disarmament.

The first of four parts in the book addresses the arms race from a global perspective — which is to say it is concerned principally with the U.S.-USSR confrontation.

In the opening chapter, the editors examine the changing nature of the international culture of violence referred to above. This change, they argue, is not only a function of the exponential growth of the destructive capacity of the superviolence of the superpowers, but also a function of the changing purposes for which nuclear weapons are deployed.

In the nuclear age it is invention that has become the mother of necessity as technological innovations in weapons capabilities drive the search for new doctrines and strategies to match new capabilities. Persuading populations to finance this culture of violence is no mean task and Simon Rosenblum's assessment of the "Soviet threat" (Chapter 2) illustrates the yeoman's service performed by the Kremlin in keeping the weapons factories of the West operating at full capacity. While the Soviet Union has built up a formidable military machine in the past four decades, it has been the West's persistence in overstating Soviet military capacity and in magnifying the Soviet threat that has served as the primary rationale for the essentially unchecked buildup of the West's own arsenals. The Soviets, in turn, have not shrunk from responding in kind, so that the term "the arms race" has earned a prominent place in modern political vocabulary.

But it is a race that is run at a great price. Noting that the arms race annually consumes goods and services equal to the total goods and services available to the poorest half of the world's population, Mel Watkins and Ernie Regehr conclude in Chapter 3 that "it is tempting to rest the case against the arms race at this point." They go on to explore the economic costs of military production and spending, debunking the myth that military activity can serve as the engine of economic recovery and growth.

Nowhere is the fear of an unprecedented nuclear threat felt more keenly than it is in Western Europe. The peace movements of Europe, described by Mark Abley in Chapter 4, were the first to bring to prominent public recognition the new character of the atomic age. And they still lead — this time in setting forth the vision of a continent freed of the threat of nuclear weapons, and sustained, if not fully by a culture of non-violence, at least by a culture of controlled and controllable violence.

Part II focuses on Canada, describing both its continuing and extensive complicity in the buildup of nuclear weapons, and the likely consequences for this country should such weapons ever be put to use in a nuclear exchange between the U.S. and USSR. Chapter 5, by Ernie Regehr, catalogues the ways in which Canada is integrated into U.S. nuclear strategies, such as component manufacture for, and the planned testing of, the cruise missile. In Chapter 6, Gordon Edwards provides a history of Canada's contribution to nuclear proliferation through the export of uranium and nuclear power technology.

The question "What would happen to Canada in a nuclear war?" is taken up in Chapter 7 by a group of researchers headed by Dr. Don G. Bates. This pioneering study points out that even if Canada was not a protagonist in a nuclear conflict, this country could not escape either direct attacks or the radioactive fallout from attacks on the United States.

Both Parts III and IV address the thorniest of all questions raised by the arms race: How can it be reversed? The focus of Part III is on the political challenges of this question and the meagre results of Canadian policy to date. In Chapter 8, David MacDonald raises the moral and political dilemmas of the nuclear age. In an environment of breathtaking technical and scientific innovation, our moral and ethical systems have failed to prepare us as a society for the fact that the technological expansion of our capacity for violence, literally to limitless possibilities, has made the use of violence as an instrument of policy obsolete.

In Chapter 9, Walter Gordon adds to the indictment of Canadian complicity in the arms race by describing the reversal, from opposition to support of Canadian involvement with nuclear weapons, by two of Canada's most prominent postwar politicians, Lester B. Pearson and Pierre E. Trudeau. Pauline Jewett follows with a critical review of Canada's recent nuclear weapons and arms control policies, and joins five colleagues from the House of Commons in a brief report describing policy changes designed to make Canada more effectively engaged in the international pursuit of alternatives to the present arms spiral.

Part IV is devoted to Canadian initiatives for peace and disarmament, which, as the above would suggest, have come principally from outside government.

While the Canadian peace movement remains fragmented and disparate, it is at the same time broadly based and representative of a wide cross-section of Canadians, as the brief description in Chapter 12 confirms. Chapters 13 through 15 are turned over to the advocates of specific disarmament proposals. As their ideas illustrate, human intelligence and ingenuity must now be employed in the search for alternatives to war with the same persistence as they have until now been employed in the search for supremacy in war.

E.R. & S.R.

PART I

The Race to Annihilation

1

The Changing Nature of the Arms Race
Ernie Regehr and Simon Rosenblum

Facing Annihilation

"Lemmings headed for the sea" is the image invoked by George Kennan, former U.S. ambassador to Moscow, in describing the nuclear weapons policies of the United States and the Soviet Union. Even lemmings, however, are obsessed with only their own destruction — the superpowers promise a much grander consequence. Concentrated in the United States and the Soviet Union, but relying on the cooperation of the allies of each, the nuclear arsenals of this planet are rapidly acquiring the theoretical capacity to achieve the annihilation, not only of their respective homelands, but of the planet itself.

In the nuclear age human society faces with new horror the possibility of its final end, brought about not by the wrath of an aggrieved deity or in the triumphant fulfilment of history, but by humankind's own destructive devices. Jonathan Schell, in his compelling examination of the character of the nuclear age, *The Fate of the Earth*, focuses particularly upon the prospect of extinction — a prospect made possible by the combination of unprecedented firepower and technological wizardry. And "the mere risk of extinction," says Schell, "has a significance that is categorically different from, and immeasurably greater than, that of any other risk ..." He concludes that "we have no right to place the possibility of this limitless, eternal defeat on the same footing as risks that we run in the ordinary conduct of our affairs in our particular transient moment of human history."

The possibility of "limitless, eternal defeat" derives from the sheer quantity of nuclear arms that have accumulated, but the increased risk that this arsenal will be unleashed derives more from the desire of the major powers to expand the areas and circumstances under which they believe that nuclear weapons can be used for the national advantage.

Indeed, the arms race has changed from the pursuit of brute superiority of firepower to the pursuit of flexibility of response — to the ability to use nuclear weapons in a variety of circumstances under which the national interest is deemed to be threatened.

The myth of deterrence has been that nuclear weapons, representing as they do the "unthinkable," have entered our security systems in order that they will not have to be used. Nuclear weapons are claimed as an effective deterrent, precisely because they are so horrific that no one will finally contemplate their use. Hence, we are said to enjoy a balance of terror.

But, as nuclear-use theories and scenarios for winnable nuclear wars proliferate, it becomes clear that, in fact, nuclear weapons have entered our arsenals because our military and political leaders believe that there are potential circumstances under which they can be detonated for our benefit. National leaders have come to the conclusion that circumstances could occur in which it would be better to fire nuclear weapons than not to fire them.

In the meantime, while we may assume there is a genuine and sincere hope that such circumstances will not occur, these same military and political leaders are still anxious to use nuclear weapons in a way in which bandits prefer to "use" their guns, by brandishing them and threatening to fire them in the hope that their objectives can be achieved without actually firing the gun. In other words, the functions of nuclear weapons have been expanded to include such things as blackmail and intimidation, a topic we will return to later.

Atomic scientists in the United States display a symbolic "doomsday" clock on the cover of their journal, *The Bulletin of the Atomic Scientists*, as a means of recording their assessment of the nearness of the hour of nuclear annihilation. In 1981, the hands of the clock were moved from seven to four minutes to midnight. "We feel impelled," wrote editor Bernard Feld, "to record and to emphasize the accelerating drifts toward world disaster in almost all realms of social activity.... We must work for worldwide reversal of the suicidal Roman dictum — 'If you want peace, prepare for war'." And it is the preparation for nuclear war that promises what the Stockholm International Peace Research Institute describes as "another great leap forward" in the Soviet-American arms race: "This new spiral in the arms race will be by far the most dangerous. Large numbers of nuclear weapons will be deployed which will be seen as useful for fighting a nuclear war but useless for nuclear deterrence. And military technology is developing a number of weapons systems which will strengthen the perception that nuclear war is fightable and winnable."

World Nuclear Arsenals

As long as nuclear weapons are assigned a broad range of functions and are required for responding to what is potentially an infinite variety of circumstances, there will remain a virtually limitless demand for new nuclear weapons. And even the most cursory examination of world nuclear arsenals suggests that, to date at least, restraint has not been a prominent feature of nuclear weapons procurement.

By any reading, the nuclear arms race has been a process of action and reaction, with the United States usually acting first and the Soviet Union reacting in an attempt to counter the perceived threat (see Table 1). After the first bomb was dropped on Hiroshima on 6 August 1945 — a four-ton device with the explosive power of 12-15,000 tons of TNT

TABLE 1
Escalation of the Arms Race

	U.S. *(Action)*	USSR *(Reaction)*
First nuclear chain reaction	Dec. 2/42	Dec. 24/46
First atom bomb exploded	Sept. 16/45	Oct. 23/49
First H-bomb exploded	Nov. 1/52	Oct. 12/53
European alliances in effect	Oct. 24/49	May 14/55
	(NATO)	(Warsaw Pact)
Tactical nuclear weapons in Europe	1954	1957
Accelerated buildup of strategic missiles	1961	1966
First supersonic bomber	1960	1975
First ballistic-missile-launching submarine	1960	1968
	(Polaris)	(Yankee)
First solid rocket fuel used in missiles	1960	1968
Multiple warheads on missiles	1964	1973
Penetration aids on missiles	1964	None to date
High-speed re-entry bodies (warheads)	1970	1975
Multiple independently-targeted re-entry vehicles (MIRVs) on missiles	1970	1975
Computerized guidance on missiles	1970	1975

Source: Jim Wallis, ed., *Waging Peace* (New York: Harper and Row, 1982), p. 34.

delivered on a slow-flying bomber — the early nuclear arms race concentrated on expanding the explosive power of the warheads themselves and on more efficient means of delivering them. Since the mid-1960s the arms race has concentrated less on the quantity of delivery systems and more on "quality," emphasizing in particular greater accuracy and the ability to strike several separate targets from a single missile.

In the process, the world's nuclear arsenal has grown to the equivalence of 16,000 million tons of TNT. In all of World War II, weapons with an explosive power equivalent to 3 million tons of TNT were used and resulted in the loss of more than 40 million lives. The destructive potential of today's nuclear arsenals is quite literally not fathomable — to describe the potential consequences of the unleashing of a destructive force of that magnitude makes all language other than that of extinction inadequate.

There are currently about 50,000 nuclear weapons under the control of the five acknowledged nuclear-weapon states: the United States, the Soviet Union, the United Kingdom, France and China. These weapons vary in size and function. Some are designed for short-range, battlefield use and are fired from artillery shells and airborne or ground-based missiles. Others are designed for intermediate-range use (up to about 2,000 miles) and are delivered by missiles and aircraft, while still others are designed for intercontinental flight via missiles and aircraft. The relative strengths of the U.S. and USSR arsenals as of 1982 are shown in Figures 1 (total arsenals) and 2 to 4 (broken out by delivery system), on pages 12 and 13.

In the category of intercontinental, or strategic, nuclear weapons, the United States has about 9,500 warheads capable of being delivered to and exploded on 9,500 separate targets in Soviet territory. Approximately 2,600 more warheads controlled by the United States are of intermediate range and can be delivered to and exploded on Soviet territory from bases in Europe and seas adjacent to the Soviet Union.

For its part, the Soviet Union has about 8,800 strategic weapons capable of being delivered to and exploded on about 8,000 separate targets in North American territory (the fact that the Soviet Union can hit fewer targets than its number of warheads is due to some Soviet missiles having multiple warheads that are not independently targeted), and an additional 2,300 intermediate-range weapons capable of being delivered to and exploded on West European territory. (For an examination of the relative strengths of the U.S. and USSR arsenals, see Chapter 2.)

Collectively, China, France and the United Kingdom are capable of delivering to, and exploding on, Soviet territory about 1,000 additional warheads. In addition, NATO and Warsaw Pact countries together possess about 20,000 tactical nuclear weapons. These are short-range weapons of a lower yield and are allocated for European battlefield use. A few hundred of the strategic nuclear warheads could kill in excess of 100 million Soviet or North American citizens and destroy the greater part of the industrial capacity of each territory.

This five-nation nuclear club has now been joined by a much larger club of near-nuclear states. Both nuclear weapons technology and nuclear weapons materials are now widely dispersed on the planet, largely through the nuclear power industry. (Chapter 6 provides a review of the relationship between nuclear power and nuclear weapons and of the role of Canada in the horizontal proliferation of weapons.) As a result at least thirty additional countries now have the means to produce nuclear weapons, with some, such as Israel, South Africa and India, quite possibly already possessing small numbers of weapons.

In the present international climate, except for the acknowledged nuclear-weapon states, the greatest diplomatic benefit probably accrues to those countries which have the clear capacity to build nuclear weapons and who reserve the right to pursue that option but have not yet officially crossed the nuclear threshold. In particular conflict situations any of these near-nuclear states may come to the conclusion that greater advantage may come from actually crossing the threshold and threatening an adversary with nuclear attack.

In each case where circumstances change to produce incentives to go from near-nuclear to nuclear, the world will once again have become a more perilous place. To this prospect must also be added the likelihood that as nuclear materials and technology proliferate even further, they will find their way into the hands of terrorist groups and criminal organizations or, as Richard Barnet puts it, "anyone who has ready cash and a strong motive to terrorize others."

The New Generations of Nuclear Weapons

From MAD to NUTS

Despite the fact that the only two instances of the use of nuclear weapons in war were not premised on the idea of deterring nuclear attack, the main post-World War II rationale for nuclear weapons has been that they are needed to deter one's adversary from using nuclear weapons. In the

FIGURE 1
Total Strategic Nuclear Weapons*
USSR 7,800; U.S. 9,536

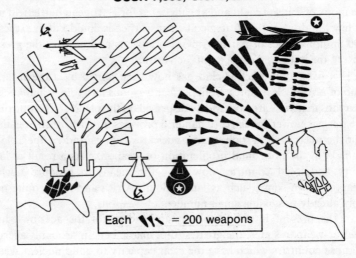

Each ⦅⦆ = 200 weapons

FIGURE 2
Nuclear Weapons on Strategic Bombers
USSR 290; U.S. 2,640

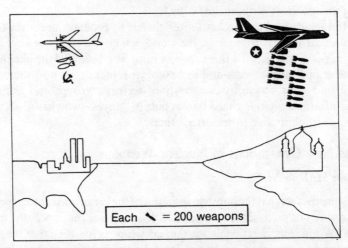

Each ＼ = 200 weapons

Note: *Including other weapons, the U.S. can explode 12,000 nuclear weapons on the Soviets: the Soviets can explode 8,000 on the U.S.

FIGURE 3
Nuclear Weapons on Land-Based Missiles (ICBMs)
USSR 5,540; U.S. 2,152

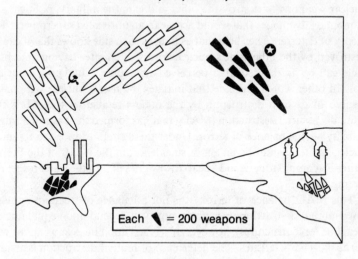

Each ◣ = 200 weapons

FIGURE 4
Nuclear Weapons on Strategic Submarines
USSR 1,970; U.S. 4,744

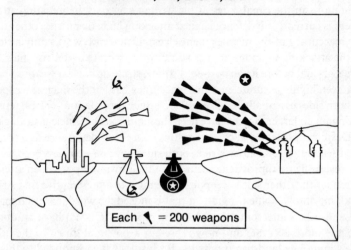

Each ◣ = 200 weapons

Source: Charts by the Center for Defense Information, Washington, D.C.,
in *The Defense Monitor,* vol. XI, no. 6

Soviet-American confrontation of the postwar years, each side has justified the buildup of its own arsenal with the argument that it is only the threat of massive retaliation with nuclear weapons that keeps each side from using nuclear weapons to destroy the other and gain the military, political and economic advantages that would accrue to an unrivalled superpower. The theory of deterrence has held that as long as each side knows that it can be destroyed by the other side's nuclear forces, even after having fired first, there can be no theoretical or perceived advantage to initiating a nuclear war. In other words, the side that initiates the use of nuclear weapons is assured of its own destruction by the other's retaliatory force. It is this mutually assured destruction (MAD) that has formed the basis of a fragile stability — the balance of terror. Under these circumstances, to initiate a nuclear attack would be an act of suicide, or, in the words of the French writer Raymon Aron, would "be to throw oneself into the water for fear of getting wet."

This MAD balance of terror (it is not a balance of weapons systems, since mutual destruction does not in any way depend upon equal nuclear weapons force structures), however, has relied upon nuclear weapons with particular characteristics. The deterrence of mutual destruction is assured only under certain conditions — and technological innovations are now altering those conditions.

In the first instance, nuclear deterrence relies upon nuclear weapons that can survive an adversary's first strike, and this has depended entirely on the limitations in the capabilities of the weapons used in the initiating attack (there is currently no defence against attacking ballistic missiles other than the inaccuracy of the missiles themselves). Deterrence works only as long as the attacking weapons are not sufficiently accurate to destroy the other side's arsenal before it can be used. To date, strategic nuclear weapons have not been highly accurate, and this inaccuracy has left the nuclear weapons of both sides essentially invulnerable to attack (population centres, representing much larger targets, have been the main object of nuclear strategies).

Despite a professed allegiance to this concept of deterrence as a threatened second or retaliatory strike, both sides have nevertheless been working feverishly to improve the accuracy of their own weapons in an attempt to render the other side's weapons vulnerable to a pre-emptive first strike. And, inevitably, some progress, if that is indeed the word, has been made.

Land-based intercontinental ballistic missiles (ICBMs) have gradually become more accurate and now represent a potential threat to the other side's immobile land-based missiles. Both sides have responded to this by "hardening" their own missile silos (essentially adding concrete in order to make them more resistant to blast), and by accelerating research into possible ballistic missile defence systems. Successive technological innovations have gradually led to the conviction on both sides that the other's ICBMs are (or will shortly be) sufficiently accurate to make their own land-based systems vulnerable. Consequently the rules of the nuclear game are gradually changing. Under the system of MAD there was no incentive to strike first, but if weapons systems are vulnerable to attack, that all changes.

Now, in an international crisis in which both sides come to the view that a nuclear exchange may be inevitable, both sides may also see advantages in going first. If nuclear weapons are going to be used, they could argue, it would be advantageous to go first and in the process destroy as many of the other side's weapons as possible and thereby limit its ability to respond. If enough of the other side's weapons are knocked out, the damage done by what is left of the retaliatory force may be kept to acceptable levels. Hence military planners have begun to calculate the circumstances under which nuclear weapons could be used to advantage. This requires judgments on such questions as, What constitutes "acceptable" damage? (can we afford to lose a million if the other side loses 10 million lives, or should the figures be 10 million of one's own lives in exchange for 50 million of the enemy's?); or, How many weapons would it take to reduce the enemy's destructive capacity to acceptable levels? Theorists thus explore scenarios in which nuclear weapons could be used — developing a body of nuclear-use theories (NUTS) — and the world is now discovering that the nuclear arms race has indeed gone from MAD to NUTS.

The Threat of a First Strike

In nuclear parlance a successful first strike is one in which the side that initiates attack destroys enough of the other side's nuclear weapons to reduce its capacity to retaliate to acceptable levels. The term "acceptable level" clearly has no technical or precise meaning. It obviously depends upon the circumstances, not the least of which being the psychological state of the person charged with making the final judgment. In the present circumstances, however, assuming a measure of rationality among decision-makers, neither side possesses such a first-strike capability or is likely to acquire one.

A myriad of technical difficulties remain to make the contemplation of a first strike a highly risky venture. The theoretical accuracy of new American and Soviet missiles remains just that as long as these weapons cannot be tested on their actual flight paths. Without actually testing the missiles on the paths they would have to follow in a real attack, the atmospheric, gravitational and magnetic effects on them cannot be known for certain.

Nor are weapons planners entirely sure of the impact of what they call the "fratricide effect" — the disabling of incoming warheads by preceding detonations (although it is this effect which was being relied upon in the famous "dense pack" basing mode to protect the proposed MX missile from being destroyed by Soviet missiles launched in a pre-emptive attack against the U.S.).

But the most persuasive current obstacle to a first strike by either side is the fact that both have submarine-based weapons, hidden in the vastness of the world's oceans, which now, and in the foreseeable future, would be extremely difficult to locate or destroy. An attack on the other's land-based weapons could obviously not be carried out with any assurance of avoiding retaliation by sea-based weapons.

Ultimately, however, whether or not there is an actual first-strike capability may be less important than whether either side perceives the other to have it. And the MX and Trident II submarine-launched missiles (see Chapter 5 for Canadian involvement in these and other U.S. nuclear weapons) in particular represent heightened U.S. efforts to threaten the Soviet Union with a credible first-strike option against Soviet land-based missiles (about two-thirds of Soviet warheads being on land-based missiles). Such a threat is fundamental to the shift in American policy, which has moved away from deterrence based on the threat of retaliation to deterrence based on the assurance of American victory in a nuclear war. Rejecting the notion that total self-destruction would be the inevitable outcome of nuclear war, the U.S. Defense Department's "Fiscal Years 1984-88 Defense Guidance" document emphasizes that U.S. armed forces have the task of prevailing in a protracted nuclear war. And Defense Secretary Caspar Weinberger in his reports to Congress speaks of the key objective of nuclear policy being "to impose termination of a major war on terms favourable to the United States and its allies, even if nuclear weapons have been used." To prevail in a protracted war, for example, the highly accurate MX and Trident missiles would be assigned the task of destroying not only Soviet nuclear forces but also Soviet command and communication networks in an attempt to prevent a Soviet order to retaliate. The policy has been named "decapitation."

This explicit statement of interest in pursuing a first-strike capacity is reinforced by the controversy over the "dense pack" and other methods of basing the MX. The "dense pack" theory is that the basing of 100 MX missiles in a cluster will protect them due to the "fratricide effect." In other words, while some of the MX could be destroyed by the first blast, subsequent Soviet attacks would have to be delayed to allow the effects of the first attack to subside, leaving sufficient time for the U.S. to launch the remaining MX missiles in retaliation. Because this claim, however, was seriously challenged in scientific circles (critics, such as Kosta Tsipis of the MIT, for example, argue that the "dense pack" will leave the MX vulnerable to attack), the Soviets are likely to infer from this uncertainty an American intention to use the missiles first (if you plan to use these weapons to initiate attack, you tend to pay relatively little attention to whether or not they are vulnerable to attack).

As weapons and destructive capacity build up, the potential costs of absorbing a pre-emptive first strike may be considered to be so high that in an international crisis leaders on either side may become convinced that any limitation on the other side's destructive capacity may be better than nothing — so that the cautious action will appear to be to shoot first. As perceptions of first-strike capabilities emerge, the other side's nuclear arsenal ceases to be a deterrent to attack and becomes an incentive.

Launch on Warning

Another and no less frightening response is to place one's nuclear forces on a "launch on warning" system. Some nuclear strategists have recommended that land-based weapons which are vulnerable to attack from the other side be committed to launch as soon as there is warning of attack. This proposal is based on the assumption that if one's land-based missiles are under attack, they will be destroyed unless they are launched during those fifteen or twenty minutes between the first warning of attack and the time of impact. If they are launched on warning, the incoming missiles will strike only empty missile silos. The danger, of course, is that the original warning will turn out to have been a false alarm. The implications of this situation were made clear by Fred Ikle, former director of the Arms Control and Disarmament Agency under President Ford and now undersecretary of defense for policy. No one, he says, can understand all the possible malfunctions, unanticipated events and human errors that could combine to confound warning systems or to bypass the "safeguards" against an unintended launch.

As nuclear weapons become increasingly sophisticated and warning times are reduced, it may become necessary to rely upon automated electronic early warning systems, not only to detect but also to respond to nuclear attack. Thus, the world faces a situation in which each superpower, fearing a first strike from the opposite side, may be putting its nuclear arsenal on much more of a hair trigger.

The submarine-launched Trident II will theoretically be accurate enough to destroy Soviet land-based missiles and will reach its target within fifteen minutes of a launch order. And the Pershing II missile scheduled for deployment in West Germany will be so accurate and fast that, in the words of Paul Warnke, it "could be in the men's room in the Kremlin in something like four minutes." Under the circumstances, any serious political crisis could have catastrophic results. Each side would be more prone to interpret a false alarm as the real thing and to launch on warning. A report by the U.S. Senate Armed Services Committee notes 3,703 alarms in the eighteen-month period from January 1979 to June 1980. Most of these were routinely assessed and dismissed, but fourteen of these false alarms were serious enough to require evaluation of whether or not they represented a potential attack. A major false alert, lasting a full six minutes, resulted when a technician mistakenly mounted on an American military computer a training tape of a Soviet attack. As British science writer Nigel Calder sums up: "When both superpowers are armed to the teeth with 'counterforce' nuclear weapons, the danger is not that either side is tempted in cold blood to make his strike, but that both are driven towards it by mutual fear. There may come a moment when, without any malice in your heart, you have frightened your opponent so badly you must hit him before he hits you."

Extending Deterrence

Gradually, this ability to attack (to "hit him before he hits you"), rather than to defend against attack, has become the cornerstone of the security systems of both the Warsaw Pact and the North Atlantic Treaty Organization. Both alliances have come to rest upon increased nuclear threat — that is, the increased ability to attack and destroy an adversary's military and industrial forces — as the basis of security (a change that was formalized in July 1980 by President Jimmy Carter's Presidential Directive 59 — namely that nuclear weapons were to be designed to threaten the other side's weapons, to strike at selected secondary military targets, and to wage a "prolonged but limited nuclear war").

It is this ability to threaten an adversary's weapons systems and control centres, by virtue of increased accuracy (which is itself a result of technological innovation), that has led beyond deterrence to first-strike scenarios, to scenarios for winning or prevailing in protracted nuclear war, and to attempts to use nuclear weapons as a means of intimidation (essentially to blackmail an adversary into acting, or refraining from acting, in a particular way). Some have referred to this phenomenon as "extended deterrence."

"Winning" in Nuclear War

Nuclear weapons as instruments of war-fighting and intimidation introduce a frightening new quality into the arms race, since both of these functions rely upon the threat of the first use of nuclear weapons. Deterrence relies upon the threat of retaliation, whereas the capacity to fight and win a nuclear war and, particularly, to intimidate, rely upon the threat of first attack. The cruise missile (see Chapter 5 for Canada's part in its development) represents a current example of the creation of a new weapons system, designed not so much for deterrence of nuclear attack as for purposes of intimidation and of fighting nuclear war.

Nuclear weapons such as cruise missiles, in addition to being instruments of extraordinary destruction, are also a rather primitive means of communicating threats and counter-threats between the two superpowers. And it has been the nature of the messages that are likely to be communicated to the Soviet Union by the testing and deployment of cruise missiles that has been a major focus of the controversy over Canada's involvement with them.

U.S. military planners and their Canadian supporters argue that the cruise carries only the message of deterrence — that is, it notifies the Soviet Union that any Soviet use of nuclear weapons against the West will be met in kind. By this reasoning the cruise missile simply represents Western modernization of its capacity to retaliate to a Soviet attack.

Some critics of the cruise insist that it carries a fundamentally different message — namely, the message of a first strike. Owing to the great accuracy of the cruise, say the critics, it can be used not simply in a general retaliatory attack, but to destroy Soviet missiles in their launching silos. In order to do this the cruise would obviously have to be used first. Hence, because the cruise would be capable of attacking and destroying Soviet weapons, the message that is carried to the Soviet Union by American deployment of the cruise is that the West is developing weapons that are appropriate for initiating a nuclear war. And, the critics of the cruise argue, when you combine this capacity with U.S. rhetoric about "winnable" nuclear wars, the message received by the Soviet Union suggests that the West is preparing for nuclear war and, in a crisis, may precipitate one.

The cruise supporters reply that it is the Soviets who have been developing the capacity to destroy American land-based missiles and that the American response to that threat is the proposed MX missile, which could launch a pre-emptive strike against Soviet missiles much more quickly. The cruise, say its supporters, is too slow (it flies slower than the speed of sound) to be used in a pre-emptive first strike. Not surprisingly, the truth lies somewhere in between.

One thing, however, is clear: the cruise is not simply a deterrent weapon, despite the assertions of Canadian and American officials. The United States has land-based nuclear weapons (about 20 per cent of which would survive even in the most extreme calculation of the results of a Soviet first strike) and many essentially invulnerable sea-based ballistic missiles which would survive any Soviet attack and could then be used in massive retaliation. These, under the present nuclear confrontation, represent the U.S. deterrent. They are not yet accurate enough to threaten Soviet weapons and so cannot be used to threaten or carry out a pre-emptive strike against Soviet weapons systems. They are confined to retaliation and are what are properly called second-strike weapons and represent the West's nuclear deterrent, indicating to the Soviets that any use of nuclear weapons against the West would be an act of suicide.

The cruise, however, has other qualities. These qualities communicate to the Soviet Union that the West is developing the capacity to hit particular military and industrial targets with nuclear weapons. Two statements by U.S. officials in 1981 most clearly indicate the war-fighting purpose of the cruise missile. In January of that year the deputy secretary of defense, Frank Carlucci, said: "I think we need to have a counterforce capability [weapons capable of attacking Soviet weapons]. Over and above that, I think we need to have a [nuclear] war-fighting capability." Then, in November of the same year, Defense Secretary Caspar Weinberger said: "We set out to achieve improved capabilities to enhance deterrence and U.S. capabilities to prevail should deterrence fail." (Weinberger, in fact, makes a distinction between "winning" and "prevailing" in war. Winning, he concedes, is a difficult concept to apply to the devastation which both sides would face in a nuclear war, but prevailing he says is something else. To prevail means only that you are in a better position to recover from the war than is your adversary.) In other words, Weinberger is calling for nuclear weapons which could be used in a nuclear war to ensure that the United States would emerge from that war in a stronger position than the Soviet Union (not necessarily to ensure that the U.S. was better off than before the war, only that its position vis-à-vis the USSR had improved). This requires highly accurate weapons that can hit military and industrial targets. The cruise missile is just such a weapon.

So while the cruise missile is not a first-strike weapon in the sense of being used to launch a pre-emptive attack against Soviet missiles, it is a nuclear war-fighting missile that, because of its high accuracy and, when launched in great numbers, its ability to evade counterattack even after being detected, is planned as a weapon to destroy fixed military and industrial targets in the Soviet Union once war has started. The objective is to ensure that the U.S. would "prevail."

Intimidation

Cruise missiles are also viewed by U.S. military planners as means by which one's adversary (read the Soviet Union) can be coerced or intimidated into taking, or refraining from, certain actions in certain circumstances. For example, the Americans would say to the Soviet Union that if the Soviets try to take advantage of the turmoil in Iran to increase Soviet influence there, they risk a limited nuclear attack. In fact, a 1979 U.S. Defense Department study, leaked to the *New York Times*, said that American conventional forces could not stop a Soviet thrust into northern Iran, and that "to prevail in an Iranian scenario, [the U.S.] might have to threaten or make use of tactical nuclear weapons."

Effective nuclear coercion would depend upon small nuclear weapons that could be launched in isolation against a specific target without thereby engaging one's adversary's strategic or massive retaliation arsenal — terms such as "limited attack" and "surgical strike" are used. Such limited strikes (or the threat of them) do not depend upon the elements of surprise or speed; rather, they depend primarily upon reliability and high accuracy, both of which are characteristic of the cruise (but neither of which, Canadians should note, can be obtained without extensive testing).

A "limited attack" or "surgical strike," of course, depends upon its remaining limited. In other words, the U.S. could not effectively threaten a limited attack on the Soviet Union to curb the latter's adventures in Iran if the Americans believed that any use of nuclear weapons would trigger a full-scale Soviet retaliatory attack on American territory. Hence, the objective in a "surgical" strike is to be precisely on target and to limit collateral damage as much as possible. A "small" nuclear attack, it is argued, would be sustained without retaliation in the hope of avoiding a full-scale nuclear exchange. (It is a measure of our growing inhumanity that today a nuclear weapon with ten times the destructive power of the Hiroshima bomb is described as "small.")

The use of nuclear weapons for intimidation purposes is, of course, not a new practice. The 1950s and early 1960s were dubbed by U.S. Secretary of State John Foster Dulles as the era of "massive retaliation." American nuclear strategy was premised on an "instant" response to

Soviet aggression even though just which Soviet provocation would bring down the nuclear storm clouds remained somewhat vague. In this era of "nuclear superiority" U.S. strategic doctrine called for the use of nuclear weapons "at times and places of our own choosing," as Dulles put it, to deter or to punish "unacceptable" Soviet actions. On several occasions senior U.S. officials considered using the atomic bomb. Daniel Ellsberg, a former specialist for the Pentagon, has noted that " . . . every president from Truman on (with the exception of Ford) has had occasion in an ongoing urgent crisis to direct serious preparations for possible U.S. initiation of tactical nuclear warfare." These preparations were in every case "leaked" to the enemy, and in several cases were accompanied by secret, explicit, official threats. Ellsberg refers to twelve instances in which the American government is known to have directly threatened the use of nuclear weapons. Of the twelve instances, ten grew directly out of Washington's efforts to defeat nationalist struggles in Asia and Latin America. These included:

- Iran in 1946, when U.S. President Truman demanded that the Soviet Union halt its support for nationalist regimes in Kurdistan and Azerbaijan;
- Korea in 1950 and 1953, against both the Korean and Chinese revolutions;
- Vietnam in 1954, when Washington secretly offered the French three tactical nuclear weapons, and again between 1968 and 1972;
- The Middle East in 1958, when Eisenhower authorized the use of nuclear weapons, if necessary, to prevent the extension of the Iraqi revolution;
- China, also in 1958, when Eisenhower directed the Pentagon to use nuclear weapons to defend the Chiang Kai-shek dictatorship's military outpost on the island of Quemoy, a few miles off the Chinese mainland;
- The Cuban missile crisis in 1962, a confrontation that grew out of Washington's attempts to crush the Cuban revolution.

Consider also this not entirely hypothetical example. War is either imminent or has broken out in the Middle East. The United States fears a prolonged war and an increase in Soviet stature in the postwar period if Soviet military aid to Arab states is significantly increased. The United States must do something dramatic to constrain the Soviet Union, so it places its nuclear forces on alert and makes it clear to Moscow that any escalation of Soviet involvement in the Middle East war will lead to the risk of nuclear attack on the Soviet Union.

To make such a threat credible, it is necessary to demonstrate two things — first, the technological capacity to carry it out, and second, the political will to carry it out.

In the matter of technological capacity, both the United States and the Soviet Union are concentrating on the development of first-use nuclear weapons. As we have already noted, first-use nuclear weapons, like the cruise, have specific technical characteristics. They are highly accurate, in some circumstances they involve a reduced warning time, and they are frequently of a much more limited yield in order to limit collateral damage. As we have also seen, deterrent weapons have no need to be very accurate (if you are aiming at New York or Moscow any strike within a kilometre or two of the centre of the target will not alter its deterrent value, while if you are aiming at a military installation you cannot afford to be more than a few tens or hundreds of metres off target).

The Pershing II missile, for example, that is planned for American deployment in Europe, is just such an accurate weapon and has a yield of about 15 kilotons (a very low yield by today's standards). It, like the cruise missile, is a first-use weapon and represents the threat of pre-emptive attack against west Soviet military targets. Similarly, the Soviet SS-20 missiles, while of a much higher yield, also emphasize accuracy and the threat of pre-emptive attack. (It is worth noting, however, that while the Pershing II can threaten part of the Soviet Union's strategic arsenal, the SS-20, due to its range and location, does not threaten any part of the U.S. strategic arsenal.)

The demonstration of political will to use nuclear weapons first is also crucial. One cannot credibly threaten a limited nuclear attack on one's adversary if one assumes that every use of a nuclear weapon will result in nuclear holocaust (since no limited objectives would be worth the risk). In the Middle East example, a U.S. threat of nuclear attack would be credible to the Soviet Union only if the U.S. had made it very clear that it believed that a limited nuclear war was in fact possible.

Hence, the U.S. administration has argued the possibility of limited nuclear war, the possibility of prevailing in nuclear war, and the possibility of launching nuclear warning shots. The United States and NATO, of course, have pointedly refused to adopt a no-first-use policy.

Posturing

The term "posturing" has been coined to describe another related function of nuclear weapons. Apart from deterrence or from issuing specific threats for the purpose of intimidation, nuclear weapons are deployed to demonstrate the resolve, assertiveness and general bearing of a super-power. The U.S. deployment of the MX missile system is, in fact, largely in this category. While supporters of the MX claim it is a response to an alleged Soviet capacity to destroy U.S. land-based missiles, the Reagan administration's eagerness to deploy the MX, even if a less vulnerable basing mode than existing silos cannot be found, suggests that it is more interested in issuing threats than in reducing the vulnerability of U.S. land-based missiles to Soviet attack. In fact, the Soviet Union's ability to wipe out American land-based missiles depends, as noted earlier, on such a wide range of factors that no rational Soviet leadership could contemplate a pre-emptive strike in the foreseeable future.

Administration officials, nevertheless, argue on two counts that the MX is essential. In the first instance, they argue that the MX missile provides a necessary advance in American first-strike capacity because within the international arena the Soviet Union is widely "perceived" to be developing a first-strike capability. From there the argument runs that if the Soviets are "perceived" to have such a capability and the Americans are "perceived" not to be responding in kind, the U.S. will then be "perceived" as lacking either the political or technological capacity to conduct itself as a superpower. In the Third World, in particular, it is said this perception will lead to a gradual shift of alle-giance away from the U.S. and towards the Soviet Union which, after all, still acts like a superpower.

In the second argument, the MX becomes a bargaining chip. In the Senate hearings Defense Secretary Weinberger said that the president had gone ahead with the dense pack, despite objections from some members of the joint chiefs of staff, because of the overriding necessity of having "a response in the ground" as quickly as possible to deter Soviet nuclear weaponry. Then, however, having declared their intent on the MX, the same administration officials began immediately to argue that any reversal on the MX would leave the U.S. in a weakened position. Bargaining chips, once put on the table become not points of negotia-tions but symbols of resolve. "If we were to waver now," said Wein-berger, "if we were to delay our peacekeeper [the president's name for the MX] program, we would be sending a clear signal to Moscow."

Nuclear Weapons and Strategic Interests

As has been suggested at several points thus far, the politics of the nuclear arms race are not confined to the direct confrontation between the superpowers, but involve the perceived economic and political interests of each around the globe.

In the nuclear age, gunboat diplomacy has reached a macabre level. Both major powers now brandish their nuclear guns in support of global political/military objectives. In the United States this intimidation, as we have noted, has become an explicit function of its nuclear arsenal. Paul Warnke, the chief of the U.S. Arms Control and Disarmament Agency in the Carter administration, speaks of disturbing signs of a growing reliance on nuclear weapons as an instrument of foreign policy — to gain political ends, not just to prevent nuclear attack. U.S. administration officials, he says, have stated categorically that the U.S. should "devise ways to employ strategic forces coercively" and that the U.S. "must possess the ability to wage nuclear war rationally." The political goal of the nuclear arsenal becomes the prevention of others from using conventional military force against U.S. interests, while leaving the latter free to use its conventional force with equanimity around the globe.

The desire to use nuclear weapons for immediate political ends stems in part from the fact that much higher stakes are now perceived to be attached to U.S. military/political/economic interests abroad. The security of the American state has become strongly identified with the protection of foreign interests and, specifically, since World War II as never before the idea of national security has become identified with secure access to energy and raw materials. The major industrial powers, which have gradually come to include the Soviet Union, have come to recognize "vital strategic interests" which, in the present age, have had to be protected by means other than the maintenance of colonial empires. Access to raw materials, access to additional markets for the surplus production of their growing industrial capacities, and places to invest surplus capital have required the progressive domination of the non-industrial regions of the globe by the industrial powers and have led inevitably to increased competition between the major powers themselves. Even as early as the turn of the century, a U.S. State Department circular recognized that the country's strategic "commercial" interests would have to become the concern of government:

> It seems to be conceded that every year we shall be confronted with an increasing surplus of manufactured goods for sale in foreign markets if American operatives and artisans are to be kept employed the year round. The enlargement of foreign consumption of the products of our mills and workshops has, therefore, become a serious problem of statesmanship as well as of commerce.

In consequence, a major feature of the international security environment has become the attempt by the industrialized powers to maintain their positions of industrial and trade pre-eminence relative to the Third World, along with an intensified push for relative advantage among the industrialized powers themselves.

Oil is perhaps the best known "strategic" resource, leading the U.S. to declare the Persian Gulf an area of its "vital interests" — even to the extent of pledging direct intervention to ensure the continued flow of oil. The same goes increasingly for other resources; particularly in the case of scarce minerals needed for sophisticated military equipment, the U.S. and its allies are heavily dependent on external sources. The Soviet Union and its allies (albeit to a lesser extent) also depend on foreign raw materials and, particularly, on foreign markets as a source of the foreign currency desperately needed to import food and Western technology.

The result is an increase in competition between the two blocs, and the main arena is the Third World. One need not go very far for evidence of this competition, and an arms deal between Zambia and the Soviet Union at the beginning of this decade provides a good example. In the $80 million deal, the Soviet Union agreed to supply the Zambian air force with Soviet MIG fighters and Zambia agreed to permit the Soviets access to Zambia's cobalt mines. Not surprisingly, the Americans were made nervous by the deal and U.S. politicians repeated fears that their vital interests were being threatened.

To this growing major-power competitition must be added a growing number of Third World countries with hegemonic ambitions, and capabilities, of their own. Taken together, in these two phenomena we have the formula for increasing tension and chaos. Increasingly, the hegemony of the superpowers is being challenged, not by each other but by emerging Third World nations, with the inevitable chaos as new power balances are sought (witness Iran and Iraq). And because resources are becoming even scarcer and the competition for them more intense, we can be sure that the world will become more, rather than less, tense — and this will continue to be the case until we find more equitable and more orderly ways of sharing the earth's resources.

In the meantime the industrial states use their bargaining advantages to exploit resources and to maintain their economic advantages. The manipulation of capital, trade barriers, and the control of technology are all used to maintain economic advantage; but lurking in the background, frequently brought into the foreground, is military force.

Military force, consisting of conventional and nuclear components, is used primarily in three ways to ensure access to resources. First, there is direct or threatened intervention in areas where interests are deemed to be threatened. Hence, rearmament programs emphasize combat readiness and highly-mobile rapid strike forces. Overseas bases are sought and maintained and occasionally, when all else fails, there is direct involvement in combat. In 1978 the French intervened in resource-rich Shaba province of Zaire to save it from the secessionist ambitions of disaffected Katanga-nists exiled in Angola. The Soviet Union entered Afghanistan in 1980 to quell a revolt on its southern flank, and maintains a massive armoured force on its western border, the main purpose of which is not to defend Soviet territory but to demonstrate the Soviet Union's ability to intervene in the affairs of its East European neighbours and, secondarily, to pose a threat to Western Europe. The United States' Rapid Deployment Force (RDF), expanded from a small, highly-mobile force to a 200,000-man interventionary force, has little to do with protecting American territory but a great deal to do with projecting force and extending American influence into various parts of the world. Both the Soviet tank force and the American RDF are designed to reach out into the world and to influence the course of events in accord with the respective interests of the sponsors of these interventionary forces. The United States, of course, wrote the book on interventionism in its adventures in Vietnam. To date, operations of this nature have not included nuclear weapons, although, as noted earlier, their use has been contemplated.

In the second use of military coercion to protect strategic interests, certain client states are armed as surrogate police forces to patrol the threatened area or region. The Americans called it "Vietnamization" in Vietnam, and the practice is reflected in the massive international arms trade, three-quarters of which involves Third World recipients. The objec-tive is to arm loyal forces within the recipient states in order to enable them to protect and look after the interests of the supplier there. Direct interven-tion is frequently costly and precluded by domestic political considerations in the supplier or industrial states, so the attempt is to get local forces essentially loyal to the supplier state to carry out a kind of proxy interven-tion. For the United States, the epitome of both the policy and its failure can be found in Iran. During the 1970s billions of dollars worth of the most sophisticated of U.S. conventional weapons systems were shipped to the Shah in the hope that he would be a bastion of American interests in that resource-rich and politically unstable region of the world. The rest, of course, is history. The Shah, despite an arsenal to challenge all comers was toppled from his throne, and now history repeats itself as the United States tries again in Saudi Arabia.

In the third instance, nuclear weapons, like conventional strike forces, are being mobilized in support of interests in the Third World. Besides deterring nuclear attack on each other, both sides seek to wring strategic advantages from their nuclear arsenals. A perceived nuclear "superiority" is itself intended to restrain the other side in its global exploits. North Americans argue that without the nuclear threat hanging over the Soviet Union, the latter would not have stopped in Afghanistan but would have taken advantage of the political and military turmoil in the Persian Gulf states and gone further to exercise greater control over countries such as Iran and Pakistan. The Soviets, for their part, argue that without their aiming a nuclear threat at the U.S., the latter would not have confined itself to conventional weapons in Vietnam but would have used nuclear weapons in order to forestall humiliating defeat.

Escalation and Domination

The balance among these three forms of military response is changing. As American (and, perhaps, Western) economic and political pre-eminence in the world is eroded, there arises a corresponding temptation to turn to nuclear and other weapons in an attempt to arrest the decline militarily. Reluctant to send hundreds of thousands of troops on permanent duty abroad, and uncertain of the stability or dependability of client states to protect American interests, Washington searches for a more compelling means of coercion. The hope is that a demonstrated willingness to back up conventional forces with the threat of nuclear forces will make U.S. military initiatives persuasive without being too costly.

As a result of the booming arms trade (in which the United States and the Soviet Union are major suppliers), Third World armies are now much better equipped than they were ten or even five years ago. This new reality obviously adds dramatically to the risks of intervention and this adds to the reasons why Pentagon officials entertain the possibility of using tactical nuclear weapons in support of forces sent abroad. Rather than become bogged down in another Vietnam, the temptation will be to turn to "small" nuclear weapons to put a quick end to any conventional war. Hence, the neutron (enhanced radiation) bomb may not be intended only for Europe.

The Pentagon's answer to the question of avoiding nuclear retaliation to its first use of nuclear weapons is that the U.S. must maintain a threat of escalating the conflict that is more credible than the Soviet threat. This means being able not only to escalate, say to a regional level, but to escalate again and again, if necessary, to a level which Soviet forces will be unable, or afraid, to match. That calls for forces that are "superior" to those of the Soviet Union at every level of nuclear conflict, up to and including a fully disarming first strike or a war of annihilation. The term for this strategy is "escalation dominance," the ability to control the level of exchange by effectively deterring the other side from escalating. This, of course, suggests a tidiness in categories of nuclear weapons and nuclear escalation processes which belong more to theoretical scenarios than to the realities of a world in crisis or at war.

To carry out escalation dominance, however, means that at every level at which one wishes to threaten a nuclear attack, there must be what Colin Gray of the Hudson Institute, a Washington strategic think tank, calls a "victory strategy." Ultimately, he says, "Washington should identify war aims that in the last resort would contemplate the destruction of Soviet political authority and the emergence of a post-war world order compatible with Western values."

Thus, the attempt by the United States to develop first-strike weapons is based, as we have argued, not on the need to deter an out-of-the-blue nuclear attack on American cities, but rather on the attempt to give the U.S. greater freedom to intervene in the affairs of states in the Third World with reduced risk of a responding challenge on the part of the Soviet Union. Explaining that strategic superiority is the key to continued U.S. pre-eminence in an increasingly turbulent Third World, Eugene Rostow, former director of the Arms Control and Disarmament Agency, has argued that "the nuclear weapon is a pervasive influence in all aspects of diplomacy and of conventional war, and in that crisis we could go forward in planning the use of our conventional forces with great freedom precisely because we knew the Soviet Union could not escalate beyond the local level."

It is clearly not the intent of the U.S. to trigger nuclear war between the United States and the Soviet Union. But America does have an objective it calls "victory," and what is meant by that is the power to organize as much of the world as possible to suit the interests of the Western industrialized world and to maintain those interests with minimum interference from the Soviet Union or its allies. The U.S. wants what Sir Solly Zuckerman, the British Nobel laureate, has described as the best kind of victory — one in which the enemy surrenders to superior force without a shot being fired. Richard Barnet, of the Institute for Policy Studies in Washington, argues that these developments greatly increase the likelihood of new U.S.-Soviet confrontations, and in future confrontations there is no guarantee that the Soviets will back down. Their record of restraint in crisis, he says, is a reflection of their relative military weakness in the past. "Having achieved rough parity with the U.S. in military power, their national-security managers are now much more likely to think like their U.S. counterparts: 'We

can't afford to back down and be exposed as a pitiful, helpless giant'."
Thus, says Barnet, "the happy accident that the world has survived the first
thirty-five years of the nuclear era is unimpressive evidence that we can
avoid nuclear war in the coming era, for world power relationships are
changing faster than we can comprehend and the arms race has become an
entirely new game."

Arms Control

When weapons are not a means of defence against attack and are instead a
means to threaten counterattack, not only is security a fragile commodity,
but arms control is virtually impossible. In the nuclear age, the major
powers consider their security to rely not on the ability to repel an attacker
but on the promise of retaliation and even pre-emptive attack. Accordingly, they have built up nuclear force structures whose main function it is
to threaten their adversaries. This applies increasingly to conventional
forces as well, the prominent function of which, as mentioned in cases such
as the U.S. RDF and the massing of Soviet troops on the USSR's western
border, is not to repel attack but to demonstrate the ability to intervene
militarily in the affairs of other states.

It is not hard to imagine that this has rather serious implications for arms
control and disarmament (there being no better evidence of this than the
paltry results of arms control negotiations to date). If one's own security
depends upon convincingly threatening one's adversary, there is obviously
little incentive to reduce one's forces — a reduction in forces would
presumably result in a reduced threat to one's adversary and, consequently, a corresponding reduction in one's own "security." Furthermore,
there can be little prospect for developing domestic political support for
force cutbacks as long as one's adversary maintains an offensive force that
remains threatening to one's homeland.

The very best that can be hoped for are arms control agreements that call
for a reasonably stable and mutual escalation of threat. And escalation is
indeed inevitable in view of the steady technological innovation of weapons systems. Weapons laboratories and test sites produce a steady stream
of refinements which must be incorporated into force structures, either in
response to known innovations by the other side or in anticipation of new
technological achievements by one's adversary.

Theoretically it would be possible to maintain a stable, minimum deterrent in which each side maintained only the minimum number of weapons
needed to threaten unacceptable damage to the other in case of attack. But
essential to such a minimum deterrent would also be the assignment of a

minimum task to nuclear weapons. If what is to be deterred is full-scale nuclear attack, according to deterrence doctrine itself, all that needs to be threatened is a full-scale nuclear attack in return. And since either the United States or the Soviet Union could be destroyed as viable societies with a few hundred nuclear weapons, any nuclear arsenals beyond that would appear to be superfluous and could be dismantled. But if the tasks assigned to nuclear weapons have gone beyond deterrence to intimidation, there can be no talk of balance; the side that seeks to use its weapons to intimidate must constantly strive for a superiority sufficient to make the other side back down in a crisis situation (in other words, escalation dominance).

Consequently, we are faced with an arms race that is getting dangerously out of control. While neither the Soviet Union nor the United States, we may assume, wishes to start a deliberate nuclear war, that unfortunately, does not preclude such a war beginning as the result of miscalculation, human or mechanical breakdown, inadequate or ineffective command control and communications procedures, or the escalation of local war.

In a world which is an amalgam of 1984 and Alice in Wonderland, not the least of the contradictions is the fact that any increase in weaponry reduces the security of everyone. George Kennan has stated the essence of the matter: "I believe that until we consent to recognize that the nuclear weapons we hold in our hands are as much a danger to us as those that repose in the hands of our supposed adversaries there will be no escape from the confusions and dilemmas to which such weapons have now brought us, and must bring us increasingly as time goes on."

Bernard Brodie, the first nuclear strategist, recognized the same thing in 1946, only a year after Hiroshima and Nagasaki, when he wrote, "Thus far, the chief purpose of our military establishment has been to win wars. From now on its chief purpose must be to avert them." Disarmament and arms control policies, therefore, have become a primary "defense measure."

Almost four decades later the danger has intensified, but the solution remains the same. In the meantime, opportunities lost in time become opportunities lost forever. We can find no better directive to begin the disarmament race than that drawn from the final statement of UN special sessions on disarmament in 1978 and 1982, both of which reiterated the 1946 wisdom of Brodie: "... the accumulation of weapons, particularly nuclear weapons, today constitutes much more a threat than a protection for the future of mankind... the time has come... to seek security in disarmament."

References

Beckett, Brian. *Weapons of Tomorrow*. London: Orbis, 1982.

Calder, Nigel. *Nuclear Nightmares*. Harmondsworth, Middlesex: Penguin Books, 1981.

Kaldor, Mary, and Smith, Dan, eds. *Disarming Europe*. London: Merlin, 1982.

Kennedy, Edward M., and Hatfield, Mark O. *Freeze!* New York: Bantam, 1982.

Lens, Sidney. *The Day Before Doomsday*. Boston: Beacon, 1981.

Lifton, Robert J., and Falk, Richard. *Indefensible Weapons*. New York: Basic Books, 1982.

Myrdal, Alva, et al. *Dynamics of European Nuclear Disarmament*. Nottingham: Spokesman, 1981.

Sanger, Clyde. *Safe and Sound*. Ottawa: Deneau, 1982.

Schell, Jonathan. *The Fate of the Earth*. Toronto: Random House, 1982.

Scoville, Herbert Jr. *MX: Prescription for Disaster*. Cambridge, Mass.: The MIT Press, 1981.

Thompson, E.P., and Smith, Dan, eds. *Protest and Survive*. Harmondsworth, Middlesex: Penguin Books, 1980.

2

Who's Ahead: The U.S. or the USSR?
Simon Rosenblum

Let us not confuse the question by blaming it all on our Soviet adversaries . . .
They too have made their mistakes; and I would be the last to deny it. But we
must remember that it has been we Americans, who, at almost every step of
the road, have taken the lead in the development of this sort of weaponry. It
was we who first produced and tested such a device; we who were the first to
raise its destructiveness to a new level with the hydrogen bomb; we who
introduced the multiple warhead; we who declined every proposal for the
renunciation of the principle of "first use"; and we alone, so help us God,
who have first used the weapon in anger against others, and against tens of
thousands of helpless noncombatants at that.

George F. Kennan
former U.S. ambassador to the USSR

Ronald Reagan describes U.S. military vulnerabilities in sweeping terms:
"In virtually every measure of military power the Soviet Union enjoys a
decided advantage." His administration vigorously declares that the
Soviets are determined to take over the world. Indeed, the last decade has
undoubtedly witnessed an upsurge in Soviet military strength which is still
continuing. This has led many in the West to agree with the Reagan
administration's claims. Indeed, the prognosis that the Soviet Union's
strategic nuclear forces are "superior" to those of the United States and
that the Soviets are aiming to fight and win a nuclear war has so pervasively
been reported in the mass media that it is rapidly becoming commonplace,
the hard-headed new realism for a hard-boiled age.

Are the Soviets stronger than the West? Differences in the composition
of Soviet and American military forces make it easy to take figures out of
context to alarm people about the military balance. The Soviets spend a
larger proportion of their GNP for military purposes than the U.S. does,
they have more missile launchers, more tanks and artillery pieces in

Europe, more ships in their navy, and their nuclear weapons have a greater total megatonnage. Does this mean that they are ahead in the arms race?

The Numbers Game

The United States has approximately 1,000 intercontinental ballistic missiles (ICBMs) and the Soviets have about 1,400. The Russian missiles are bigger than the American ones. The U.S. and the Soviets have approximately equal numbers of strategic weapons, but Soviet warheads, too, are bigger. Such facts are cited as if they were deciding factors in the "who's ahead" debate, but they are virtually meaningless. Actually, a closer look at American military capabilities leads to the opposite conclusion (see Table 1 on page 36).

A familiar charge used by those who warn of impending or present danger is that the Soviet Union has more strategic delivery vehicles than the United States (2,490 to 2,032 in 1982). The number of missiles meant something in the days before multiple independently-targeted warheads. Now that figure, at least as an indicator of offensive strength, has very limited utility. More relevant is the number of warheads and bombs (which, after all, actually kill people and demolish targets). The United States has 25 per cent more of these.

Yet beyond this, measuring nuclear forces in numbers of missiles and warheads ("bean counts") doesn't really mean all that much. Weapon systems must be related to specific missions, i.e., their accuracy, speed and vulnerability, as well as the strategic doctrines of the superpowers. The Soviet advantage in the number of ICBM launchers, upon which Washington now bases its claims of Soviet superiority, has always been a sign of Soviet weakness rather than strength. That is why the Nixon administration explicitly conceded to the Soviet Union's higher number of ICBMs in the SALT I agreement. Henry Kissinger considered the treaty a major coup for America. The United States, he told Congress, was interested in warheads, not launchers. "This was the theory behind SALT, which froze numbers of at-that-time single warhead systems in the Soviet Union against multiple warhead systems in the U.S.," he explained. The U.S. was able to develop solid fuel and precision multiple warhead missiles before the Soviet Union, which made it less dependent both on land-based ICBMs and on comparable numbers of heavy weapons. To make up for its lack of accurate multi-warheaded lighter missiles, the Soviet Union relied on heavier land-based ICBMs.

Another charge is that the Soviet Union's weapons possess greater "throw-weight" than those of the United States. This is a misleading comparison, because in the mid-1960s the U.S. Defense Department made a conscious and deliberate choice to trade in throw-weight for accuracy. Soviet missiles are bigger because they are built in a style American missile designers regard as extremely old-fashioned. Ninety-five per cent of Soviet missiles are powered by liquid fuel, which the U.S. stopped using for new military missiles some twenty years ago. The "throw-weight gap" exists because the Americans decided in the 1960s that there was no point in building big missiles, a fact that has not stifled heated warnings since over the Soviet lead in "heavy" missiles. The question is irrelevant, because the size of a missile's warhead does not necessarily bear any relation to the size of its blast. For example, the latest American ICBM warhead, the Mark 12-A, is just 2 per cent heavier than its predecessor, the Mark 12; yet its explosive blast is twice as large. So the U.S. doesn't need heavy throw-weight to perform its strategic missions. Moscow on the other hand has long had to compensate for inferior accuracy by increasing missile yields. Since a near tenfold increase in yield equates to only a twofold improvement in accuracy, this was less than ideal. By 1980, Moscow was finally able to test accuracies equal to those of the U.S. Minuteman 3 force (deployed since the early 1970s). Of all those who complain about the Soviet SS-18, the only "heavy" missile in either superpower's arsenal, nobody proposes that the U.S. should, or needs to, build anything so huge. "In megatonnage, the Soviets are way ahead; it doesn't make a damn bit of difference," former SALT negotiator Paul Warnke says. "The fact that they might have a two-megaton warhead compared to our modest ones of something like 400,000 tons of TNT only makes one difference: How big is the hole going to be where the high school used to be?" In comparison with the SS-18, the MX has a higher chance of destroying missile silos because of its superior accuracy. In short, throw-weight tells little about a warhead's capacity to destroy area or hard targets. According to retired U.S. Admiral Eugene LaRocque:

> Comparing the sizes of American and Soviet missiles is like comparing the sizes of our calculators. Bigger doesn't mean better. We build our missiles smaller because our technology is more advanced. Our ICBMs have miniaturized, computerized guidance packages, more efficient rocket engines, thinner but more effective heat shields, greater accuracy and more compact, efficient hydrogen weapons.

The crucial advantages held by the U.S. over the USSR are rarely mentioned in Washington today. The U.S. is ten to twenty years ahead of

TABLE 1
The U.S.-Soviet Strategic Arms Race*

	ICBMs		Submarine-Launched Ballistic Missiles		Long-Range Bombers		Total Strategic Delivery Vehicles		Total Warheads		Total Megatons**	
	U.S.	USSR	U.S.	USSR	U.S.	USSR	U.S.	USSR	U.S.	USSR	U.S.	USSR
1990***	1,350	1,700	720	1,300	450	200	2,550	3,200	18,000	20,000	7,100	13,000
1985****	1,052	1,500	664	1,100	348	140	2,064	2,740	13,300	10,000	4,200	9,200
1982	1,052	1,400	632	950	348	140	2,032	2,490	11,000	8,000	4,100	7,100
1980	1,054	1,400	640	950	348	140	2,042	2,490	10,000	6,000	4,000	5,700
1978	1,054	1,400	656	810	348	140	2,058	2,350	9,800	5,200	3,800	5,400
1976	1,054	1,500	656	750	390	140	2,100	2,390	9,400	3,200	3,700	4,500
1974	1,054	1,600	656	640	470	140	2,180	2,380	8,400	2,400	3,800	4,200
1972	1,054	1,500	656	450	520	140	2,230	2,090	5,800	2,100	4,100	4,000
1970	1,054	1,300	656	240	520	140	2,230	1,680	3,900	1,800	4,300	3,100
1968	1,054	850	656	40	650	155	2,360	1,045	4,500	850	5,100	2,300
1966	1,054	250	592	30	750	155	2,396	435	5,000	550	5,600	1,200
1964	800	200	336	20	1,280	155	2,416	375	6,800	500	7,500	1,000
1962	80	40	144	20	1,650	155	1,874	290	7,400	400	8,000	800
1960	20	a few	32	15	1,650	130	1,702	150	6,500	300	7,200	800

Notes to Table 1

*   Discrepancies between figures cited here and in Chapter 1 reflect differences in methods of tabulating weapons systems.

**   The figures shown are for "equivalent megatons," the most commonly used measure of aggregate explosive power. This is obtained by taking the square root of weapons yields above one megaton and the cube root of weapons yields below one megaton.

***   Assumes no SALT Treaty limiting strategic offensive weapons. The numbers shown are extrapolations of official U.S. estimates provided in congressional testimony on the SALT II Treaty.

Source: Ground Zero Collective, *Ground Zero Nuclear War: What's in it For You?* (New York: Pocket Books, 1982), p. 267.

---

the Soviet Union in microelectronics and increasing its lead, three or four weapon generations ahead in precision-guided weapons systems, ten to twenty years ahead in surveillance techniques. America is at least five years ahead in computerization in general and is increasing its lead in war gaming, anti-submarine warfare, signal processing and early-warning systems. The U.S. is also about a generation ahead on anti-tank and anti-aircraft missiles and is at work in several areas that the Soviets have hardly touched. Dr. William Perry, President Carter's undersecretary of defense for research and engineering summed up this American supremacy in military technology: "In precision-guided weapons . . ., the most significant application of technology to modern warfare since the development of radar, the United States has a substantial lead." In fact, the superiority of American military technology has made it far less expensive for the U.S. to modernize its strategic weapons systems. To improve the accuracy of the delivery systems of their strategic nuclear warheads, the Soviets have had to introduce a whole new generation of ICBMs, while the U.S., by merely improving its guidance system and by introducing the Mark 12-A warhead, has achieved the same result at one-sixth the cost.

The following dialogue from the Senate Foreign Relations Committee (29 April 1982) reveals that the Reagan administration is fully aware of America's supremacy in nuclear weapons technology:

> Senator Charles Percy: "Would you rather have at your disposal the U.S. nuclear arsenal or the Soviet nuclear arsenal?"

> Defense Secretary Weinberger: " . . . I would not for a moment exchange anything because we have an immense edge in technology."

The new scenario in Washington (and mirrored in Ottawa) imagines a "limited" Soviet attack on all U.S. land-based missile forces and missile submarine bases. With a portion of their own ICBM forces, the Soviets could (this "window of vulnerability" scenario assumes) destroy most of the U.S. forces. In retaliation, the U.S. could not strike Soviet nuclear forces because American sea-based missiles are supposedly not sufficiently accurate and its bombers too slow. Nor could the U.S. attack Soviet cities for fear of retaliation against those U.S. cities which had hitherto been spared. The U.S. deterrent would thus itself be deterred, and the U.S. would be compelled to back down in a confrontation with the Soviets. Indeed, with this scenario clearly understood, the Soviets would not actually have to undertake the attack in the first place to achieve their aims. The vulnerability of the U.S. land-based missiles would provide the Soviets with important political advantages.

But this scenario actually is based on extremely dubious premises. Critics retort that this script is, in the words of Paul Warnke, former U.S. chief arms control negotiator, "inherently implausible." First, Soviet planners could not be confident that all U.S. ICBMs would be destroyed in a first strike. Indeed, as physicists Bernard Feld and Kosta Tsipis from the Massachusetts Institute of Technology state: "... the assertion that the U.S. Minuteman force can now or in the future be destroyed with any degree of assurance by an all-out Russian counterforce attack [on Minuteman silos] seems to us to be a careless over-simplification, if not a deliberate exaggeration." Second, the U.S. would not have to respond to a "limited" Soviet attack on its land-based missiles by an all-out assault on Soviet cities. On the contrary, a whole range of Soviet military targets could be struck — there are over 20,000 such targets in the U.S. strategic operational plan — causing damage to the Soviet Union commensurate with that suffered by the U.S. Desmond Ball, an authority on strategic policy, points out:

> In any case, on that second strike, after they have knocked out your ICBMs, which is going to use up most of their ICBMs, what are you going to need accuracy for? The targets you are going to go after at that point are other military targets: airfields, army camps, tank concentration, or urban industrial areas. Neither of those require high accuracy. In any case, the accuracy of sub-launched missiles these days is approaching that of the ICBMs. It is certainly good enough to do a lot of hard-target operations that in the past could not have been done by submarines.

But perhaps most important, after such a "limited" attack with thousands of nuclear warheads causing between 8 and 20 million casualties (according to the American Office of Technical Assessment), it is hardly logical to suppose that Soviet strategists could count on a cool decision by the United States to do nothing in retaliation. Common sense suggests that Soviet leaders could not possibly contemplate a first strike against U.S. land-based missiles unless they had gone collectively insane. As Nobel physicist Hans Bethe argues, "Only madmen would contemplate such a gamble. Whatever else they may be, the Soviet leaders are not madmen."

In spite of fears about the Soviet Union's potential ability to destroy America's land-based missile force, the fact is that U.S. missiles are more reliable and accurate than Soviet missiles. While the USSR places most of its strategic eggs in one basket — increasingly vulnerable land-based ICBMs — the U.S. is relying increasingly on invulnerable submarine-launched ballistic missiles (SLBMs). The United States has forty-one nuclear submarines, ten of the older Polaris class and thirty-one Poseidons, plus new Tridents coming onstream. The Polaris carries sixteen missiles with one to three warheads apiece. The Poseidon carries sixteen missiles each with nine to fourteen warheads, each one three times as powerful as the Hiroshima bomb. One or two Poseidon subs, which are invulnerable to attack at this time, could destroy most or all of the 218 Soviet cities with a population of 100,000 or more.

There is "no doubt" the United States could stage a massive nuclear counterattack even if the Soviet Union struck first, according to a recent independent study by the Carnegie Endowment for International Peace. Rebutting Ronald Reagan's assertion that the Soviets hold a "margin of superiority," the study concluded that the U.S. arsenal "is not now vulnerable" and that the Soviets would be "very" vulnerable if their land-based missiles were knocked out first. The Boston Study Group similarly concluded that the Soviet nuclear buildup does not jeopardize the U.S. ability to carry out "assured destruction" in case of nuclear attack:

> A careful analysis of each of the [Soviet military] trends under consideration has led us to the conclusion that the degree of change ... is often exaggerated; and that the overall impact of current and likely future developments in Soviet forces does not warrant any new or special concern for the security of this country or its allies.

George Kistiakowsky, the American scientist and presidential science advisor, who was responsible for devising the implosion system of the first atom bombs, has published a record of his days in which he tells how President Eisenhower's policies were always frustrated by those who consistently exaggerated the Soviet military threat. Today he does not hesitate to declare that any analysis of the predictions that have been made of the Soviet military threat over the past twenty years will show that they have always been exaggerated. In the present context, Admiral Eugene Carroll

(Ret.) has drily commented: "The window of vulnerability is the son of the missile gap." Leslie H. Gelb, head of the U.S. State Department's Bureau of Political and Military Affairs under President Carter, points out that just as Defense Secretary Weinberger would pick U.S. technology over Russian:

> I have yet to meet a senior American officer involved in this subject who would trade the American arsenal for the Soviet one. Only those experts who focus exclusively on Soviet superiority in land-based missiles think otherwise. And here the debate among the experts ascends to the level of theology.

While the USSR is modernizing its military capabilities — and doing some things earlier and more quickly than the West had anticipated a few years ago — this buildup does not and will not, for the forseeable future, jeopardize the United States' ability to respond flexibly and selectively, or all out, to Soviet strikes. Even if it were true that the Soviet Union was now spending more money than the U.S. on military weapons, it must be remembered that there is no strict relationship between money and effectiveness in strategic weapons — or, for that matter, in anything. The Soviets are doing more, and they have become a formidable military power; but their methods are far more inefficient than America's; they get far less "bang for the buck" (or "rubble for the rouble"). Therefore, comparing military spending — in dollars or in roubles — does not bring us anywhere close to the essence of the military balance.

Hardliners in the West, however, insist that the Soviets are now making a clear bid for superiority. There can be no doubt that the USSR is striving very hard to achieve overall parity with the United States, but the assumption that it is the pacesetter in the arms race is incorrect. The United States still enjoys a significant lead in the qualitative measures of strategic power (e.g., in the accuracy, reliability and survivability of its nuclear delivery systems). What has occurred is that the growth in the size of the USSR's nuclear arsenal has diminished America's perceived advantage in strategic weaponry. This is not to say that America's nuclear war-making potential has in any way been reduced: both superpowers have long possessed sufficient firepower to destroy the world many times over, and both continue to expand their arsenals at rapid rates. What has changed is that the gap between U.S. and Soviet capabilities has narrowed over the last fifteen years. As Michael W. Johnson, formerly a senior analyst for the U.S. army, noted, "Although much is made of the projected Soviet deployment of SS-18s and SS-19s and their capability of destroying all American land-based ICBMs, these Soviet ICBMs will merely be capable of doing in the 1980s what American ICBMs could do in the 1960s."

In short, there are few grounds for complacency about the Soviets: they are improving their forces more, and more quickly, than intelligence analysts had predicted. But, neither are there grounds for panic. The American deterrent force is still capable of devastating the USSR, and notions of impending Soviet "strategic superiority" have no operational meaning. The U.S. is still able to carry out its strategic missions, can still deter the Soviets from attacking, and can respond in limited fashion to limited strikes. As long as this is so, there is a "strategic balance." After all, as President Carter said in his January 1979 State of the Union address, "Just one of our relatively invulnerable Poseidon submarines, comprising less than 2% of our total nuclear force, carries enough warheads to destroy every large and medium-sized city in the Soviet Union."

Arthur Macy Cox, who worked on Soviet and East European affairs for the CIA for many years, makes the point that the current U.S. concern about perceived changes in the international balance of military power has little to do with real military changes and nothing at all to do with Soviet understanding of the political implication of military power. A number of U.S. commentators now argue that the renewal of the image of the "Soviet threat" in the U.S. has much more to do with American internal political trends than with objective Soviet actions. Several sectors of American political life have traditionally used the Soviet spectre to strengthen their own hold on policy (for an examination of the role of the military-industrial complex in this regard, see Chapter 3). By exaggerating Soviet abilities and intentions these groups prejudice public debate on East-West relations at precisely those moments when détente is most urgently needed.

The Soviet Threat

Although the scenarios pertaining to supposed Soviet military capabilities are relatively easy to demystify on the basis of plain facts, the newest arguments focus on the more subjective plane of Soviet intentions. Richard Pipes, an important Reagan advisor and a pacesetter among this new school, has asserted that the USSR "thinks it could fight and win a nuclear war." Pipes assures us that the Soviets would take the risk because, having lost tens of millions in World War II, the Soviet leadership would not value life as we do in the West:

> The Soviet ruling élite regards conflict and violence as natural regulators of all human affairs; wars between nations, in its view, represent only a variant of wars between classes... Soviet doctrine emphatically asserts that while an all-out nuclear war would indeed prove extremely destructive to both parties, its outcome would not be mutual suicide; the country better prepared

for it and in possession of a superior strategy could win and emerge a viable society....

...There is something innately destabilizing in the very fact that we consider nuclear war unfeasible and suicidal for both, and our chief adversary views it as feasible and winnable for himself.

Such bold conclusions, however, must be examined closely. The burden of Pipes's (and others') case is that the USSR, believing it could fight and survive a nuclear war, would be prepared to launch one under certain circumstances. Of course, the Soviet Union is no innocent party in all this. It has added some innovations to the nuclear arsenal. Its repressive political system fosters an unsentimental attitude towards the use of power. But one need not have any illusions on that score in order to maintain that the Soviet Union does not desire nuclear war. Raymond L. Garthoff, a former American diplomat, recently studied Soviet perspectives on the nuclear arms race and concluded: "The Soviet leaders believe that peaceful coexistence — with continued political and ideological competition — is the preferable alternative to an unrestrained arms race and to recurring high-risk politico-military confrontation; that détente and a relaxation of tensions is in the interests of the Soviet Union; and that nuclear war would not be."

There is nothing in Soviet behaviour, history or ideology to suggest that the model of the Soviet leader waiting by the button until the computer predicts an "acceptable" casualty level is anything but a Pentagon rationalization to support a continuing arms race. Soviet leaders have committed some monumental crimes in the name of national security, mostly against their own people. And they have invaded countries on their borders. But the historic preoccupation with the defence of their homeland, and above all the uncertainties any leader faces about limiting the danger in a nuclear war, make a holocaust by design implausible. (This is not to say that the same result could not arrive thanks to adherence to nuclear-use theories or an accident.)

George Kennan, the historian and former American diplomat, feels that the view of the Soviet Union in "our governmental and journalistic establishments" is so distorted and exaggerated that it imperils the chances for a "more hopeful world." He now maintains that the view of the Soviet Union prevailing in the United States is "so extreme, so subjective, so far removed from what any sober scrutiny of external reality would reveal, that it is not only ineffective but dangerous as a guide to political action." It might be said that all this is a harmless (but expensive) fantasy, a kind of insurance policy against Armageddon. But unlike an insurance policy, the arms race directly affects the risk. By preparing for an implausible war the United States now makes other scenarios for nuclear war — wars by accident and miscalculation — far more probable. "So far as nuclear war is concerned, we and the Soviet Union are in the same boat," Professor Roger Fisher of the Harvard Law School observed. "You can think of that physically. There is no way that we can make our end of the boat safer by making the other end more likely to tip over."

The American Search for First-Strike Capability

I must reluctantly conclude from the evidence that the United States is ahead now and is rapidly approaching a first-strike capability — which it should start deploying by the mid-1980s. The Soviet Union, meanwhile, seems to be struggling for a second best. There is no available evidence that the USSR has the combined missile lethality, anti-submarine warfare potential, ballistic missile defense, or space warfare technology to attain a disabling first strike before the end of this century, if then.

Robert Aldridge
former Lockheed nuclear engineer

American strategists have recently introduced the "counterforce" doctrine, which envisions "limited" nuclear strikes against Soviet missile forces — thereby calling into question the survivability of the USSR's second-strike deterrent capability (thus increasing Moscow's perceived vulnerability, and enhancing America's presumed bargaining position). If anti-ballistic missiles (banned by treaty) are not permitted to interfere with missiles in flight or spoil the enemy's ability to destroy you, neither should your missiles be able to destroy his missiles before he even launches them. Yet the counterforce options call for exactly the kinds of accurate weapons that could in principle serve in a disabling first strike.

Confidence that one can destroy a missile in its silo, which is "hardened" against attack by steel and concrete construction designed to withstand all but a direct hit, is a function of the reliability of the incoming missile, the size of its warhead, and its accuracy. The chances of hitting a missile in its silo are improved more by the accuracy than by the size of a warhead. The MX missile system would theoretically possess just such a "silo-killing" capability. The U.S. president's 1980 arms control impact statement said the following about the MX missile, which in its advanced version is said to be accurate to within 100 yards and have a 92 per cent probability of destroying the hardest (most blast-resistant) Soviet missile silo:

...if the M-X were deployed in substantial numbers, the U.S. would have acquired, through both the Minuteman and M-X programs, an apparent capability to destroy most of the Soviet silo-based ICBM force in a first-strike.

... under crisis conditions, Soviet leaders, concerned that war was imminent, and fearing for the survival of their ICBMs if the United States struck first, nonetheless might perceive pressures to strike first themselves. Such a situation, of course, would be unstable.

With the MX, in combination with the accuracies soon to be achieved by warheads on the new Trident submarines, and the deployment of Pershing II and cruise missiles, the U.S. would be able, theoretically, to wipe out Soviet land-based ICBMs, leaving only missiles based on submarines and bombers (an obsolete and vulnerable delivery system) to contend with.

As was pointed out in Chapter 1, this superiority would have a destabilizing effect. The unprecedented range, accuracy and speed of the Trident II missiles, which can reach Soviet targets from virtually anywhere in the world within fifteen minutes, might impel the Russians to launch their vulnerable land-based ICBMs "on warning," thus increasing the danger of a nuclear war by miscalculation. At the Trident submarine commissioning ceremony, U.S. Admiral Rickover declared: "No enemy can feel other than fear or terror with this ship at sea." He might have added: "And neither can we." If the United States continues in the planned deployment of the Advanced Trident II missile in 1989, it will have the first survivable submarine force with, at minimum, a plausible capacity for an effective attack on Soviet land-based missiles. This is being made possible largely through the development of new global positioning satellites called Navstars. When the full constellation of Navstars are in orbit and receiving equipment installed on Trident missiles, accuracy will be increased from ¼ nautical mile CEP to 300 feet CEP (CEP refers to circular error probability, meaning the radius of a circle centred on the target in which half the warheads will hit). The new Trident is so deadly that the fiscal year 1980 arms control impact statement (a report the American president is required to submit to Congress along with the military budget) described it thus:

> The addition of highly accurate Trident-2 missiles with higher yield warheads would give the U.S. SLBM forces a substantial time-urgent hard-target-kill capability for a first-strike.
>
> ... the countersilo capability of a [deleted] KT Trident-2 missile would exceed that of all currently deployed U.S. ballistic missiles. Moreover, the additional effects of two potential advances (Trident-2 and M-X) in U.S. countersilo capabilities by the early 1990s could put a large portion of Soviet

fixed ICBM silos at risk. This could have significant destabilizing effects. . . .

The American government repeatedly says that it does not want a first-strike capability yet goes on equipping itself with precisely the weapons it needs for that purpose. The U.S. starts off with a key advantage in the new missile duel: at least three-quarters of all Soviet strategic warheads are carried on silo-based ICBMs which are becoming more vulnerable to U.S. missiles. Only one-quarter of U.S. warheads are so based. Moreover, at least 50 per cent of all American warheads are in submarines which cannot be destroyed by any of the ICBMs or SLBMs the Soviets are developing or have deployed.

American naval chiefs seem certain that the Russians cannot seriously threaten their missile submarines in the forseeable future. According to American navy intelligence analysts, the Soviets have never successfully tracked a single U.S. nuclear-missile submarine. But are the Soviet missile submarines (SSBNs) safe from a pre-emptive strike by the U.S. navy? The Soviet submarine missile force is somewhat more vulnerable than that of the United States, since U.S. anti-submarine warfare (ASW) in the Atlantic is far superior to that of the Soviet Union. Not only is American surveillance and information-processing technology more advanced, but a large number of Soviet submarines, the Yankee class, are equipped with missiles with ranges of the order of 1,300 nautical miles, forcing them to operate in the Atlantic Ocean to be able to hit even the Eastern United States. Here they are especially vulnerable to U.S. anti-submarine warfare. The United States has large sonar towers off the coast of Norway, off the Azores, and (in the Pacific theatre) off the Japanese islands. These are attached by cable to a giant computer processing centre, which can dampen out all of the other noises in the ocean and leave in only the noises of Soviet submarines. It is widely agreed that U.S. attack submarines, though outnumbered by their Soviet counterparts, are far more effective in locating and following Soviet ballistic missile submarines than vice versa.

This Soviet weakness will decrease as more and more of their submarines are equipped with missiles having ranges greater than 4,000 miles, which can thus be launched in the Arctic and Far Pacific. Nevertheless, even in such waters, the Soviets must be concerned about their submarine survivability since their ships are noisier and easier to detect and track than American submarines. To understand better the entire picture, let us review the number of Soviet submarines that would have to be instantaneously destroyed. In mid-1979, the USSR had about sixty-four missile submarines. It is a reasonable assumption that by the mid-1980s, the Soviets would have approximately eighty SSBNs capable of running submerged for extended periods. That number may pose no problem for the techniques the U.S. is developing. And the job of destroying them is made easier by the fact that only 15 per cent are away from port at any time; most could be hit in their pens.

Aggressive pursuit of anti-submarine warfare capacity by the United States (with Canadian cooperation, as outlined in Chapter 5) has serious implications for a first-strike strategy. While a primary aim of ASW capacity ostensibly is the protection of shipping lanes, to the extent that this threatens the invulnerability of the Soviet Union's retaliatory force, and therefore contributes to Soviet perceptions of a U.S. counterforce strategy, it represents a destabilizing activity. An American Library of Congress report concludes:

> The United States engages in a wide range of ASW activities. Not only are the various components being upgraded, but they are being coherently and systematically integrated. Indeed it is the achievement of mutually reinforcing relationships among the individual elements, rather than the incremental improvements to particular programs, that accounts for the rapid overall increase in ASW effectiveness.

The report further states:

> If the United States achieves a disarming first-strike capability against Soviet ICBMs, and also develops an ASW capability that, together with attacks on naval facilities, could practically negate the Soviet SSBN force, then the strategic balance as it has come to be broadly defined and accepted would no longer be stable.

The usual argument for the adoption of a "war-fighting" strategy is that the Soviets have one. The Soviets, indeed, are developing a counterforce capability of their own. As in the case of every major technological development of the postwar arms race, they have started far behind the United States but have striven to imitate U.S. technological achievements — usually lagging about five years behind. Jimmy Carter's Presidential Directive 59 of July 1980 officially recognized the intention of the United States government to widen its options to include the possibility of "limited nuclear wars" and counterforce strategy. The American major rearmament program will undoubtedly stimulate a Soviet response in kind. If these new weapons systems truly are meant to respond to Soviet moves, they are futile and dangerous gestures — futile because the USSR would soon be able to counter them, dangerous because rather than enhancing stability, they foster instability. The spiralling arms race is fuelled by — and, in turn, promotes — mutual fear and uncertainty between the East and the West. The introduction of counterforce pushes the world closer to the brink of nuclear catastrophe.

"Voodoo Arms Control"

President Reagan's news conference on 31 March 1982 was the occasion for unveiling the official response to the worldwide protest against the nuclear arms race. Reagan set the tone at the outset: We all want peace, he said, and we all want to "lower the level of armaments" — but first the United States has to catch up with the Russians. Senator Mark Hatfield immediately labelled that approach "voodoo arms control" — meaning that you must have more in order to have less.

The contradictions in Reagan's approach have just been challenged on their own terms. Of course, a more fundamental consideration is the illogic of debate about superiority or inferiority when each superpower possesses such enormous overkill capacity. If the only aim of American nuclear strategy were to deter a Soviet first strike, the present U.S. arsenal could be diminished by at least 75 per cent — instantly. If, on the other hand, Washington wants to achieve a first-strike potential of its own — without risking Soviet retaliation — it clearly has a way to go. This appears to be exactly what the U.S. administration's alarms are really about. When Reagan speaks of a "window of vulnerability," he is not referring to American vulnerability to a Soviet first strike, but to U.S. vulnerability to Soviet retaliation. After intensive interviewing of President Reagan and his chief nuclear weapons advisors, journalist Robert Scheer suggests that the American public is being deceived:

> Instead of going to the people and saying, "Hey, listen, we want to get back to the good old days of superiority," they pretend that we have actually fallen behind and are simply trying to catch up. Instead of talking openly about nuclear-war-fighting as they did in the first year of their Administration — before their poll-takers advised them to soften their rhetoric — they now stress the need for credible deterrence against the Soviet nuclear-war-fighters. But the neo-hawks have already said too much and written too much to conceal their true intentions.
>
> If this attempt to deceive were simply a matter of special interest lobbying in some relatively unimportant area of our national life, then one might shrug and say, "So what's new about political chicanery?" But the danger is that these people are dealing with more than commonplace matters, even though most of the violence has so far been verbal. Because of their role in an Administration in which the President sympathizes

strongly with their point of view, they have already profoundly affected the commitment to new weapons systems, systems that will make the world far more dangerous, while at the same time they have abandoned the possibility of arms control no matter how many hours we are willing to spend in negotiations with the Soviets.

The Third World Connection

As we saw in Chapter 1, the superpowers can get into World War III not just by accumulating nuclear weapons but through involvement in a conflict that could spiral into a confrontation of central nuclear systems. With the two sides unwilling to back down, and heading further and further up the escalatory spiral, eventually nuclear weapons could be used though neither may have intended to do so at the beginning. The growing link between conventional arms and nuclear war reflects the fact that recent technological innovations in armaments design — particularly the development of new explosives and of "smart" weapons with near-100 per cent "kill probability" — have made conventional arms far more lethal and destructive than ever before. And given the inclination of the major nuclear powers to intervene in local Third World conflicts, the chances are increasing that one side or another may feel tempted or compelled to use nuclear weapons.

The United States is a declining power that still possesses considerable clout and seeks to retain its influence and control over the political and economic future of much of the world. This substantially increases the possibility of such a nuclear development. Unable or unwilling to construct a meaningful political-economic approach to revolutionary upheavals and North-South conflicts, Washington seeks, through its military power, to reorganize the agenda, establish new political boundaries, and impose solutions that basically reflect overwhelming U.S. economic interests — American direct corporate investments in the Third World countries are over $30 billion.

Chapter 1 showed that as the broader American economic and political position in the world is being eroded, the tendency is to re-emphasize the role of nuclear weapons. The U.S. is seeking to use the muscle of its nuclear weaponry to compensate for the loss of real influence. Washington can't count on sending 500,000 or more troops abroad and can't necessarily rely on the stability or dependability of Third World allies to protect American interests. Consequently, the view in Washington is that there must be a much earlier and more effective use of American firepower backed up — in places that, unlike Central America, are far from the U.S.'s logistical base

— by the clear threat and the willingness to employ tactical nuclear weapons to support American military initiatives.

At U.S. government hearings in 1982, General Ellis, speaking for the Strategic Air Command, believed that it was no longer possible to draw a line between nuclear and conventional weapons. He was devising possible U.S. responses to Soviet activity in South Asia and Africa. Such contingency planning involved limited and regional nuclear options and called for combat missions by heavy bombers that could be flown west over the Pacific and Indian Oceans to the Middle East. There is no way to interpret such military strategy other than as a warning to the Soviet Union that America now has plans to respond to a conventional attack on an area it considers vital with a limited nuclear strike. In this sense, Presidential Directive 59 can be read at least partly as a response to the lack of credibility of President Carter's commitment to defend the Persian Gulf, if that commitment is to be met with conventional forces in areas far closer to Soviet soil. Zbigniew Brzezinski told reporters in background briefings that the United States could defend its commitment with nuclear weapons; now that intention has been officially embodied in the targeting plans for U.S. nuclear forces.

It is increasingly probable, therefore, that the cruise missile will be targeted against Africa or the Middle East. These locations are flashpoints where an American military presence might consider escalating quickly to "small" nuclear weapons to put a swift end to any conventional war. And it must be realized that the neutron bomb is not only intended for deployment in Europe. U.S. Secretary of Defense Caspar Weinberger has said that the neutron bomb could be used on battlefields outside Europe. Defense Department officials mentioned the Gulf region, the oil fields in Iran and Saudi Arabia as possible areas for the use of the bomb. Hence, any area in the world could be a target for the neutron bomb.

In a sense, this is not a new strategic doctrine. In the days of John Foster Dulles's threats of "massive retaliation," the United States enjoyed a decisive nuclear superiority and made first-strike threats, often against nations with no nuclear weapons of their own. According to the Brookings Institute, a private think tank in Washington, the United States threatened to use nuclear weapons no less than eighteen times between 1946 and 1970 against the Soviet Union and its allies. American nuclear strategy is meant to intimidate as well as deter, and without first-strike superiority its policy of threatening to start a nuclear conflict becomes in effect suicidal and therefore not credible. In a showdown, Soviet leaders might be tempted to call the U.S. nuclear bluff. Paul Nitze, a top-level Reagan arms negotiator, has compared the situation to "a game of chess. The atomic queens may never be brought into play; they may never actually take one of the opponent's pieces. But the position of the atomic queens may still have a decisive bearing on which side can safely advance a limited-war bishop or even a cold-war pawn."

Zbigniew Brzezinski justified Presidential Directive 59 in the following manner: "I assumed that our pre-existing doctrine of threatened mutual destruction only made sense while we were in a superior position over the Soviets. We could scare them with this doctrine because in practice it meant: We will destroy you, but you cannot destroy us. As the situation grows more equal, this doctrine became less convincing." American defence analysts fear that if the United States cannot dominate the escalation process on every rung of the ladder, the U.S. nuclear arsenal will be rendered useless by what Reagan advisor Colin Gray called "the paralyzing impact of self-deterrence." In other words, without flexible nuclear superiority, Washington would not be able to use its nuclear forces as a trump card in superpower conflicts. When asked if this new policy of "flexible response" included limited nuclear war, Brzezinski replied: "If necessary that includes limited nuclear war... It could escalate, would probably escalate... But when one side is capable of carrying it out and the other isn't, then the side that has that capability is in a better position to negotiate in a crisis situation." In the Reagan era, this might best be called supply-side militarism. As Richard Perle, the man whom President Reagan appointed assistant secretary of defense for international security policy, concludes: "I've always worried less about what would happen in an actual nuclear exchange than the effect that the nuclear balance has on our willingness to take risks in local situations."

Such deliberate arms policies are effectively making it all too possible that sooner or later — unless U.S. threats always work perfectly, which is highly improbable — a U.S. president will turn a non-nuclear conflict into a nuclear one, or a local nuclear exchange into a global one. The conventional notion of deterrence had always been wrapped in swathes of assurances by its proponents that the actual use of nuclear weapons was unthinkable. This had been apparently borne out during the Cuba crisis, when, as one American commentator put it, "we were eyeball to eyeball with the Russians, and they blinked." But in today's world, the superpowers' nuclear forces are closer to parity, so that nowadays *Time* magazine offers up the pious hope that, next time, both parties might blink at once. To which, Paul Warnke, former U.S. chief arms control negotiator appropriately asks: "Do we want to re-enact High Noon with nuclear weapons?" It comes down to the question of how the U.S. can ensure that its use of tactical nuclear weapons, or its threatened use, would remain one-sided, rather than leading to a two-way exchange, the prospect of which would deter it in the first place. If the United States launches a limited attack in real conflict, Edward Luttwak, a top advisor to President Reagan, assures us that Moscow will "know what the U.S. is up to and will show restraint." The off-the-cuff opinions of such strategists provide a fragile basis upon which to rest world security.

The whole panoply of new nuclear arms and deployments serves to implement presidential directives to connect hot spots such as the Middle East to what amounts to an American Doomsday Machine. E.P. Thompson, a leading spokesman of the European peace movement, made an accurate appraisal when he wrote:

> The Russian state is now the most dangerous in relation to its own people and to the people of its client states. The rulers of Russia are police-minded and security-minded people, imprisoned within their own ideology, accustomed to meet argument with repression and tanks. But the basic postures of the Soviet Union seem to me, still, to be those of siege and aggressive defence... The United States seems to me to be more dangerous and provocative in its general military and diplomatic strategies, which press around the Soviet Union with menacing bases. It is in Washington, rather than Moscow, that scenarios are dreamed up for "theatre" wars; and it is in America that the "alchemists" of superkill, the clever technologists of "advantage" and ultimate weapons, press forward the "politics of tomorrow".

Soviet Expansionism in the Third World

> Soviet advances notwithstanding, the United States is generally superior to the Soviet Union in those types of combat forces that are most appropriate for rapidly projecting power to areas remote from either homeland.
>
> U.S. Joint Chiefs of Staff, 1982

In order to back up their demands, Western rearmament advocates frequently rely upon charges of massive Soviet expansionism in the Third World. Since 1975, when the U.S. retreated from Vietnam, the USSR has expanded its military power. It has used its allies' conventional forces, mainly Cubans and East Germans, and/or its own troops and advisers, to spread revolution to Angola, Ethiopia, South Yemen and Afghanistan, and to control strategic areas or chokepoints. Without doubt, the Soviets are increasingly prepared to use military means to protect "socialist" regimes from external or internal challenges.

Cold War interpretations of Soviet foreign policy have been given a new lease on life by recent developments in Africa. In Angola, the Horn of Africa and Mozambique, Moscow and its Cuban proxies, it is claimed, have spurned the spirit of détente in a determined effort to subvert and infiltrate the African continent. Communist military intervention in Africa on this scale is indeed unprecedented. Moscow, at one and the same time, proved it had now developed the capacity to deploy men and equipment thousands of miles from their home base and the willingness to play an active part in areas distant from its traditional sphere of influence. However, Soviet goals in Africa can be presented in a much less disquieting manner. Africa is increasingly an arena in which the USSR and the West (and also China) are competing for power and influence. This marks less a new, more ambitious phase in Soviet expansionism than an appraisal, in Moscow, that political developments on the continent have weakened Western control and created opportunities for the extension of Soviet influence. Moscow is staking out a claim for itself and trying to ensure that its weight can be brought to bear, and its objectives taken into account, when decisions pertaining to Soviet interests are arrived at.

Whatever their motives, the entry of the Soviet Union into African affairs has, by balancing Western hegemony, enabled African governments to play off one against the other, hence widening their room for manoeuvre. The American assessment of the Angolan conflict — the Soviets launching a massive airlift of armaments to Angola, along with 10,000 Cuban troops, to give the Popular Movement for the Liberation of Angola (MPLA) a decisive edge in the civil war there — reflects a pronounced tendency to squeeze the most disparate situations into the familiar and simple mould of Cold War thinking. It overlooks the fact that the Portuguese were only able to maintain their grip on their African empire for so long because of aid from NATO powers. Indeed, the Soviet Union had, throughout this period, been the only major power to afford material help to the liberation movements, in particular the MPLA which had been in the forefront of the battle against Portuguese colonialism. The U.S. and the U.K. only discovered their new roles as disinterested friends of Angolan freedom and independence after the overthrow of the Caetano dictatorship in Lisbon. President Nyerere of Tanzania, made some pertinent observations on Western responses to Communist activities in the continent. He defended the role of the Cubans and Soviets and accused the U.S. of using Africa in the Middle East conflict and concluded that "current developments show that the greatest immediate danger to Africa's freedom comes from nations in the Western bloc." The past invasion and current subversion of Angola by U.S.-aided South Africa is a case in point.

Another assertion is that the Soviet invasion of Afghanistan is a first step toward their eventual goal of gaining control of Middle East oil. A look at the map reveals that the Soviets would not need to go through Afghanistan to get to the Persian Gulf. The Soviet Republics of Azerbaijan and Turkmen and the Soviet-controlled Caspian Sea provide much closer and more direct access to Middle East oil fields than the treacherous passes of Afghanistan. The Soviet invasion of Afghanistan can better be explained by purely parochial concerns — political instability in a border country — rather than designs for control of the Gulf. Any presumption of a Soviet "blueprint" for control of Middle East oilfields, moreover, is contradicted by Moscow's alliance with Ethiopia. Ethiopia provoked a split with Somalia and, according to Keith Dunn of the U.S. Army College, the consequence was that the Soviet Union "damaged its geopolitical situation in the Horn of Africa and caused it to lose access to the best port facilities in the area."

Many Pentagon officials concede there is a very low probability of a Soviet drive on the Persian Gulf. What worries them much more, in fact, is an internal conflict or regional dispute that jeopardizes the flow of oil. Afghanistan provided an opportunity for Washington's plan to reassert U.S. military force in the Third World. President Carter pledged to use "any means necessary, including military force," to protect American oil supplies in the Persian Gulf. In an ominous development, the Pentagon has deployed seven cargo ships — filled with equipment, supplies, fuel and water to support a marine amphibious brigade of 12,000 men — in the Indian Ocean, where they will serve as a floating arms depot for combat forces sent to Iran or elsewhere in the area. As we saw in Chapter 1, Washington has also created the Rapid Deployment Force (RDF) which may be used to "deter" conflict — by physically occupying the battlefield before the battle gets fully under way — as well as to counter aggression by others. This non-nuclear equivalent of what might be called a "first-strike" deployment doctrine was unveiled in a little-noticed address by Zbigniew Brzezinski to the Economic Club of Chicago: the RDF, he said, "will give us the capacity to respond quickly, effectively, and even pre-emptively in those parts of the world where our vital interests might be engaged and where there are no permanently stationed American forces." And given the growing tendency of conservative American leaders to exploit the "Soviet threat" issue for political gain, it is increasingly likely that Washington will engage in military "show of force" operations to demonstrate that it has the "will" to "stand up to the Russians" in contested areas abroad. Many top American policy-makers have been contemplating intervention in places like El Salvador, Guatemala, South Yemen, Oman and the Western Sahara.

All in all, the USSR has not built a large empire in the years since 1945. It has failed to control Yugoslavia and Albania; it has lost its influence over and incurred the subsequent enmity of China; it has suffered defeat in Indonesia, a defeat of insurgencies in Malaysia and half a dozen other countries, and loss of influence in Algeria, Sudan and Somalia; it has written off major military and political investments in Iraq, Uganda and Guinea; it has seen the transformation of Egypt into a U.S. ally. The extent of Soviet expansion is much less impressive or daunting compared with the prodigious growth of America's economic reach during these same thirty-five years. Besides, in the struggle to maintain and enlarge its world position and ensure a hospitable environment for American corporations, the United States has resorted to many of the same violent methods of foreign intervention as the Soviet Union. It has also installed or propped up authoritarian governments that are at best different in degree rather than in kind from the Soviet Union's totalitarian satellite and client states.

Since 1945, according to the Brookings Institute, the U.S. has used military force 215 times to gain political or economic ends. Many believe that the U.S. has engaged in such military and economic commitments for the main purpose of preserving freedom and democracy. But the reality is that the top ten recipients of U.S. military and economic aid, according to Amnesty International, are also the world's top ten dictatorships or viola-tors of human rights: South Korea, The Philippines, Indonesia, Thailand, Chile, Argentina, Uruguay, Haiti, Brazil and Iran (under the Shah). Is there any way to justify U.S. support to these governments as "defending freedom"? According to testimony by Senator Alan Cranston, fifty-one countries or 60 per cent of the nations receiving military grants from the U.S. are classified as "repressive regimes." These governments allow U.S. air and naval bases on their soil and offer a "favorable investment climate" for U.S. multinational corporations: low wages, no unions, no strikes, cheap raw materials and no government regulations.

Because the United States has historically been allied with Third World economic "imperialism," and the USSR has not, the tendency has been for liberation struggles in the Third World to turn to the East for military and material aid. These alliances are as much due to a mixture of pragmatism and ideology in the Third World movements themselves as they are the work of Soviet expansionism. The tendency in the West simply to blame Russian meddling for developments in the Third World that are unfavou-rable to Western interests fails to appreciate the legitimate resentment against the West felt increasingly in the less developed countries.

At the same time, the record of Soviet diplomatic successes shows that Third World countries safeguard their own sovereignty. It is very dubious, for example, whether the many African liberation movements that have accepted Soviet arms have by this fact become Soviet satellites. It would be easy to argue from historical precedent that these movements seek nothing so much as national independence and ultimately find themselves hostile to both superpowers. Zimbabwe is an example. After years of bloody civil war, the black majority regime, led by Robert Mugabe, makes it clear that even though it received some military assistance from the Soviets, it seeks close economic relations with and aid from the West. The Angolan regime, likewise, has been recognized by all NATO powers except the United States, and is striving to reduce its links to the Eastern European and Soviet bloc. And although they did everything they could to promote the destabilization of America's model client state in Iran, the Soviets soon discovered that, despite their geographic advantage, the religiously charged upheaval in Iran was as much beyond their control as Washington's.

The bottom line is not very favourable to the Soviet Union. According to the Center for Defense Information headed by Rear Admiral Eugene LaRoque, the USSR can command the allegiance of only nineteen countries (out of 155). The Center's careful 1980 study, "Soviet Geopolitical Momentum," found that Soviet influence, in fact, has actually decreased since the late 1950s and their setbacks dwarf marginal Soviet advances in lesser countries. Robert McNamara, U.S. secretary of defense from 1961 to 1968 serving under Presidents Kennedy and Johnson, concurs:

> I, myself, believe they've gotten weaker. That may sound naive when one says it in the face of what has clearly been an increase in the number of their conventional forces — not nearly as great, by the way, as many say, but still an increase. But I think they've gotten weaker because, economically and politically, there have been some very serious failures. In my opinion, they are in a weaker position today than they were fourteen to fifteen years ago.

Yet, of late, there has been an adventurist turn in Soviet foreign policy. At the same time as it was closing the gap in strategic weaponry, the Soviet Union was also expanding its conventional (i.e., non-nuclear) arsenals. More and more voices can be heard alerting the West to a massive and frightening growth in Soviet naval forces. Again, the extent of this expansion has been exaggerated. Soviet naval growth has been proportionately greater than the West's but started from a much lower base line. Although the Soviet bloc does deploy more submarines, it has fewer nuclear-powered ones than the West, its fleet is technologically inferior, and it lags behind in anti-submarine warfare. The United States has five amphibious assault ships which are gigantic: like small carriers, they weigh 40,000 tons and carry 25 helicopters and 15 VTOL (vertical take-off and landing) planes.

The U.S. has another forty amphibious landing ships which weigh over 10,000 tons. The size of the ship determines its range, that is, the distance and time over which it has the fuel and supplies to operate. With one exception, the largest amphibious landing ships in the Soviet Union weigh 4,000 tons. These small ships are designed to carry landing craft in the enclosed seas near the Soviet Union: the Baltic, the Mediterranean, the Sea of China, and the Sea of Okhotsk. Much of the growth of the Soviet navy has been devoted to protecting its vulnerable nuclear submarines, according to Michael McGwire, an expert on the Soviet navy at the Brookings Institute. Nevertheless, the Soviets have, for the first time ever, created a navy of impressive dimensions. The Soviet navy has been transformed from a coastal defence force into a true ocean-going fleet. The Soviets have built a massive naval force which, according to the authoritative "Janes Fighting Ships" Report for 1980, "goes far beyond the needs of defense of the Soviet sea frontiers."

There is no question that there has been a Soviet naval buildup. The controversial issues have to do with its extent and significance. The Soviets do not have naval military bases abroad to give them the logistical flexibility they need to develop their navy further. They have port facilities in Angola and Vietnam where they can dock and refuel. However, unlike the base in Somalia which the Soviets lost, these are not real bases where they can store weapons, or set up an air bridge to bring in weapons to re-arm the Soviet navy.

Although the Soviets have in recent years been building the Kiev-class aircraft carrier, guided-missile aviation cruisers, and other surface ships designed to project power at a distance or to attack U.S. ocean supply lines to Europe and Japan, they have virtually no capacity to land an expeditionary force by sea. Because of the tremendous expense, the United States is the only country in the world that operates a fleet of aircraft carriers with modern supersonic aircraft. The Soviet navy still lacks true aircraft carriers which can accommodate high-performance combat planes with a deep-penetration attack capability, like the U.S. carrier-borne A-6s and A-7s. The approximately 800 combat planes in the Soviet naval air force are no match for the combined U.S. navy and marine corps airforces which have twice that number of planes and most of which can be launched from aircraft carriers. Soviet air-cargo planes have shorter range and cannot be refuelled in the air. As the U.S. Joint Chiefs of Staff noted in their 1982 "Military Posture Statement," "the lack of sea-based tactical air support greatly limits Soviet ability to carry out amphibious landing against navy opposition." Thus, while there is no doubt that the Soviets have a greater capability for intervention abroad than they had a decade ago, it falls far

short of what the United States can bring to bear and, given Moscow's lack
of true aircraft carriers, could not be used against any well-armed opponent. For these reasons, the Rand Corporation concluded that "gross
Soviet capabilities to project power abroad do not remotely equal the
U.S.'s" and could not sustain an occupation/invasion beyond its own
immediate border-state areas.

The chief object of Soviet naval policy is to counter Western naval
forces. According to a Brookings Institute study: "The primary mission of
the Soviet navy continues to be defensive to protect the Soviet Union from
Western sea-based strike forces and to deter the latter from intervening in
regions, like the middle East, close to Soviet shores." As a result, the high
seas cannot anymore be thought of as an exclusive Western possession.
Soviet naval forces are being used to "show the flag" and demonstrate
Moscow's resolve to protect its new-found allies in Africa and Asia. By
restricting America's capacity to use the threat of force to intimidate Third
World governments, the Soviet navy has deprived Washington of a
favoured instrument of coercion and thus further diminished America's
perceived global power. For instance, the U.S. would probably be more
hesitant to embark on a 1958 Lebanon-style marine landing now that
Western control of the Mediterranean is no longer undisputed.

Concern among NATO policy-makers has been directed at the loss of
"overwhelming authority" on the world's seas and the freedom of action
which went with it. As American military critic Michael Klare has argued:
"It is not western shipping that is threatened by Soviet naval deployments,
but Washington's strategy for continued Western hegemony in remote
Third World areas." All one can say authoritatively at this point is that the
USSR's military buildup (especially after the Soviet-built airbase in South
Yemen is completed) has given it the means to play a global role and
enhanced its ability to further its interests outside Europe. The upshot is
that Moscow can now begin to contemplate the type of action which
Washington has taken for granted for a generation.

The Resurgent American Empire

The dynamics of American foreign policy are quite suggestive. After
Vietnam the U.S. government concluded that it could no longer afford to
pay the cost, economically or politically, of massive military intervention
of the Vietnam type. The American public adopted a "never again" stance
(sometimes called the "Vietnam Syndrome"), barring the use of direct
military force to control Third World conflicts. The shift in America's
relative power position led its leaders to impose much tighter "cost-

effectiveness" controls over the employment of U.S. forces abroad, and, as in the case of Angola, to accede to the loss of marginal interests wherever the political-economic costs of continued involvement outweighed any political gains.

As we saw in Chapter 1, under the Nixon-Kissinger doctrine, many U.S. soldiers were withdrawn from potential combat zones in the Third World while massive shipments of U.S. arms were used to convert selected clients into regional "police" powers. These "surrogate gendarmes" were countries like Iran, Indonesia, Brazil, South Africa, Greece and Israel — countries charged with the responsibility of maintaining order in critical Third World areas. Washington was to be left free, as it was in Chile, to conduct covert operations and destabilization of governments it disapproved of.

In the past few years events have altered the American game plan. Most important was the Iranian revolution of 1978-79, which toppled the Shah and thus shattered the strategy of relying on client states to control the Third World. In March 1979, *Business Week* published a special issue on "The Decline of American Power" which summarized the belligerent outlook shared by influential business and political leaders. "Between the fall of Vietnam and the fall of the Shah," the issue began, "the United States has been buffeted by an unnerving series of shocks that signal an acccelerating erosion of power and influence." And because America's economy is so dependent on foreign markets and raw material, its leaders have become convinced, as *Business Week* put it, that "a reassertion of U.S. influence around the world" is needed to protect "the way of life built since World War II." American leaders have campaigned to reverse the Vietnam Syndrome and to rehabilitate intervention as a legitimate means of coping with domestic "turbulence" in the Third World. And in order to sell America on an interventionist policy it was convenient to heat up the Cold War. American policy-makers differ over the precise boundaries of the United States' core interests — there is some disagreement, for instance, as to whether they include the preservation of white minority rule in South Africa. Most, however, now view the Vietnam Syndrome as an intolerable constraint on U.S. power at a time of growing challenges to American "interests" abroad.

The U.S. government has declared that it intends to reassert its world leadership — in the 1950s sense. "Never since World War II," foreign policy analyst and advisor George Kennan wrote in February 1980, "has there been so far-reaching a militarization of thought and discourse in the capital ... An unsuspecting stranger could only conclude that the last hope of peaceful, non-military solutions had been exhausted — that from now on only weapons, however used, could count."

The world now faces an explosive combination: declining relative American power, increased Soviet military mobility, and rising insurgent popular movements. The danger of a U.S. first strike in some future Third World crisis becomes particularly frightening when we consider the dissimilarities of the present world environment and the world that faced Washington in the early 1960s. First, of course, there is the expansion of Soviet power. While Pentagon rhetoric of the 1960s was no less vehement in its portrayal of the "Soviet threat" than that of the 1980s, the actual military situation was quite different — whereas in 1960 Moscow had almost no capacity to conduct military operations outside of the immediate Soviet bloc, today the USSR has a true ocean-going navy and some air-transport capability. Furthermore, because Soviet territory stretches so deeply into Central Asia, Moscow can move large forces overland to potential conflict zones in the Middle East. And while no one can, at this point, predict Soviet moves in a future African or Middle East crisis, it is obvious that the likelihood of Soviet military involvement must be factored into any calculations of possible conflict. Consequently, there is more temptation for the U.S. to jump the gun. However rational such strategies may appear to Pentagon officials, it is obvious that they increase the risk of nuclear Armageddon. When a crisis arises, the levels of tension and uncertainty on both sides will quickly escalate, making negotiations more difficult while increasing the risk of miscalculation, thus bringing the world closer to the brink. The urge to build "useable" nuclear weapons is the attempt to threaten one's adversary with a limited nuclear attack as a means of preventing that adversary from "overstepping his bounds" elsewhere in the world. Colin Gray of the Hudson Institute, one of the most articulate and forceful members of the school of strategic thought currently dominant in Washington, advocates the MX for precisely these reasons:

> The United States has a fundamental foreign policy requirement that its strategic nuclear forces provide credible limited first-strike options . . . Overall, MX should be thought of as a weapon system that is essential for the support of forward-placed allies, in that supportive limited first-strike options could be threatened credibly, secure in the knowledge that the United States has a residual ICBM force that could deter attack upon itself.

None of the above is to suggest that Washington and Moscow are locked into a rigid timetable for the onset of World War III. Rather it is to say that the world situation now increasingly presents the possibilities for such a conflict. In the long run, peace will only be safeguarded if the division of the world into rival blocs is ended and peoples are allowed to determine their own destinies. So long as empire and hegemonic policies characterize the U.S.-Soviet relationship and their actions in their spheres of influence in the Third World, resistance and the risk of war will remain with us. And so long as a major part of humanity is doomed to starvation and oppression, there can be no real peace.

Conclusion: Towards Disarmament

> Despite of all that has happened, I feel that the questions of war and peace and disarmament are so crucial that they must be given absolute priority even in the most difficult circumstances. It is imperative that all possible means be used to solve these questions and to lay the groundwork for further progress. Most urgent of all are steps to avert a nuclear war, which is the greatest peril confronting the modern world.
>
> Andrei Sakharov
> Soviet dissident

Most of the alarm about the "decline" of American military power rests upon an alleged loss of strategic superiority to the Soviet Union. However, the constant Reagan administration assertion that the United States is inferior to the USSR in overall strategic power is simply not borne out by the facts. Under close scrutiny, much of that assessment has been shown to be based on questionable assumptions, and sometimes on questionable facts, taking individual facts and events out of their larger contexts and ignoring the limits on Soviet power and the setbacks encountered by Moscow. Not only critics of the Pentagon are aware of America's military might. General David C. Jones, past chairman of the Joint Chiefs of Staff, expressed the opinion in his 1980 annual report to Congress that "I would not swap our present military capability with that of the Soviet Union nor would I want to trade the border problems each country faces." When asked if he would consider making such a trade, Jones's successor, General John W. Vessey Jr., simply replied: "Not on your life."

The present is a replay of history, albeit a more dangerous one. The past has been replete with "gaps." There was a bomber gap in the early 1950s that was later proven false — but only after U.S. production of B-52 bombers was well under way. In the late 1950s and early 1960s, the West was warned of a missile gap, and it was later shown to be fictional — but only after the Pentagon had accelerated production of ICBMs and SLBMs. Herbert York, who had been associated with both President Eisenhower

3

The Economics of the Arms Race
Ernie Regehr and Mel Watkins

Military Spending and Human Needs

World military spending has now reached in excess of $600 billion per year, an amount roughly equivalent to the Gross National Product of Latin America or twice that of the continent of Africa. Each passing minute close to $1.5 million is spent on military forces and their equipment. About $100 billion of the annual total is spent on nuclear weapons. Another $50 billion is spent on military research and development and nearly 500,000 scientists and engineers are engaged in that effort.

At the same time, the world economy is in the grip of widespread recession and the poorest half of the world's population (about 2 billion people) struggles to survive on a collective total income that is no more than the world spends for military purposes. In thirty-two countries governments spend more for military purposes than for education and health care combined. Even in the United States, one of the two largest military spenders, one person in seven lives below the poverty threshold, while in the Soviet Union, the other of the two largest military spenders, the infant mortality rate is twice the average of other developed countries.

Canada, though invariably described as a low military spender, in fact ranks within the top 20 per cent of military spenders in the world when measured on a per capita basis. In total terms (in fiscal year 1982-83 Canada's military budget was just over $7 billion), Canada ranks closer to the top 10 per cent, and is within the top third of the top thirty industrial countries in military spending. In recent years Canadian military spending has been increasing at the rate of between 15 and 20 per cent per year, while at the same time the federal government indicates it is considering further cuts in various universal social programs as a means of slowing the rate of

---

This chapter is based in part on an article by Mel Watkins in *This Magazine*, July 1982.

government spending and of controlling what has almost become a run-away budget deficit.

It is tempting to rest one's case against the arms race at this point. Future civilizations will surely judge us harshly for such wanton disregard of real needs — assuming, of course, that we do not by our insanity preclude that judgment ever being made.

One hardly needs to be an economist, then, to recognize the economic effects of the arms race. Those effects are largely matters of common sense, and their proper understanding requires, more than anything else, a concern for humanity. And while the issue has been much neglected by the mainstream of the economics profession, there has nevertheless developed extensive research into the subject, showing that the economic effects of the arms race are uniformly unfavourable and are getting worse. Of course, even if the economic effects of the arms race were somehow favourable, we ought most certainly still to oppose the arms race on moral grounds.

Military Spending as a Public Good

Exercising Consumer Choice

Economists distinguish between private goods, which are purchased by consumers and are presumed to satisfy private needs, and public goods, which are purchased by governments and are presumed to satisfy public needs. Economic orthodoxy regards the supplying of both kinds of goods as reflecting consumer choice, the former as registered via the marketplace and the latter as registered via the ballot box.

Military spending is a public good that is intended to meet the public need of greater security. But, does the consumer, in the case of the public good of military spending, actually get what is paid for? And does he or she actually exercise choice?

As regards the first question, much of the public debate over levels of military spending, in the United States in particular and in Canada as an alliance partner of the U.S., is focused precisely on the question of whether higher levels of military spending do in fact deliver higher degrees of national security. The Reagan administration clearly thinks it does, and the Trudeau government appears to concur. Public opinion polls, on the other hand, suggest that the average consumer has a different view. A fundamental perception that is spreading in Europe and North America is that increased spending, at least on nuclear weapons, decreases, rather than increases, security, a viewpoint argued in Chapter 1. In the fall of 1981, 68 per cent of Americans declared themselves to be in support of a nuclear freeze and Canadians in a large number of muncipalities voted 70 per cent and more in favour of nuclear disarmament (see Chapter 13). The United Nations, in special sessions on disarmament in 1978 and 1982, declared reduced military spending and disarmament to be the most reliable means to security.

In other words, military spending as an economic transaction is in question because there is spreading doubt that the consumer actually receives what he has sought to purchase. Nuclear arms spending, in particular, is increasingly perceived as a peculiar kind of spending such that the less you spend on it, the better off you are. In the memorable words of Nikita Khrushchev (1960): "Missiles are not cucumbers, one cannot eat them, and one does not require more than a certain number in order to ward off an attack."

This raises the second question. Given that consumers are becoming increasingly sceptical that they are getting good value for their taxes in support of military spending, how effective is the ballot box as a means of articulating consumer choice? For example, the popularity of Ronald Reagan at the ballot box can hardly be translated into American support for militarism when the polls just referred to, not to mention the variety of voting motives, are taken into account. Indeed, levels of military spending continue to increase rapidly, in spite of consumer preference clearly being elsewhere.

Furthermore, and notwithstanding economic orthodoxy, it is by no means clear that consumer sovereignty reigns even with respect to private goods; there is much evidence of what can rather be seen as producer, or corporate, sovereignty. Who *really* decides that we need yet another brand of light beer? And when it comes to arms spending as a public good, the case of the reality of corporate control, interlocked as well with state control, is overwhelming. It is what Dwight Eisenhower had in mind, regrettably only at the end of his presidency, when he warned the American people about the existence and power of the military-industrial complex. Decisions about arms spending are essentially the monopoly of the latter.

The implications of this cut deeply, even for the economist. It should be an elementary requirement that public goods have public support. An arms race that proceeds without respect to public opinion ultimately raises the most troubling questions about the existence of democracy.

The American political scientist Alan Wolfe has cast considerable light on the way decisions are actually made with respect to military spending in the U.S. A major element in determining military security needs is the assessment of the "Soviet threat." The nature and extent of the Soviet threat in turn depends substantially upon who makes the assessment — in other words, the Soviet threat rises and falls according to which special interests within the American political economy manage to make their particular perspective the dominant one. Wolfe argues that "in the past, U.S. perceptions of hostile Soviet intentions have increased, not when the Russians have become more aggressive or militaristic, but when certain constellations of political forces have come together within the United States to force the question of the Soviet threat onto the American political agenda." Perceptions of the Soviet threat have peaked on three occasions since World War II: five or six years immediately following the war; at the end of the Fifties and beginning of the Sixties, culminating with the Cuba missile crisis; and the present period since 1976 and the beginning of the anti-SALT II campaign. Domestic political rivalries, presidential competition with Congress, inter-service rivalries, new foreign policy initiatives, and domestic economic policies are the important factors in U.S. perceptions of the Soviet threat.

U.S. perceptions of the Soviet threat impact on Canada both pervasively through the media and specifically through the integration of Canadian military production with that of the U.S. To the extent that weapons technology influences military organization and the perception of conflicts, Canadian reliance upon U.S. weapons systems tends to move the Canadian military establishment towards uncritical acceptance of U.S. descriptions of the strategic environment.

The Military-Industrial Complex

Seymour Melman has described a "new economic system" that he says operates the U.S. war economy. The governing institution is an industrial management network installed in the federal government under the secretary of defense which controls the country's largest network of industrial enterprises. He notes that a list of the 100 largest corporations in the U.S. is essentially also a list of the 100 top military contractors. "With characteristic managerial propensity for extending its powers," says Melman, "limited only by its allocated share of the national product, the new state-management combines peak economic, political, and military decision-making."

Private management extends its sphere of control by means of investing capital, making a profit, and then reinvesting the surplus — thereby adding to its sphere of control and "decision-power," which is the main management objective. State management, however, operates independently of the profit-making procedure, drawing its capital from increased funding from the federal budget. Because the objective of the military-industrial state-management system is to maintain and increase the inflow of capital available for conversion to "decision-power," new spending programs are developed with the needs of the management system in mind, not the equipment needs of the military establishment. Hence, new weapons systems are developed less for some strategic objectives such as security, and more to get funding from the Defense Department budget.

Robert Aldridge, a former aerospace engineer with the Lockheed Corporation, has shown that military contracting is related more to corporate security than to national security. When a particular contract nears completion, and the product is about to be delivered, the company must start looking for future sales prospects. While in the civilian market this might call for an increase in advertising, in the military market the process takes a different twist. Since it is the armed forces who are the customers, it is their interest which must be stimulated. Employees are assigned to discovering new "ventures." An improved version of an existing weapon or even something dramatically new is proposed to the military by the weapons contractor.

In fact, Aldridge says, "with regard to keeping the business going, the weapons industry has learned a lot from Detroit." He examines the progression of sea-based ballistic missiles through yearly (or bi-yearly) model changes. For example, the Polaris A-1 missile with a range of 1,200 nautical miles was lengthened two and a half feet to reach out another 300 miles. It came out two years later as the Polaris A-2 model. Next came the A-3 — still the same diameter but with improved propulsion and triple header bomb-load — and it was deployed after two more years. The next model change enlarged the circumference and carried multiple re-entry vehicles (warheads) which could be directed to different targets.

Weapons strategies are then rewritten to fit the new models, rather than the reverse. The Poseidon, for example, with its multiple independently-targeted re-entry vehicles (MIRVs), was ostensibly needed to confuse Soviet anti-ballistic missile defences. But Pentagon planners foresaw that existing deterrence theory, based on second-strike retaliation against such vulnerable targets as cities and industrial parks, would not hold up as a credible excuse for making fancier weapons. Stronger justification was needed; the Pentagon supplied it, ominously, in the form of a new strategic "counterforce" doctrine, which emphasizes flexible strategic responses and "winning" nuclear war — which implies the first use of nuclear weapons (see Chapter 1).

The military industry would have radically different dimensions if strategic/military considerations were exclusively the basis of production (just as the automobile industry would be radically different if consumer needs, and not the needs of the industry, were the motive for production). The military production corporations do not respond competitively to externally perceived needs; rather, these corporations are the means which Melman's state management uses to gain control over as much of the national budget as possible.

A vast literature on the military-industrial complex in the United States has demonstrated that the mutual interests of the military establishment and the military industry in the United States — both dependent on growing military budgets for their expansion — have led to monopoly control rather than consumer choice in setting both the level and the nature of military spending.

Is the same true for Canada? Clearly, Canada is not possessed of a military-industrial complex after the model of that in the United States. Special circumstances do, however, obtain which exert special influence on both the level and nature of military spending in Canada. In the process, consumer choice in the purchase of the public good of military spending may be just as surely subverted here as it is in the United States.

In 1958, Canada and the United States entered into Defence Production Sharing Arrangements (DPSA) whereby Canadian industry was given essentially unrestricted access to the U.S. weapons market. (Minor restrictions remained and over the years others have been added, but the DPSA remain a kind of "auto pact" in defence trade across the Canada-U.S. border.) Under these arrangements the United States serves as the designer and manufacturer of major weapons systems, and Canada, with a few exceptions, concentrates on supplying components for these U.S.-designed and -built systems. As a result the Canadian military commodities industry is export-oriented and heavily dependent upon a single market.

The Canadian military industry now exports well in excess of $1 billion worth of commodities annually (see Table 1). The industry's significance within the Canadian economy can be measured in a number of ways. As a proportion of the country's Gross National Product (GNP), military production for Canadian use and for export represents less than one-half of one per cent. About 80 per cent of military production in Canada is exported, and this represents about 1.5 per cent of total merchandise exports. Within particular segments of the Canadian economy, however, military production in Canada is rather more significant. As a proportion of total exports of manufactured goods, military-related exports approach 5 per cent, and as a proportion of manufactured goods exported exclusive of trade under the Canada-U.S. auto pact, military-related exports reach 10 per cent. Within particular industries, notably the aircraft and avionics industry, military production is rather more important. The Air Industries

TABLE 1
Canada-United States Defence Production Sharing Procurement
(C$ millions)

	1959-1969	1970	1971	1972	1973	1974	1975	1976	1977	1978	1979	1980	1981
United States Procurement in Canada													
Prime Contracts	1,450.6	105.5	107.5	80.1	115.4	87.0	96.3	74.6	113.1	103.2	194.9	174.1	340.7
Subcontracts	968.2	121.0	108.8	94.9	83.4	63.0	92.2	116.5	201.0	163.8	172.8	307.6	485.9
TOTAL	2,418.8	226.5	216.3	175.0	198.8	150.0	188.5	191.1	314.1	267.0	367.7	481.7	826.6
Canadian Procurement in the United States													
Prime Contracts	579.4	92.1	32.0	49.1	100.1	149.9	83.4	739.9	76.9	137.4	84.5	197.6	507.8
Subcontracts	1,334.4	130.8	148.6	144.4	131.9	131.5	149.3	139.1	222.6	178.2	210.1	291.7	526.0
TOTAL	1,913.8	222.9	180.6	193.5	232.0	281.4	232.7	879.0	299.5	315.6	294.6	489.3	1,033.8

Source: Compiled by Defence Programs Branch, Department of External Affairs.

Association of Canada reports that estimated Canadian aerospace sales in 1982, including aircraft and avionics, were $3 billion, 80 per cent of which were exported. Given military exports of $800 million, roughly one-quarter of total production and one-third of total exports in these industries were military related.

For Canada, the motives for entering the DPSA were and remain essentially commercial. The U.S. market has been a substantial one, and back in 1958 the Canadian government saw the DPSA as an opportunity to recapture some of the hi-tech jobs in the aerospace industry which had been lost through the cancellation of the Avro Arrow, the Canadian-built and -designed jet fighter, and as a chance to improve its balance of payments position. The United States, on the other hand, sought control over continental defence policy, correctly assuming that integration of the military industries of the two countries would ultimately serve the interests of policy integration (some aspects of the industrial integration are discussed in Chapter 5).

In 1963 the two countries added the significant provision that weapons trade between the two countries should be kept in "rough balance." Canada must buy from the United States as much as it sells to the U.S., which means that Canadian access to the U.S. military market is ultimately determined by the extent of Canadian procurement in the United States. Consequently, just as in the United States, the procurement decisions by the Canadian Department of National Defence may not reflect consumer choice via the ballot box as much as the needs of the Canadian weapons industry. The structure of that industry is such that it depends ultimately for its survival on continued access to the U.S. market, and that access in turn depends essentially on continued Canadian procurement in the United States.

For example, during the Vietnam War, Canadian military sales to the United States increased sharply and Canada built up a substantial trade surplus (see Table 1). In the early 1970s, a combination of a decrease in direct U.S. involvement in the war in Vietnam and mounting U.S. international balance of payments deficits led to sharp cutbacks in U.S. military procurement in Canada. The Canadian military commodities industry experienced a serious surplus capacity, and unemployment to go with it, but could not expect to regain substantial access to the U.S. market until Canada had done something to redress the imbalance in trade across the border. Not only did Canada subsequently order major pieces of military equipment from the United States, but in the case of the long-range patrol aircraft, the U.S. put substantial, and now documented, pressure on Canada to buy a particular kind of aircraft. Subsequently, aided by the Reagan arms boom, Canadian sales to the United States have gone up dramatically, increasing by more than 100 per cent (in current dollars) in the two years from 1979 to 1981. While a myriad of factors came together to increase Canadian spending on military equipment (e.g., the aging equipment itself, and NATO pressure to increase overall military spending), the military trade surplus and the importance of offset arrangements in equipment orders suggest that the needs of the weapons industry in Canada, rather than Canadian security needs, are a central factor in deciding government purchases of the public good of military spending.

Military Spending and Productivity

The Economics of Waste

Quite apart from the question of "who decides" and whether the goods purchased (weapons) produce the desired effect (security), there have always been major costs or consequences to arms spending — most obviously, the use (meaning misuse) of scarce scientific, engineering and technical skills, and the allocation (meaning misallocation) of research and development spending. In effect, we have taken the most advanced and potentially productive technological skills of our society and wantonly used them to "produce" unproductive waste. Seymour Melman calls this "the looting of the means of production" and whatever growth results "parasitic economic growth."

True, it is sometimes alleged that military technology creates major benefits for the civilian economy. The evidence, however, suggests the opposite. Military research produces not technology in general but military technology in particular. The fact of the matter is that the concentration of a large proportion of scientific resources on weapons research impoverishes civilian technology.

Ruth Sivard, in her annual survey of *Military and Social Expenditures*, gives us some revealing statistics on this effect, comparing nine developed countries (U.S., U.K., France, West Germany, Sweden, Italy, Denmark, Canada and Japan) in the period 1960 to 1979 with respect to the relationship between military expenditures (as a percentage of GNP) and the annual rate of growth in productivity in manufacturing. What is evident is a striking inverse relationship: the more a country spends on arms, the less productive its economy. Thus Japan had the lowest military expenditures and the best industrial productivity record, while the U.S. and the U.K. had, respectively, the highest and second highest military expenditures matched with the worst and second worst productivity gains.

Of the nine countries, it so happens that the only one that does not fit the pattern is Canada. We had the second lowest military expenditure relative to GNP (tied with Denmark) but the third worst productivity growth. Why does Canada not get the economic gains that might be expected from low resource diversion to the waste of armaments? It is reasonable to infer that the anomaly results in part because the Canadian economy, being closely linked to the American economy, shares in the inefficiency of the latter, which in turn is a consequence of *its* high diversion to the waste of armaments.

Melman cites various specific examples of the "industrial-technological depletion" of the United States caused by virtue of its concentration of technical manpower and capital on military technology and in military industry:

- United States industry operates with an antiquated stock of metal-working machinery.
- No United States railroad has anything in motion that compares with the Japanese trains.
- The United States merchant fleet ranks very low in age of vessels.
- While the United States uses the largest number of research scientists and engineers in the world, key United States industries, such as steel and machine tools, are in trouble in domestic markets, with the U.S. frequently importing more machine tools than it exports.
- U.S. companies have had increasingly to acquire licences to produce European-developed technology in high-technology industries such as chemicals and electrical equipment.

While acknowledging the presence of some "spillover" to civilian areas from technology developed in pursuit of military-oriented goals, Lloyd Dumas points out that what is developed is obviously most strongly influenced by what is sought. Advances in civilian technology, whether they be improved techniques of power generation or food preservation, will typically be found faster and at a much reduced expense if they are pursued directly. It should also be true, incidentally, that if there is spillover from military research that is beneficial for civilian purposes, the opposite should also be true; but, in fact, military planners are most reluctant to depend to any significant degree upon spillover.

Nor has the presence of military production in Canada proven to be a major boon to civilian industrial sophistication. A major part of the Canadian military industry's work is subcontracting to U.S. defence contractors. This implies, and represents in fact, an industry geared to performing short-run tasks according to specifications provided by the U.S.

prime contractor. This tends to preclude indigenous design and development of commodities that can ultimately go into mass production and then compete, on the basis of lower per-unit production costs, in an international market.

If we had data on the Soviet economy analogous to that for capitalist economies, there is no doubt it would fit the overall pattern being outlined here. Specifically, it would show that the Soviet Union had a higher ratio of military expenditure to GNP *and* a lower rate of productivity growth than any of the nine countries mentioned above. As Emma Rothschild of MIT has written: "The Soviet economy, of course, is a poor example of the economic benefits of militarization." Ruth Sivard points out that it has been estimated that the U.S. and the Soviet Union, the top two military powers, rank seventh and twenty-third respectively among 141 nations in economic-social standing. "History's most expensive arms race," she tells us, "contrasts with the steady deterioration of the civilian economy. Both military superpowers, tied up in an intense arms competition, have lost status in the commercial market, as well as within their own military alliances." Or as Lord Zuckerman, former chief scientific advisor to the British government, has put it: "The arms race is a luxury which not even the superpowers can afford any longer."

The contradictions that manifest themselves in the American economy are only too evident. The United States has the technical capacity to end Western civilization tomorrow but cannot produce a car competitive with Japanese imports. The syndicated American columnist, Nicholas von Hoffman, in reviewing the movie *The Deer Hunter*, invited us to contrast the ultramodern military technology used to fight the war in Vietnam (this was even more evident in *Apocalypse Now*) with the ancient steel mill in Pennsylvania, shown in the early part of the movie, that looked like a relic from Britain's Industrial Revolution.

The result of all this is summarized by Sivard: "In striking contrast to the robust expansion of military force is the pervasive malaise of the world economy." If arms spending was good for the economy, why hasn't there been a recovery since the mid-Seventies and into the Eighties in the midst of the new arms boom? This is no rhetorical question, given the reality of Ronald Reagan and his commitment both to increase U.S. military spending and to get the U.S. economy moving again, to re-industrialize America. He is already delivering on the former; we await the latter.

Emma Rothschild sees the military industries as the leading sector of the U.S. economy in the long period of expansion from the Forties to the Seventies. In effect, during this period, the economic costs of militarism were not intolerable. But, she argues, this expansion spent itself, becoming unproductive (in ways already argued). Rather than moving on, however, the U.S. has intensified arms spending. Even before Reagan was elected, Rothschild wrote ominously: "The U.S. may buy itself two things with its $1 trillion defense budget of 1981 to 1985. The first is an economic decline of the sort that comes about once or twice in a century. The second is nuclear war."

Mary Kaldor sees modern weapons systems as "baroque," dysfunctional even on their own terms (like the breakdown of the American helicopters in the Iran hostage fiasco) and, further, dysfunctional for the economy. She specifies how the latter happens:

> Baroque military technology artificially expands industries that would otherwise have contracted. It absorbs resources that might otherwise have been used for investment and innovation in newer, more dynamic industries. And it distorts concepts of what constitutes technical advance, emphasising elaborate custom-built product improvements that are typical of industries in the decline instead of the simpler mass-market process improvements which tend to characterise industries in their prime.

She draws a powerful conclusion: "It has thus contributed to the slowdown of capital investment and productivity growth and to the gradual degeneration of the American economy."

Arms and Jobs

To speak of the economic effects of the arms race is necessarily to conjure up, immediately and properly, the issue of jobs. It is an issue that matters so very much to people, particularly today when there is already such widespread unemployment. As we have just seen, in the longer term, job creation is adversely affected by the impact of military spending on the productivity of the civilian economy and thereby on the overall growth of the economy. Nevertheless, it will be insisted, military spending must, in immediate terms, surely create jobs.

Indeed, there has been an undeniable correlation historically between arms spending and economic prosperity. The Great Depression of the Thirties was ended by World War II. This conflict was followed with indecent haste by the Cold War. We are entitled to note that the brief interlude between the two was marked by a successful conversion to a peacetime economy. Still, what was never tested was the ability of the system, and specifically the American capitalist system, continuously to generate full employment without military spending. The real economic philosophy that emerged from this economic upheaval of the Thirties was not so much about more public spending in general as about more arms

spending in particular; Keynesianism as a theory became military Keynesianism in practice. Perhaps that is why Richard Nixon was able to say as
president that "we are all Keynesians now." Certainly, even Ronald Reagan — we should say, above all Ronald Reagan — very much likes that
version of Keynesianism.

But, it will be objected, while spending on arms creates jobs, so — to use
what was once a favourite example of the conservative mind — would
digging holes and filling them in. This is true: any kind of spending creates
jobs. The essential point, however, is that some kinds of spending are more
efficient than others in creating jobs. How does arms spending rank in that
regard?

A U.S. study by the Michigan Public Interest Research Group (PIR-
GIM), "The Empty Pork Barrel: Unemployment and the Pentagon,"
found that military spending creates *unemployment* rather than *employment*. Spending on weapons is highly capital intensive and draws spending
away from sectors of the economy that are labour intensive. An analysis of
the years 1968 through 1972 indicated that the net annual job loss nation-
wide, when the military budget averaged about $80 billion per year, was
about 840,000 jobs. This resulted from the negative impact of military
spending upon major sectors of the U.S. economy: durable goods, non-
durable goods, residential and non-residential construction, state and local
government expenditures, services, exports, imports, federal civil purchases, and producers of durable equipment. It was found that when
spending on the military went up, expenditures on these civilian categories
went down by certain definite percentages. During the period under
review, twenty-six states, containing 60 per cent of the U.S. population, lost
more jobs than they gained from military spending. Every major industrial
state in the nation, with only the exceptions of Texas and California, lost
jobs — most very heavily. New York alone suffered a net loss of 426,000
jobs. Michigan, Illinois and Ohio together lost 492,000 jobs. Most of the
New England, all of the Middle Atlantic, and all of the North Central states
lost heavily. These losses occurred in spite of the fact that some of these
states had substantial military contracts and large military bases. The
negative impact of Pentagon spending upon their industrial base far outweighed the jobs they gained through military contracts and bases. The
loss in employment was most pronounced in highly industrialized areas
that did not have large numbers of bases and therefore not many military
personnel stationed there. "In addition to the reallocative effects of military spending," says the PIRGIM report, "there is also the fact that for
every dollar spent in that direction there are fewer jobs created than if the
money were spent by consumers and the private sector including state and

local government. Where military expenditures go for military hardware, the labor input is a small component compared to the product of civilian goods and services."

Whether the cut meant that money went from military contracts to civilian industry, or that military personnel were cut and state and local government had a rise in employment, a reallocation would mean a net increase of jobs for the economy. Another American study of the direct and indirect effects on employment of $1 billion of spending showed spending on the military yields a pay-off of 76,000 jobs, compared with 100,000 for construction, 139,000 for health services, 187,000 for education, and 112,000 for tax cuts to consumers.

A recent study by Stuart Elliott using U.S. Commerce Department figures indicates that employment in U.S. defence industries declined by 25,000 from January 1981 to June 1982. During the same period of military spending increases, the number of military personnel increased by 45,000 and civilian personnel in the Defense Department increased by 78,000 — making an overall net increase in employment of 98,000. Defence spending during the same period increased by $33 billion, which means that only one new defence-related job was created for every $330,000 spent. If, by generous estimate, one were to conclude that another 200,000 jobs were indirectly created by the military buildup, it would still mean that each new job costs about $100,000.

In Canada military production, and in particular military exports, are lauded as important job-creation enterprises. But the example of Canada's single largest military export sale is less than convincing. In 1982, General Motors of Canada, with the benefit of a minimum of $26 million in grants and interest-free loans from the federal government, received a contract to supply at least 900 light armoured vehicles (LAV) for the U.S. armed forces for $625,000,000 (Canadian). Company officials say that the contract has Canadian content of about 30 per cent (the rest is imported components from the United States), which will mean a net export of about $187,500,000. Because Canada-U.S. military trade must be kept in rough balance according to the DPSA, the export of $187,500,000 in military commodities to the United States ultimately means the import of military goods of the same value.

The contract, again according to company officials, will generate 3,500 direct man-years of work in Canada, with additional jobs being created among Canadian suppliers of components and other materials. It is interesting to calculate the amount of public expenditures required to generate these 3,500 direct jobs. In the first instance there are the Defence Industry Productivity grants of $26 million paid to the company (or about $7,500 of public money per job). In addition, the contract will generate $187,500,000 worth of military (i.e., non-productive or, in economic terms, waste) equipment imports from the United States (or about $53,000 per job). Clearly, the sale represents major public expenditures, directly through grants and indirectly through increased military procurement, in exchange for relatively few jobs. The same funds properly channelled directly into the Canadian economy could be expected to generate more jobs.

Rather than saying that arms spending creates jobs, we say that, relative to alternatives, arms spending destroys jobs — and that way of looking at things, in terms of forgone opportunities, is the correct way to assess the employment impact of any kind of spending.

The economics of waste manifests itself not just in stifling productivity and job growth: We will now turn to some of the other effects, in particular those arising from Canada's military-industrial integration with the U.S.

Reaganomics

Yet another way in which arms spending destroys jobs has become manifest in very recent years; some commentators believe that it may haunt us for some time. It is an aspect of the particular mix of policies that flows from Washington that has been dubbed Reaganomics. It consists of very high interest rates that choke off economic growth, pushing the economy into recession and creating a crisis of unemployment.

Why the high interest rates? One plausible explanation runs in terms of the massive U.S. federal government deficit at the same time as Washington is committed to fighting inflation through restraint. In the context of what is really an *easy* or loose fiscal policy, all the burden of that restraint falls on monetary policy. The result is very *tight* monetary policy, meaning high interest rates.

But why the large deficit? The biggest single reason is the increase in military spending in the U.S., which is currently running at an annual growth rate in *real* terms (after allowing for inflation) of 11 per cent. No other factor so clearly contributes to the abnormally high interest rates that, in turn, bear the chief responsibility for the protracted recession of the early 1980s. High interest rates crippled the American economy. Canadian policy-makers made Canadian interest rates follow the American rates upwards and crippled the Canadian economy.

As we write (in early 1983), there has been at least a momentary reprieve in interest rates — instead of being ridiculously high they are now simply high — and it may be, though this is far from certain, that the American and Canadian economies are now moving into a recovery phase. But the best guarantee, perhaps the only guarantee, that interest rates in the U.S., and hence in Canada, will not rise again and force us into another recession, if not a real depression, is a cut in arms spending in the U.S.

Richard Lipsey of Queen's University, a very distinguished mainstream economist, speaking at a *Financial Post* Conference in the latter part of 1982, described what he called "one possible scenario for disaster." It consisted, he said, of much bigger deficits in the U.S., resulting from arms spending, that could push us back to 20 per cent-plus interest rates, and down into a deep depression. He concluded that the U.S. *must* cut back on arms spending. An increasing number of American economists are saying the same thing: that military spending is growing at several times the rate that tax revenues can possibly be expected to grow; that as recovery begins, the increasing private demand for funds will have to compete with escalating demands from the public sector to finance the deficit; and that interest rates will rise, choke off the recovery, and recreate the recession, or worse.

Foreign Ownership

At first glance the Canadian military industries' export orientation appears to make them an exception to the branch plant Canadian pattern, in which the manufacturing sector (particularly that part of it that is foreign owned) tends to be largely confined, by its inefficiency, to servicing the domestic market. Through the Defence Production Sharing Arrangements, however (as with the provisions of the auto pact), the U.S. market has essentially been redefined as a domestic market, in which Canadian-based firms, regardless of nationality of ownership, receive government assistance to help them compete with U.S.-based firms. Just as tariffs have the effect of protecting particular products and markets, and not Canadian-owned firms per se, the DPSA protects a market, not an indigenous industry.

Figures are currently unavailable to measure the extent to which Canadian military sales to the U.S. under the DPSA are actually carried out by subsidiaries of U.S. companies. It is probable, however, that the DPSA actually reinforce trends towards U.S. ownership. If a U.S. parent firm sets up a subsidiary in Canada, it receives Defence Industry Productivity grants from the Canadian government to cover certain retooling and pre-production costs; it then supplies components to the parent, in the process maintaining low levels of taxable income in Canada through payments by the subsidiary to the parent of special licence and management fees and through special pricing arrangements.

Balance of Payments

Another unfavourable characteristic of Canada's manufacturing sector may also be duplicated in the DPSA. Canadian manufacturing in general, and foreign firms in particular, as the authors of the Science Council's study report *The Weakest Link* have noted, receive large flows of manufactured components and production equipment from U.S. suppliers. The implications for Canada's balance of trade are obvious and similar consequences obtain in military trade.

Although Canada did, during the late Sixties and early Seventies, build up a substantial trade surplus with the U.S. in high-technology military commodities, the 1963 agreement that there should be a "rough balance" in trade under the DPSA meant that the U.S. would make special efforts to eliminate the trade surplus and restore the balance. This not only increased pressure on Canadian defence procurement, it also effectively precluded the use of the DPSA to redress Canada's overall imbalance in manufacturing trade. In fact, a foreign exchange loss due to military procurement may be effectively institutionalized through the DPSA. According to the 1974 Canada Input/Output model, Canadian production in aerospace and electronics (where military production in Canada is concentrated), generates, on average, direct and indirect imports of about 20 per cent of the value of production. Since the indirect imports, comprising roughly one-third of the total, are not tabulated in the DPSA trade proper that is to be kept in balance, they represent *additional* imports that constitute a permanent foreign exchange drain as long as the DPSA trade is itself in balance.

A more specific illustration of this import dependence was provided by an advertisement placed in a Canadian financial newspaper by Lockheed Corporation announcing that since its receipt of the contract to supply new long-range patrol aircraft to the Canadian armed forces, Bristol Aerospace of Winnipeg had already begun work on wing components. The ad pointed out that "the tools and fixtures needed to help build key elements of Aurora's wings have reached Bristol Aerospace Ltd. in Winnipeg from one of Lockheed's subcontractors in the U.S." The deal to purchase long-range patrol aircraft from the United States involved not only the import of the aircraft itself, but also the import of equipment and components in order to permit Canada to participate in industrial offsets.

Industrial Truncation

Industrial truncation (i.e., the capability to carry out only specific limited functions within the total range of functions required in order to develop, produce and market a product) is part of the design of the DPSA. An informal element of the DPSA was the concession by Canada to permit a specialized division of labour between the arms industries of the two countries. Following the cancellation of the Avro Arrow, Canada was inclined to conclude that, given American refusal to buy major weapons systems from foreign sources and given the fact that Canadian armed forces requirements could not on their own sustain the massive outlays for research and development required to design, develop and build major weapons systems, the domestic weapons industry would be most viable if it specialized. This led to a Canadian emphasis upon the production of components for American-designed systems. As a result, the U.S. Department of Defense became the *de facto* design authority for the Canadian defence industry, the latter producing military commodities to American DOD specifications. As one Canadian official put it: "In order to have a defence industry you have to have a Department of National Defence that does its own planning and that puts out military specifications." But after 1959 military planners in Canada could not plan their own requirements because they were committed to buying off-the-shelf from the U.S. There are in effect now few Canadian requirements to which the Canadian industry must work; rather, it must meet American requirements.

Government Subsidies

The Canadian arms industry is also substantially dependent upon government funding for research, development, plant modernization and retooling. Of grant programs administered by the Department of Industry, Trade and Commerce and the Department of National Defence during the ten years ending with fiscal year 1977-78, 46 per cent were explicitly designed to serve the weapons industry. So-called defence pre-production grants throughout the 1970s amounted to about 15 per cent of total arms sales, although this does understate the yield of military research since it ignores civilian sales that result from these grants.

In response to the contract to purchase a new fighter aircraft, the Air Industries Association declared a need for substantial increases in government support if Canadian industry was to participate fully in the new fighter aircraft subcontracts. Subsequently, funding under the Defence Industry Productivity program has been increased threefold to about $150 million per year.

Military Spending and the Economic Fate of the West

It has been said that the revival of the Cold War is highly functional for the U.S. (and for the Soviet Union), especially as a way to keep the American economy going. A Western government wanting to get the economy moving again cannot get involved in useful production; that, says Noam Chomsky, is to be reserved for private enterprise. That leaves waste production. But how do you get taxpayers to pay for waste? Till now, the answer has been to confine spending to a particular kind of waste, namely armaments, while alleging that it is not waste at all by spooking the hell out of us with stories of Soviet superiority.

This record has been played for a long time, virtually since the end of World War II. In spite of heavy military spending, somehow the most urgent priority remains more military spending. At some point we have to face the fact that heavy military spending has tended to create a militaristic society that, by its nature, denies (and increasingly so) the possibilities of pacific spending alternatives.

Of course, it comes as no surprise that certain elements within an economy benefit from the production of military commodities. And that in turn raises the larger question of the relationship between military spending and the maintenance of the capitalist West. Growth in production, according to some critics of capitalism, leads to an excessive production capacity that soon outstrips aggregate demand, causing the rate of profits to fall. Military spending is said to be well-suited ideologically to be used as a corrective measure because it effectively raises aggregate demand and profit rates. In addition, while military spending consumes the system's economic surplus, this appropriated surplus is not then used by the state to enter into competition with private capital; rather, it is effectively removed from the system, thereby permanently dealing with capitalism's propensity to create surplus capacity that outstrips demand.

But, we have argued here, the economic effects of military spending are uniformly unfavourable for Western economies. Is there any way to square these views? One way is to focus on the *strategic* rationale for military spending, namely, that the vital strategic interests of a hegemonic power, like the United States, demand high levels of military spending in order to maintain that hegemony abroad and, ultimately, to maintain order at home. For it will be evident from a moment's thought that this strategic logic contains a powerful economic rationale. Indeed, Harry Magdoff argues convincingly that in the U.S., national security and commercial interests have merged to the point of being indistinguishable. The size of the "free" world, he says, and the degree of its "security," define the geographic boundaries where capital is relatively free to invest and trade. Military power, including overseas military bases, serves these merged security and commercial interests in a variety of ways: by protecting present and potential sources of raw materials, safeguarding foreign markets and investments, protecting commercial sea and air routes, and establishing spheres of influence in which U.S. business enterprises enjoy a competitive advantage.

This perspective, however, only highlights the fundamental contradiction for the American economy: high levels of military spending undermine the strength of the economy via mechanisms previously argued, while that same economy ultimately depends for its continued strength on high levels of military spending in order to protect such vital strategic interests as access to foreign sources of raw materials and energy and access to foreign markets for American goods.

It needs to be noted that the same fundamental contradiction is characteristic of the Soviet economy. While there is much that distinguishes the United States and the USSR, both are hegemonic powers pursuing strategic interests and both spend massively to "deter" the other. Consequently, both have high levels of military spending that are also destructive of their economies.

In Canada this contradiction manifests itself in the integration of Canadian arms spending and production with that of the U.S. through military alliances. That integration, in turn, is destructive of the pursuit of autonomous Canadian economic and political interests.

Military Spending, Degeneracy and the Logic of Exterminism

The massively expensive weapons systems favoured by the West are, in the language of Mary Kaldor, increasingly baroque, gargantuan (like the MX missile system), inflexible and dysfunctional — except in risking a holocaust, if one can think of that as functional! For Kaldor, this degeneracy of the weapons system has fuelled a broader degeneracy. With regard to both the U.S. and the Soviet Union, she writes:

> In the past, the armament sector may have worked quite well in blunting some of the contradictions in each society. This is no longer true. The declining military effectiveness and growing cost of armament are gradually undermining the political weight of the superpowers and sapping their economic strength. The crisis of the armament sector has thrown up new forms of conflict and protest. New political and economic rivalries in the West, and the consumer dissatisfaction, dissidence and increased repression in the Soviet Union are all elements of a wider breakdown of the postwar international system of which the armaments sector is a vital part.

For E.P. Thompson, the economic effects of the arms race must be seen within the context of what he calls "the deep structure of the Cold War." Wars, and Cold Wars, are about violence. Deterrence is repressed violence, preferable of course to real violence, but not without its terrible consequences. Being repressed, not actualized externally, the violence works its way back into the internal system. "Superpowers which have been locked for thirty years in the posture of military confrontation increasingly adopt militaristic characteristics in their economies, their polity and their culture." The same point is made by former Swedish Minister of Disarmament Alva Myrdal: "The competitive race between the two superpowers has steadily escalated, and the militarization of the economy and national life of almost all countries has intensified." She has called for an end to the arms race so as "to bar a complete militarization of the whole world," a not unrealistic possibility when consideration is given as well to the frightening proliferation of nuclear weapons. The "logic" of all this is, in the powerful language of Thompson, "the logic of exterminism." It is that spectre that has now been forced to our consciousness, in all its awesome and awful dimensions, by Jonathan Schell's *The Fate of the Earth*.

What is constantly at risk, in the face of this terrifying technology, is the closing of the circle, the curtailment of freedom, perhaps ultimately the loss of all life. A leading economic effect of the arms race is the Western military-industrial complex centred in the United States — and whatever you want to label it in the Soviet Union. These then become the cause of further arms production. And so on. Years ago C. Wright Mills said it all: "The immediate cause of World War III is the preparation for it."

But there is hope exactly because this logic of exterminism cannot avoid creating its own contradictions. The arms race is causing more and more people to see the enormity of what is at risk, and following E.P. Thompson, to proclaim: "We must protest if we are to survive." If enough of us do that, we will find a growing interest not only in understanding the economics of armament but also its necessary sequel, that reverse side of the coin, the economics of disarmament.

These are troubled times in terms of the shape of the economy and the prospect for jobs. They are also troubled times because of the very real possibility of a nuclear holocaust. This is surely a surfeit of bad news. The thrust of this chapter, however, is that these two pieces of bad news, if properly put together from a disarmament perspective, become good news. That good news is that less arms spending, a movement towards disarmament, would be both good for peace and good for the eonomy. The case for disarmament is doubly compelling.

References

Dumas, Lloyd. "Economic Conversion, Productive Efficiency and Social Welfare." *Journal of Sociology and Social Welfare*, Winter 1977.

Kaldor, Mary. *The Baroque Arsenal*. New York: Hill and Wang, 1981.

Melman, Seymour. *The Permanent War Economy: American Capitalism in Decline*. New York: Simon and Schuster, 1974.

Regehr, Ernie. *Making a Killing: Canada's Arms Industry*. Toronto: McClelland and Stewart, 1975.

Regehr, Ernie. *The Utilization of Resources for Military Purposes in Canada and the Impact on Canadian Industrialization and Defence Procurement*. United Nations Document 80-15587, 1980.

Rothschild, Emma. "Boom and Bust." *New York Review of Books*, April 3, 1980.

Watkins, Mel. "An Economist Looks at the Arms Race." *This Magazine*, July 1982.

4

The European Disarmament Movement
Mark Abley

> Wars commence in our culture first of all, and we kill each other in euphemisms and abstractions long before the first missiles have been launched...
> The deformed human mind is the ultimate doomsday weapon — it is out of the human mind that the missiles and the neutron warheads come.
>
> E.P. Thompson[1]

It began in the fall of 1979, and since then it has become the most vocal and dynamic movement on the European continent. The small nations were the seedbed. Within six weeks in 1979, a peace campaign in Norway gathered 69,000 signatures for disarmament. On 24 November 1979, more than 20,000 people marched through the streets of Utrecht to protest against any deployment of new nuclear missiles in the Netherlands. Two weeks later, nearly 70,000 marched in Brussels. In Belgium and the Netherlands, the Christian pacifist organization known as Pax Christi has enjoyed considerable support for many years. But these early protests were in vain, for on 12 December 1979, NATO decided to "modernize" its nuclear armoury. At that meeting West Germany formally agreed to take 108 Pershing II missiles, as well as 112 Tomahawk cruise missiles; Britain promised to accept 160 cruise missiles; Italy agreed to harbour ninety-six cruise missiles, and Belgium and Holland forty-eight each. NATO's warlike decision had an unforeseen effect, however: the peace movement did not look back.

It was a warlike decision because that innocuous verb, "modernize," fails to describe weapons that are qualitatively new. Cruise and Pershing II missiles will, so the argument goes, fill a gap in the NATO arsenal; as of early 1983 NATO had no land-based missiles with a range greater than 1,000 miles. The new Soviet missiles known as SS-20s, and their old SS-4s

An earlier version of part of this chapter was published in *Canadian Forum*, August 1981.

and SS-5s, fit this category, and the NATO weapons are now said to be needed to counter the threat posed by the SS-20. Yet the official justifications and warnings are selective: they provide only a fragment of the truth. Aside from its large number of short-range missiles, NATO has chosen to rely on long-range bombers and on missiles launched from virtually invulnerable submarines. Indeed the English economist Dan Smith, using information from the International Institute for Strategic Studies in London, found the apparent gap in NATO's arsenal to be a carefully nourished illusion. By some adroit work with statistics, Smith could even claim that "NATO has a numerical superiority... in precisely that category into which Tomahawk cruise missiles and Pershing IIs will fit."[2] But the outrage that followed the NATO decision to "modernize" had little to do with such quantitative analysis. Europeans know that their continent is already encrusted with weapons (the nuclear explosives that are permanently kept in Britain alone have a power equal to about 200 million tons of TNT) and for many people in 1979 and 1980 the threat of cruise missiles served primarily as a spur, a catalyst that helped them break out of weariness and bitter resignation.

Cruise missiles and Pershings IIs have no defensive capacity. They are lethal offensive weapons that carry the arms race one stage further. For, whereas the SS-20s can reach nowhere near the U.S., the new NATO missiles can penetrate deep into Soviet territory, and the Pershing II will be able to hit Russian targets less than five minutes after launching. It's not surprising, then, that the USSR has been worried by NATO's decision to deploy these weapons in Europe; from the Soviet point of view, they would change the whole nature of the nuclear balance in Europe. But the people of Western Europe are worrying too: "The tactical nuclear weapon would be employed in the view of NATO to limit the war to Europe. Europe is to be transformed into a 'nuclear Maginot line' for the defence of the United States."[3] These are the words of Nino Pasti, an Italian senator and a former deputy supreme commander for NATO nuclear affairs. Rear Admiral Eugene LaRocque, a former strategic planner in the Pentagon, puts it even more bluntly: "We fought World War I in Europe, we fought World War II in Europe, and if you dummies let us, we'll fight World War III in Europe."[4] In the eyes of American planners, the new missiles enhance the possibility of a limited nuclear war, a war from which U.S. territory would escape undamaged. Neutron bombs and other "mini-nukes" offer similar possibilities. A war confined to the European "theatre" has understandable appeal for Pentagon strategists; the appeal is not so obvious for residents of Europe.

Acceptance of a theatre war in Europe is the logical result of a gradual change in United States policy over the past twenty years. In the 1960s, American planners tended (publicly, at least) to admit that any nuclear war with the USSR would cause slaughter on both sides, and that efforts to limit its scope stood little chance of success. But as President Nixon remarked in his State of the World address in 1971, the U.S. needed to develop "alternatives appropriate to the nature and level of the provocation... without necessarily having to resort to mass destruction."[5] As we saw in Chapter 1, the technological advances in weaponry have created such alternatives, in the shape of precise military options, so that nowadays the "unthinkable" is constantly programmed. While President Kennedy once pledged that the U.S. would never again initiate the use of nuclear weapons in war, NATO's strategy of "flexible response" relies on a readiness to do exactly that, and successive U.S. presidents have refused a no-first-use pledge. Nuclear war has come out of the closet. Yet is the USSR willing to accept the altered rules of this monstrous game? Lawrence Freedman, director of policy studies at the Royal Institute of International Affairs, has (with no sense of irony) commented: "Recent moves in NATO have encouraged plans for selective, discrete strikes rather than all-out exchanges.... Unfortunately, the Soviet Union has shown little interest in Western ideas on limited nuclear war."[6]

That Soviet reluctance is understandable. Fortunately or unfortunately, the USSR is a European as well as an Asiatic state, and any theatre war that wiped Moscow and Leningrad off the stage forever would be, for the Soviets, not so much an edifying morality play or a black comedy as the climax of a tragedy. We might also consider a warning issued by Lord Zuckerman, formerly the chief scientific advisor to the government of Britain: "I do not believe that nuclear weapons could be used in what is now fashionably called a 'theatre war'. I do not believe that any scenario exists which suggests that nuclear weapons could be used in field warfare between two nuclear states without escalation resulting. I know of several such exercises. They all lead to the opposite conclusion."[7]

Cruise and Pershing II missiles, scheduled for deployment in late 1983, would undoubtedly increase the destructive power of NATO. Together with America's MX system, they threaten the Soviet Union with a devastation more absolute and immediate than it has ever faced. But power and security mean very different things. New Zealand and the Malagasy Republic are a trifle less powerful than the U.S.; they are also a good deal more secure, for they don't have thousands of nuclear warheads aimed at their territory. In this sense the new missiles threaten the security of Western Europe, for they increase the probability that, if nuclear war begins elsewhere on the earth, Europe would immediately be caught up in it. As the prime minister of Sweden, Olof Palme, has observed: "A war can simply be transported here, even though actual causes for war do not exist. Here there is a ready theatre for war. Here there have been great military forces for a long time. Here there are programmed weapons all ready for action."[8] The campaigners for European disarmament are convinced that only a massive reduction in weaponry can lead to true security, the security that grants the continent a future.

The New Impetus for Disarmament

Europe has seen various proposals for disarmament during the past thirty years. In 1956 the foreign secretary of Poland, Adam Rapacki, took to the UN General Assembly a plan to outlaw nuclear weapons from Czechoslovakia, Poland, East Germany and West Germany; NATO rejected the scheme (for failing to limit non-nuclear or "conventional" weapons, and for doing nothing to re-unify Germany). Other Polish initiatives in 1958, 1962 and 1964 were also turned down. Until recently the most promising scheme for regional disarmament came from Scandinavia, which sought to establish a nuclear-free zone in the Baltic. Sweden and Finland are neutral already, while Norway and Denmark, despite their membership of NATO, have refused to allow nuclear weapons to be stationed on their soil in peacetime. Many Scandinavians hope that if these nations were to agree to dismantle all nuclear stockpiles and bases, the USSR would agree to remove missiles aimed at the region from its own Baltic territory. However, the discovery of a nuclear-tipped Soviet submarine in Swedish waters in 1982 quenched much of the enthusiasm for the idea. At present there is more hope of establishing a nuclear-free zone in the Balkans, thanks to the 1981 election victory of the socialist party PASOK in Greece, whose prime minister, Andreas Papandreou, is a public supporter of the international peace movement. On three occasions in the past, Romanian proposals to "de-nuclearize" the Balkans have come to nothing; with PASOK in power in Greece, agreement may not be far away. Such a move might seem to count for little (though not to residents of Romania, Greece, Bulgaria and Yugoslavia); but if progress towards disarmament is really to be attained, such piecemeal gestures may well be the most effective means.

The impetus for a formal campaign for European nuclear disarmament (END) came primarily from Britain, where the Thatcher government's ardent support for cruise missiles caused rapid, widespread anger. The most prominent figure in the movement has been E.P. Thompson (author of *The Making of the English Working Class*, *Writing By Candlelight* and many other books), a historian who, in his radical iconoclasm and his moral fury, strikes many people as a kind of Cobbett or Orwell for our time. Thompson, however, has resisted attempts in the press to cast him as an overseer or godfather of the END movement. The campaign needs to adapt to local pressures and local causes; it requires local leaders. Yet through all the languages of Europe it shares a vision: a continent free of nuclear weapons, a continent of peace.

The initial appeal was launched on 28 April 1980. "We must," it says, "commence to act as if a united, neutral and pacific Europe already exists. We must learn to be loyal, not to 'East' or 'West', but to each other, and we must disregard the prohibitions and limitations imposed by any national state."[9] By September, hundreds of signatories had been found in twenty-six countries (mostly European, but with representatives from Japan, Australia, Canada and the U.S.). Perhaps most important, the appeal quickly gained signatories in Poland, Czechoslovakia, Hungary (Andras Hegedus, a former prime minister) and the USSR (Roy Medvedev, a dissident historian). For the campaign will stand no chance of success if it cannot eventually influence policies in the Warsaw Pact nations as well as NATO; the Pentagon is not the only source of nuclear escalation. As E.P. Thompson has written: "To allow the Western peace movement to drift into collusion with the strategy of the [Soviet-influenced] World Peace Council — that is, in effect, to become a movement opposing NATO militarism *only* — is a recipe for our own containment and ultimate defeat." [10] Despite the geographical presence of Russia on the continent of Europe, END tacitly excludes the Soviet Union from its immediate campaign; by promoting a zone of peace "from Poland to Portugal," it hopes to hasten eventual reconciliation between the superpowers as well.

The uneven growth of the European peace movements since 1979 has been very much a reflection of differences in the national political cultures. In France, for example, relatively little headway has been made, as all the main political parties are determined to maintain the country's independent nuclear force. It might also be observed that hostility to the peace movement among the media has been unusually pronounced in France (even in reputable journals such as *Le Monde*) and that the French are notoriously suspicious of any movement which they see as coming their way from Germany. But in many countries, progress has been little short of spectacular. Demonstrations held in four nations in 1981 (Italy, Holland, Britain and West Germany) were each attended by more than a quarter of a million people. In Norway, Britain, Iceland and other parts of northern Europe, peace campaigners have managed to create alliances among groups who might normally have little in common: doctors, feminists, liberals, church people, socialists and so on. The peace movements of southern Europe tend to be structured in a more directly political way, close to the usual party lines; what they gain in cohesiveness over their northern counterparts, they perhaps lose in a narrowness of base. In short, the continent's peace campaigners suffer from formidable difficulties of unity and structure; END is more an idea than an organization. Alternatively, it is the dream towards which many organizations strive.

The national movements share certain problems as well as certain goals. One charge regularly made against peace workers is that they are giving comfort and joy to the Soviet Union; indeed, NATO apologists and politicians of the right have often claimed that the peace movements are in the pay of the KGB. Bruce Kent, the Roman Catholic monsignor who serves as general secretary of Britain's long-standing Campaign for Nuclear Disarmament (CND), once silenced such voices by offering £100 to the first person who could show that a single rouble had ever been knowingly accepted by CND. It is true that most of the energy and righteous fury of European peace campaigners has been directed against NATO, the indigenous militarism. But it is also true that very, very few in the movement have been drawn into the trap of whitewashing the USSR. Most would point out that, for instance, the "Soviet threat" is over-stated in most of the Western media,[11] and that all but a few technological developments in the arms race have been initiated by the U.S. But to say this is not in any way to excuse, apologize for or deny the Soviet Union's often tyrannical behaviour.

The imposition of martial law in Poland and the suppression of the independent union Solidarity were greeted with sorrow and anger in the European peace movement; but these events did not, as some observers had expected, signal the end of END as a mass campaign. Even in West Germany, where the shock of martial law was felt most keenly and where the electorate was already moving firmly to the right, the peace movement recovered so fast that less than six months later, in June 1982, about 400,000 demonstrators marched through Bonn, greeting President Reagan with living proof that END was anything but a spent force. The Polish crisis, moreover, can be seen as providing glum confirmation of the analysis of international relations given by such commentators as Noam Chomsky. In Chomsky's words:

> The Cold War has been highly functional for the superpowers, which is one reason why it persists despite the danger of total destruction if the system misbehaves. When the US moves to overthrow the government of Iran or Guatemala or Chile, or to invade Cuba or Indochina or the Dominican

Republic, or to bolster murderous dictatorships in Latin America or Asia, it does so in a noble effort to defend free peoples from the imminent Russian (or earlier, Chinese) threat. Similarly, when the Soviet Union sends its tanks to East Berlin, Hungary, Czechoslovakia or Afghanistan, it is acting from the purest motives, in defense of socialism and freedom against the machinations of US imperialism and its cohorts. The rhetoric employed on both sides is similar.[12]

Nuclear weapons do not emerge from a political vacuum; it is the unmended fracture of Europe by the Cold War that has made adversaries out of neighbouring peoples, and has placed us all at risk.

Ever since the Cold War began, the regimes in Eastern Europe have proclaimed their devotion to peace, while Western governments have lavished attention on the cause of freedom. The contention of E.P. Thompson (explained in his brilliant essay "Beyond the Cold War"[13]) is that regardless of the justice in these respective claims, peace and freedom must now be seen as indivisible and mutually dependent. Given the official rhetoric in Eastern-bloc nations about their stewardship of international peace, it is not altogether surprising (though nevertheless sad) that no mass movements for peace have sprung up there. There are, it is true, officially-sanctioned peace campaigners, but these are to a large extent apologists for Warsaw Pact activities. The few independent peace workers in the USSR, like their compatriots in Amnesty International, have been harassed and threatened by the Soviet authorities. It seems clear, however, that the government of East Germany — and to a lesser extent Hungary and Czechoslovakia — has become alarmed at the growing support for an unofficial peace movement there. A Protestant Youth organization in East Germany has adopted the slogan "Swords Into Ploughshares," and in the spring of 1982 a group of thirty prominent East Germans launched a campaign entitled "The Berlin Appeal: Peace Without Weapons." END workers elsewhere in Europe were encouraged by such developments; they also hoped that political dissidents in Eastern Europe would sense a kinship with Western protesters, rather than with NATO governments. Thompson has insisted that "the Western peace movement (which can scarcely be cast convincingly by Soviet ideologists as an 'agent of Western imperialism') should press steadily upon the state structures of the East demands for greater openness of exchange, both of persons and of ideas."[14] Whereas international tension can help to justify domestic repression — another means by which the Cold War serves Soviet interests — peace and détente erode that justification, thereby increasing democratic possibilities within the nations of the Warsaw Pact.

Sustaining the Momentum

Throughout Western Europe, the vision of a healed continent has proved attractive to enormous numbers of people in many walks of life. The demonstration that sprawled over Hyde Park in central London in June 1982 was characteristic; its speakers included a scientist, a schoolgirl, a union leader, a Methodist minister, an Australian aborigine, a poet, a housewife, a journalist, Labour and Liberal politicians, a high-ranking officer in the Dutch army(!), and an American Quaker. Such people are moved by an awareness that the practice of deterrence has failed to produce a stable peace, and that (as Pope John Paul said in his New Year's message of 1980) a mere 200 of the 50,000 nuclear weapons in existence would be enough to wipe out the major cities of the world. They remember the words of an experienced military commander, Lord Mountbatten: "There are powerful voices around the world who still give credence to the old Roman precept — if you desire peace, prepare for war. This is absolute nuclear nonsense ... The nuclear arms race has no military purpose. Wars cannot be fought with nuclear weapons. Their existence only adds to our perils because of the illusions they have generated."[15] Intellectually and emotionally, the European peace movement has done well. But in practical terms, how can it harness the rage, hope and love of its millions of supporters? How can its momentum be sustained?

One possibility is simply to maintain the pressure about certain essential issues (though these vary, to some extent, from nation to nation): the arrival of cruise and Pershing II missiles, for instance, and the creation of nuclear-free zones. On some points, peace campaigners have already won a majority of public opinion; a good example concerns the British government's determination to buy four astronomically expensive Trident submarines so as to maintain an independent nuclear force. According to an Opinion Research Centre poll conducted in February 1982, only 23 per cent of the British public were in agreement with this £7 billion (or £10 billion) scheme; 63 per cent disapproved, and the rest felt unsure. But few people in the peace movement are content to wait for such specific, limited issues to catch the public eye. Many of them seek a broader platform, one from which positive ideas of their own can be engendered and discussed. One current of thought, especially strong in Denmark, Holland and West Germany, prefers to link disarmament with such wider issues as social-use production, industrial democracy and economic internationalism. Millions of jobs in Western Europe depend on the arms trade, and without a coherent, thoughtful policy for assuring employment and living standards, the peace movement may find it hard to gain mass support among industrial workers. Yet many of the people now glad to lend their voices and their feet to a movement against nuclear weapons would be deeply suspicious of anything smacking of political manipulation. If peace campaigners try too hard to capture new areas of support, they may find that some of their original following has drifted away.

The question is related to the most difficult problem now confronting the European movement: how to respond to limited manoeuvres towards arms control, particularly those emanating from the Soviet and American governments. The greatest damage to the peace campaign in the past few years may well have been inflicted by Ronald Reagan at his most pacific, in his proposal, made in the fall of 1981, for a "zero option" on medium-range European missiles. This idea, swiftly and totally rejected by the USSR, balanced an offer to dispense with the stationing of cruise and Pershing II missiles in Europe with a demand that the Soviet Union withdraw all its SS-20s; it thus seemed in exact accord with END's most famous early slogan, "No Cruise Missiles, No SS-20s." Much of the peace movement appeared bewildered by the sudden offer, and its eventual hostility to the plan was hardly designed to dispel suspicions about the impartiality of peace campaigners with respect to the two superpowers. Representatives of the movement did not always make the best job of explaining to the public why the "zero option," in President Reagan's form, was unacceptable. (In brief, it called on the USSR to withdraw hundreds of missiles already in place, in return for a promise by NATO not to site any *new* missiles on European soil; it also made no mention of future developments in intermediate weaponry, or of nuclear missiles in the adjacent seas.) In any event, not everyone in the peace movement believes that its time and energy should be devoted to public arguments about the (inevitably confusing and detailed) statistics of violence; moral passion can easily be lost in a forest of charts and graphs. Arms control has been preached for decades, and with little result. Yet if the movement reacts with instant hostility or sublime indifference to official proposals aimed at limiting nuclear weapons, it runs the risk of appearing simply negative, or absurdly idealistic. Romanticism can be a subtle danger.

The European and North American peace movements have, until now, experienced relatively little direct contact. But as Daniel Ellsberg has pointed out, in one important respect their demands interlock neatly. The focus of American energy has been on attaining a global nuclear "freeze" at present levels of weaponry, whereas Europeans have directed their attention to ridding the continent of nuclear arms. Yet even if END should succeed in its original objective, that of preventing the placement of cruise and Pershing II missiles on European soil, it may find that the victory was hollow. For in October 1981, shortly before President Reagan's "zero option" speech, the U.S. Congress authorized the production of more than 6,000 cruise missiles, both air-launched and sea-launched. If the sea-launched weapons were stationed on giant decks in the ocean (one idea that has been advanced), two such platforms could hold more missiles than are due to be based in all the European states. Thus Europeans may find that the Atlantic and Mediterranean waters off their shores could be loaded with the very weapons which they struggled so hard to prevent from blanketing their land. If, however, END's call for a comprehensive reduction of nuclear weaponry on the continent were to be combined with the North American demand for a total freeze on the development and installation of new armaments, the result would be a proposition well worth pursuing. Although the peace movements cherish their own diversity and their independence of spirit, greater coordination would seem to be highly desirable.

The peace movement has often been characterized as "unilateral." But this old stereotyping is no longer, if it ever was, accurate. In past decades, as nuclear stockpiles grew towards their present grotesque dimensions, disarmers were commonly dismissed as unrealistic. But now that the major powers possess more than enough weapons to bring about the extinction of our entire species (not to mention much of the rest of the animal kingdom), "realism" scarcely seems an appropriate word to use with anybody who opposes disarmament. Besides, almost everyone, including General Secretary Andropov and President Reagan, can claim to support multilateral disarmament. Peace workers agree that the construction of lasting stability cannot be a one-sided pursuit; they are unilateralist only in the sense that they want a multilateral process to begin by example. They want to see the pious speeches translated into action. In the long run, of course, efforts to create a European tract of peace must necessarily be incomplete; in a nuclear age, there can be no such thing as a refuge of absolute safety. Proponents of END say that a start must be made somewhere, and that a nuclear-free Europe would provide a practical moral example to peoples in other parts of the world: a multinational domain, exerting peaceful pressure towards a general disarmament. (Nonetheless, the establishment of a nuclear-free zone in Europe need not entail a necessary reduction in conventional weapons, or the immediate abolition of the two opposing alliances.)

One further difficulty that the movements face, in Europe and everywhere else, is that of forcing us all to confront the facts of nuclear war. The horrific details of radiation sickness, for example, are easily available, but no healthy mind can contemplate for long the consequences of a single nuclear explosion, let alone a hundred or a thousand. Silent, inert acceptance is often hard to escape. The phenomenon has been examined in detail by the Cambridge University psychologist Nicholas Humphrey: "When someone tells me — and I tell you — that a war between the United States and Russia will now mean a Second World War every second, and that the equivalent of 5,000 Hiroshima bombs will land on England, my imagination draws a blank. It is not just that I cannot bear the thought; I cannot even *have* the thought of 5,000 Hiroshima bombs..."[16] Humphrey's conclusion, however, is optimistic: that despite the psychological forces of incomprehension, denial, embarrassment, helplessness and even latent admiration that nuclear weapons can so readily provoke in us, steadfast public anger may yet lead us to disarm. The armaments are not our masters; we need not be accomplice to our own death. Enough changes of heart cannot fail to bring a change of policy.

In certain ways, indeed, the influence of the peace movement has already been profound. Admittedly it has not removed a single warhead from its place. But it has succeeded in altering the stance and tone of President Reagan's administration; the belligerent rhetoric heard in his election campaign of 1980 and in the early months of 1981 has been discarded under the pressure of peace. Foreign Secretary Gromyko's conciliatory speech to the UN General Assembly in June 1982 provided clear evidence that the Soviet Union also pays close attention to the Western peace movement. And the superpowers are now at least holding intermittent meetings at Geneva. To take a smaller example, the British Home Office (i.e., Department of Justice) has been eager to promote "civil defence" as a useful means of preserving civilization in the event of nuclear war. Its booklet *Protect and Survive*, outlining such charming measures for survival as the consumption of rinsed frogs, was issued in 1980. But as a host of scientists and doctors were quick to point out, effective civil defence against nuclear attack is a delusion, and those who promote it are guilty of shoving our intellects and emotions away from the truth. Even the strongest fallout shelter is useless against a direct hit. The happy result of *Protect and Survive* was that interest in disarmament grew throughout Britain (the title of E.P. Thompson's most famous polemic, "Protest and Survive," makes punning reference to the Home Office pamphlet), while the concept of civil defence against nuclear bombs was dealt a severe blow. "Operation Hard Rock," a national exercise in civil defence intended for October 1982, had to be cancelled ignominiously thanks to public scepticism and the refusal of local councils to participate; but for the strength of the peace movement, "Hard Rock" would surely have gone ahead.

It began in the fall of 1979, and in a few years the European peace movement has come a long way. It has stepped, in a sense, far beyond the immediate rage provoked by cruise and Pershing II missiles, into an attempt to find new ways of thinking and feeling about our world. For the Cold War has left its scars in the minds of human beings as well as in the soil of Europe and the military bases scattered over the planet. If Europe suffers from a deformed political culture, then every citizen of the continent has a responsibility to heal the sickness in himself. And when *Pravda* or the *Daily Telegraph* invite their readers to think of the other half of Europe as alien, barbarian, other, then spiritual resistance becomes a moral duty. To accept the prospect of World War III is to confess a desperate failure. The challenge posed by END is to think in peace.

"Let us place loyalty to each other above loyalty to the armourers! Do not allow anyone to divide us!" The words are those of the European Declaration, launched at a demonstration in London in June 1982 and repeated days later in Central Park, New York. "We are already, in our movements, creating a new kind of politics, an international fellowship of resistance and of friendship, which refuses advantage to either 'side' because it refuses to acknowledge any 'side' except that of our common future: a future which will never come unless we, in this living generation, honour our trust."[17]

Notes

1   E.P. Thompson, "Protest and Survive," in *Protest and Survive*, ed. E.P. Thompson and Dan Smith (London: Penguin Books, 1980), pp. 51-52.
2   Dan Smith, "The European Nuclear Theatre," in ibid, p. 119.
3   Quoted in *Sanity* (the journal of CND), July-August 1979.
4   Quoted in *New Statesman*, 31 October 1980.
5   Quoted in Ken Coates, *European Nuclear Disarmament* (Nottingham: Bertrand Russell Peace Foundation, 1980), p. 11.
6   *The Times* (London), 26 March 1980.
7   F. Griffiths and J.C. Polanyi, eds, *The Dangers of Nuclear War* (Toronto: University of Toronto Press, 1980), p. 164.
8   END, *Bulletin of Work in Progress*, no. 1 (1980), pp. 10-11.
9   Thompson and Smith, eds, *Protest and Survive*, p. 225. The appeal is quoted in full, pp. 223-26. Lists of signatories can be found at the end of Coates, *European Nuclear Disarmament* and in END, *Bulletin of Work in Progress*, no. 3.
10   *The Guardian* (London), 23 February 1981.
11   Cf. "The Soviet Megalith under a Microscope," an important article by Richard Stubbing, assistant provost of Duke University and formerly the deputy chief of the national security division in the U.S. Office of Management and Budget, published in *The Guardian* (London), 22 February 1982. Stubbing analyzes in detail the claims made by the Pentagon about Soviet military spending, power and war-readiness, and demonstrates how the alarmist rhetoric wildly exagger-

ates the facts. It is true, for example, that the USSR has recently completed two KIEV-class aircraft carriers, the largest ships it has ever built; it is also true that the U.S. navy has eighteen ships of equal or greater capability. Stubbing observes that not only does NATO have a slight edge in total military manpower over the Warsaw Pact, but also "the United States and its NATO allies outspent the Soviet Union and its Warsaw Pact allies on defence by more than $300 *billion* in the past decade." (Italics mine.)

12 END, *Bulletin of Work in Progress*, no. 1 (1980), p. 7.
13 Originally published as a pamphlet by Merlin Press and END (London, 1982), and reprinted in Thompson's collection of peace essays, *Zero Option* (London: Merlin Press, 1982).
14 E.P. Thompson, *Beyond the Cold War* (London: Merlin Press/END, 1982), p. 33.
15 Quoted in *Sanity*, August 1980, and in Coates, *European Nuclear Disarmament*.
16 Nicholas Humphrey, "Four Minutes to Midnight," the Bronowski Memorial Lecture, broadcast on BBC-TV and printed in *The Listener*, 29 October 1981, pp. 493-99. This quotation comes from p. 494.
17 *Sanity*, June-July 1982, p. 24.

PART II

Canada's Part in the Arms Race

5

Canada and the U.S. Nuclear Arsenal
Ernie Regehr

Since the final days of World War II, Canada has had continuous, direct involvement with the nuclear weapons of the United States — as a supplier of raw materials, as a potential nuclear combatant (with either nuclear weapons themselves or surveillance and guidance tasks assigned to Canadian armed forces at home and abroad), as a producer of component parts, and as a site for the testing of nuclear weapons delivery vehicles.

At the same time, Canada is to date virtually unique among states as a country which is capable of building its own nuclear weapons but which has nevertheless clearly and consistently disavowed any interest in acquiring its own nuclear arsenal. And therein lies a continuing contradiction (some would say hypocrisy) in Canadian defence policy: while disavowing nuclear weapons, Canada has at the same time pursued defence and industrial policies based upon intimate involvement with nuclear weapons (in fact, about as intimate an involvement as is possible without actually becoming defined as a nuclear-weapon state).

A major source of this contradiction was Canada's emergence from World War II with the assumption that future Canadian security would depend upon "collective" security rather than on independent or strictly nationally-defined security measures. And while Lester B. Pearson, as minister of state for external affairs in the 1950s, pressed repeatedly for collective security arrangements under, if at all possible, the aegis of the United Nations, the particular collectivities which Canada ultimately joined were rather more restricted (not to mention restrictive) than the United Nations. Inevitably, given the bi-polar nature of the postwar world and Canada's close physical proximity to one of those poles, and given the intensity with which both sides of that bi-polar world were pursuing nuclear defence strategies, Canada found itself in regional alliances dominated by nuclear weapons and strategies.

Indeed, on the North American continent there was considered to be no realistic option to "collective" (now meaning continental) security. With an almost coy understatement, a 1945 government policy document allows that "the pressure which would be brought to bear on Canada by the United States in the event of Canada seeming reluctant or refusing to co-operate with (the United States) in continental defence would be very substantial and might be difficult to resist." The document briefly considers the desirability of an independent defence policy in the interests of playing a mediating role between the United States and the Soviet Union, but concludes that Canada was unlikely to exercise much influence over Soviet behaviour and that therefore a mediation role was not realistic. On the other hand, cooperation with the United States "would ensure that Canada was provided with information about U.S. plans and intentions which would give her an opportunity to express her views regarding the urgency of any situation and the necessity of proposed defence measures." An earlier document on northern defence is more to the point and less concerned with producing high-minded rationalizations for Canada's satellite status: ". . . in the event of a threat against this region, failure on the part of Canada to undertake defence measures in Northwest Canada on a scale considered by the U.S. to be adequate, or to co-operate adequately with the U.S. in its defence, would probably lead to the infringement of Canadian sovereignty by the United States" (in other words, the Americans would do it for us). General Maurice Pope put it even more bluntly in 1944: "To the Americans the defence of the United States is continental defence and that includes us, and nothing . . . will ever drive that idea out of their heads."

Accordingly, Canada was compelled, at least in the minds of the policy-makers of the day, to provide defence forces, not commensurate with Canadian assessment of an external threat, but commensurate with Canadian perceptions of the level of forces required to produce in the United States sufficient confidence and assurance that Canada was committed to the common defence.

While Canada's close alliance with the United States has always been, and continues to be, based on much more than geographical proximity (e.g., largely shared values and culture), the essential domination of Canadian security considerations by the United States led, particularly in the immediate postwar years, to a Canadian search for European ties that could mitigate American influence on Canada. To a large extent, therefore, Canada entered into its two defence alliances (NORAD and NATO) more in the attempt to salvage at least the formal conditions of sovereignty than as a conscious act of abdicating independence in security matters (although the former has by no means prevented the latter). In the case of NORAD, then the North American Air Defence Agreement, entered into in 1958, Canada sought a formal agreement as a means of retaining a formal role in North American defence planning — on the assumption that defence planning for the entire continent of North America would emanate from Washington, with or without a formal alliance with Canada. Participation in NATO (entered into in 1949), on the other hand, was based on the hope of developing a defence policy relationship with Europe in the hope of introducing some countervailing influences into Canadian security policy formulation.

In such a policy environment, Canadian defence equipment procurement decisions (including those related to nuclear weapons) have tended to be highly symbolic events, concerned less with building up a particular Canadian military capability than with sending messages to alliance headquarters. Major equipment purchases have thus been a means of access, in the case of NORAD, to the club that would, with or without Canadian membership, decide the continent's security posture; and in the case of NATO, to the club that would, it was hoped, enable Canada to broaden the base of its foreign relations. Canadian perceptions of the Soviet threat are, therefore, of little consequence in Canadian procurement decisions. More to the point have been Canadian perceptions of Canada's obligations to and relationships with its allies. Hence, the fundamental question of post-World War II Canadian defence policy has really been, How does Canada most efficiently (i.e., for the greatest political return at the least cost) demonstrate to Europe and particularly the United States that Canada's commitment to collective security is serious and credible? The important matter for Canada is to be seen to be buying aircraft or tanks — and because the Canadian contribution to the collective military apparatus will of necessity always be small by the standards of the alliance leadership, neither Canada nor the alliances have attached great importance to the types of equipment that have ultimately been acquired by Canada. (The long-range patrol aircraft purchased in the late 1970s from Lockheed Corporation in the United States are perhaps the one major exception. In this case the United States Defense Department took a keen interest in the purchase, encouraging Canada not only to buy a particular type of aircraft but also to buy it from a particular company. Even here, however, the U.S. interest was premised less on concern for the military role which Canada would be playing than on improving the fortunes of an ailing Lockheed Corporation.)

Aircraft and ground forces are the items most directly related to the general interests of the alliances. In the case of aircraft Canada is effectively obliged to buy American, given Canadian industry's dependence on sales to the United States and given the provisions under the Defence Production Sharing Arrangements by which Canadian access to the U.S. market is dependent upon Canadian purchases from the U.S. (see Chapter 3). That leaves ground forces and equipment purchases for those forces as the primary means of demonstrating solidarity with European NATO. Most recently this has taken the form of purchasing German tanks.

The purchase of German tanks was not unrelated to the fact that the government's attempt to establish more formal trade links with Europe a few years earlier had been met in Europe with pointed questions as to the nature of Canada's commitment to European common security. Canada quickly set about demonstrating that commitment — besides buying German tanks, new fighter aircraft were promised and ordered for Canada's European forces, and the NATO request for a 3 per cent annual growth rate (after inflation) in the defence budget was also accepted.

Given its preoccupation with membership or acceptance, with the minimum payment of dues, in its two military clubs, Canada has paid only secondary attention to the policies those clubs actually pursue. Having only minor influence over the shape of those policies, Canada also feels only a minor compulsion to take direct responsibility for them. This is particularly the case regarding nuclear weapons policies.

It is, in fact, the exception when government representatives rationalize or defend Canadian involvement with nuclear weapons by arguing the merits of the nuclear strategies those weapons represent. The more common tactic is to argue that Canadian involvement is too marginal to be worth worrying about, or that such involvement is a matter of commitment to collective defence and a necessary deference to the will of the majority in the collectivity.

At no time has this been more clearly demonstrated than it was during initial government justifications of its intention to permit the United States to flight-test the cruise missile on Canadian territory. The most prominent argument advanced was that such permission was simply a normal part of Canada's contribution to the collective defence efforts of the West. When the issue was raised in the House of Commons by the New Democratic Party foreign affairs critic, Pauline Jewett, the government responded through the parliamentary secretary to the minister of state, David Berger, who pointed out that Canada's security policy rested on a commitment to the peaceful settlement of disputes, the pursuit of verifiable arms control, and on "deterrence of war through the collective security arrangements of NATO and NORAD." By way of introduction he told the House that "the Canadian decision in principle to permit such testing... demonstrates Canada's support for NATO."

Later, the then minister of external affairs, Mark MacGuigan, also sought to justify the testing decision as a matter of commitment to NATO rather than on the specific merits of the cruise missile. Again replying to a question by Pauline Jewett, Mr. MacGuigan said: "We are doing this for ourselves and the alliance to which we belong. I can well understand the honourable member, who leads her party in rejecting the NATO alliance, that she would not be interested in the protection which that alliance gives us in its reliance on nuclear weapons."

The minister's general reference to the "protection" which derives from the "reliance on nuclear weapons" suggests the only argument in support of Canadian involvement with nuclear weapons that even approaches the nature of a strategic rationale. From time to time Canadian officials make a general appeal to the doctrine of deterrence, but given the radical changes this doctrine has undergone in the past half-dozen years (see Chapter 1), this only serves to confirm the fact that Canada has become a largely uncritical participant in the evolution of U.S., and alliance, nuclear strategy.

Even in private conversations, the Canadian officials advising the government do not acknowledge the changes in strategic thinking which have led the United States to view nuclear weapons as a means, not only of deterring Soviet use of nuclear weapons, but also of regaining international American pre-eminence. The current U.S. nuclear weapons program will result in 17,000 new nuclear weapons (some replacing existing weapons) in the assembly of a nuclear arsenal capable of fighting nuclear war at every level of conflict, from local to global. This buildup is premised (as U.S. government documents such as the Department of Defense report on "defense guidance for fiscal years 1984-88" show) on the assumption that it is possible to emerge out of any such nuclear conflict as the prevailing power in possession of political and strategic advantages that were not available immediately prior to the conflict. Yet Canadian officials continue to insist that American statements about the possibility of "winning" a nuclear war are simply rhetoric (albeit somewhat embarrassing to America's allies) and that they have nothing to do with American military planning.

Currently, Canada has points of involvement with the full range of U.S. nuclear weapons, ranging from tactical (short-range, battlefield) to intermediate-range to strategic (intercontinental). In the past this involvement has included the supply of raw materials for nuclear weapons.

Canada as a Supplier of Nuclear Materials

While at no time has there been any serious Canadian consideration given to Canada's developing its own independent nuclear weapons, neither has there been any serious Canadian consideration given to the question of whether or not Canada should be a supplier of uranium to the nuclear weapons programs of its allies. This aspect of Canada's part in the arms race is discussed fully in the next chapter, but we should still note here that although Prime Minister Pearson announced in 1965 that Canada would reverse its earlier policy of supplying uranium for nuclear weapons and research, Canada remains a major exporter of uranium and there can be no final assurance that none of this will end up in weapons programs. Saskatchewan researchers, for example, have identified direct links between Saskatchewan uranium and overseas companies and countries that are engaged in the manufacture of nuclear weapons. The Saskatoon-based Interchurch Uranium Committee has concluded that uranium received by France from the Cluff Lake mine in Saskatchewan contributes directly to the French weapons production and testing capacity. The Cluff Lake mine is 20 per cent owned by the government of Saskatchewan and 80 per cent by a consortium of French companies. This French consortium is in turn 30 per cent owned by the French Commissariat de l'Energie Atomique (CEA), which manufactures and tests nuclear weapons. CEA operates the "Centre of Experiments" in the South Pacific, where regular bomb tests have taken place since the mid-1960s.

West Germany also has contracts with both Cluff Lake and Rabbit Lake mines. A West German, government-owned company controls 49 per cent of the Rabbit Lake mine and a portion of Maurice Bay. West Germany, in turn, has been linked to the transfer of nuclear technology to South Africa, one of the acknowledged near-nuclear states which many believe has already tested nuclear devices (at any rate, South Africa has already acquired, with the clandestine help of Space Research Corporation of Quebec and Vermont, sophisticated artillery technology suitable for firing tactical nuclear weapons).

About 85 per cent of uranium mined in Canada is sold abroad, some of which goes to the Soviet Union for enrichment. Much of the rest goes to enrichment plants in the U.S., France and Britain. In addition, uranium from other countries comes to Canada for refinement into a chemical form suitable for enrichment.

In effect, the uranium exported from Canada goes into a large international pot— a pot from which nuclear power and nuclear weapons programs both draw. Under the circumstances it is not possible to guarantee that nuclear weapons do not draw any Canadian uranium from that pot.

Canada as a Nuclear Combatant

In the first two decades following World War II it was Canadian policy to supply materials directly to the nuclear weapons program of the United States, and it was also during this period that Canada confronted most directly the question of whether or not Canadian forces should be equipped with nuclear weapons.

In 1954 the Liberal government of Louis St. Laurent in Ottawa concurred with the NATO decision to adopt officially the strategy of relying upon tactical nuclear weapons to meet conventional attack in Europe. With land and air forces in Europe, it was inevitable that Canada would have to face the question of whether to place some of those tactical nuclear weapons with Canadian forces. The same was true in North America. Having already entered into cooperative air defence arrangements with the United States through the Distant Early Warning (DEW) line in northern Canada, it was also inevitable that Canada would face the question of whether or not to go beyond warning to join the Americans in a continental air defence system and whether to use tactical nuclear weapons in such a system.

The problem of what to do with nuclear weapons presented itself to Canadian policy-makers in the form of three questions identified by Jon B. McLin: Should Canadian forces have nuclear weapons under their exclusive control, whether acquired by manufacture or international agreement? In what ways and to what extent should Canada contribute to the U.S. nuclear deterrent by taking measures under its control, such as allowing the storage of American weapons and/or carriers on Canadian territory? Should Canadian forces in North America and/or Europe be provided with nuclear weapons that are not under their exclusive control?

The controversy came quite early to focus on the last question, and the story of the Diefenbaker government's faltering attempts to deal with it, and the Liberal Party's about-turn on it (see Chapter 9 for the latter), remains one of the great controversies in postwar Canadian political history.

Inasmuch as Canada had the capability of conducting an indigenous nuclear weapons program, it is not surprising that the possibility of an exclusively Canadian nuclear force would be considered, however briefly. Aside from an obvious reluctance to incur the cost of a nuclear weapons program, involving delivery systems as well as warheads, and, perhaps, a cultural disinclination to aspire to military prominence, there were no compelling strategic grounds for an independent nuclear arsenal in Canada. Whatever Canadian perceptions of the Soviet threat, Canadian policy-makers could distinguish no particular threat to Canada which would require a military response independent of that of the United States. Similarly, there were no compelling strategic reasons why U.S. strategic weapons should be either stored in or operated from Canadian territory. With permission to use Canadian air space and refuelling facilities, long-range bombers, for example, could operate effectively from U.S. bases (later, not even Canadian refuelling facilities were needed). Land- or sea-based ballistic missiles, of course, did not require the use of either Canadian land and sea territory or airspace.

There developed, however, for the decision-makers of the day, compelling reasons, given the state of weapons technology and NATO strategy, for tactical nuclear weapons controlled by the United States to be assigned to Canadian forces in Canada and Europe. In North America, U.S. interceptor squadrons, assigned the task of intercepting a Soviet bomber attack, operated from two Canadian bases, Goose Bay, Labrador and Harmon Field, Newfoundland. These U.S. interceptor forces were assigned tactical nuclear weapons, but Canada never did grant the U.S. permission to keep the nuclear warheads at the Canadian bases. As part of the NORAD agreement, however, Canada agreed to assist in the task of maintaining forces to counter the threat of attack by manned nuclear bombers. The weapons systems eventually acquired for this purpose were short-range ground-to-air missiles (the Bomarc) and interceptor aircraft (the CF-101 Voodoos). Both of these weapons systems were acquired by the Progressive Conservative government of John Diefenbaker without nuclear warheads, although his government clearly knew that the full military effectiveness of these weapons depended upon their being armed with nuclear warheads.

In Europe the Canadian brigade group on the NATO front line was equipped by the Diefenbaker government with Lacrosse and, later, Honest John missiles, both of which were initially provided with conventional warheads, but both of which were acknowledged to depend upon nuclear warheads to perform the role assigned to them with NATO. Canada's air division in Europe was given a strike reconnaissance role and equipped with CF-104 aircraft. Both the role and the aircraft were acknowledged to require nuclear weapons. Ultimately, the Liberals under Lester Pearson, who had earlier insisted that Canada not accept nuclear weapons roles, argued that the Diefenbaker-acquired equipment made no sense without nuclear weapons and thus called for, and after their election arranged for, the acquisition of nuclear weapons for these North American and European systems.

From the start, the Diefenbaker government gave little indication that it objected to Canadian involvement with nuclear weapons. In 1957 the government gave unqualified support to NATO plans to stockpile nuclear weapons in Europe and subsequently to the development and articulation of the strategy of a "flexible response." NATO, through the United States in particular, came to the view that a policy of massive retaliation with nuclear weapons did not provide the necessary flexibility to respond to Soviet initiatives at various or appropriate levels. The introduction of tactical nuclear weapons, it was argued, would enable NATO to respond to Warsaw Pact incursions with nuclear weapons, but without immediately engaging the strategic arsenals of the major powers.

Publicly expressed reservations on the part of the government began with the appointment of Howard Green as secretary of state for external affairs. John McLin points out that the government, including Howard Green, did agree in principle to accept nuclear weapons in 1959, but implementation of that agreement was variously delayed and over the following two years the government managed to avoid committing itself one way or the other. Howard Green took a particular interest in disarmament negotiations throughout the period and frequently indicated that Canadian acquisition of nuclear warheads might have detrimental effects upon the outcome of these talks.

The Liberal Party, under Louis St. Laurent and, later, Lester Pearson, approved of the placement of tactical nuclear weapons in Europe, but Pearson, at one point also citing disarmament negotiations, was opposed to Canadian forces acquiring nuclear weapons. The 1961 Liberal convention maintained the party's opposition to nuclear weapons, but the position was qualified in two ways according to McLin — it acknowledged that in certain circumstances Canadian forces in Europe might need nuclear weapons, and it did not preclude the possibility that Canada might accept nuclear weapons under exclusive American control. Subsequently Pearson came to argue the qualifications more forcefully and at the beginning of 1963 completed his reversal by announcing that Canada should accept nuclear weapons as a fulfilment of the commitments it had entered into in acquiring equipment that was designed to carry nuclear warheads. He went on to call for a thorough re-evaluation of defence policy and referred to the possibility of Canada's then assuming non-nuclear roles in the buildup of NATO's conventional forces.

An election followed in 1963, and despite the fact that the Liberals formed a minority government, by mid-August they announced that Canada would acquire nuclear weapons for the Honest John missiles and CF-104 fighter aircraft in Europe and for the Bomarc missiles and CF-101 (Voodoo) fighter aircraft in Canada. The weapons were accepted under joint control arrangements.

By 1967, Pearson had come to the conclusion that Canada should end its nuclear role in Europe. When Pierre Trudeau assumed leadership of the Liberal Party in 1968, he announced a general review of foreign policy, and Canada's relationship to NATO in particular, and by 1970 the government announced its intention to denuclearize Canada's miliary role in Europe by the end of 1972. The Canadian Bomarc missile sites were also dismantled, and the replacement of the CF-101 interceptor aircraft in Canada will be complete by the mid-1980s. With that, the last nuclear weapons will have been removed from Canadian territory and the Canadian forces inventory at home and abroad.

This will not, however, mean the end of Canadian forces participation in preparations for, and potentially the conduct of, nuclear combat.

Nuclear weapons systems are precisely that — systems. Frequently they are systems that to be effective, must span large portions of the globe and as such depend upon a myriad of communications links in order to make them operational and effective. The superpowers, in fact, depend upon communications facilities outside of their own jurisdiction and rely upon the cooperation of allies. Through NORAD, now renamed the North American Aerospace Defence Agreement, Canadian involvement in helping to provide the necessary international infrastructure for U.S. nuclear weapons has been institutionalized.

It is now obvious that in the event of all-out nuclear war between the United States and the Soviet Union, the Arctic region would represent the front line of combat. Most bomber and missile traffic would pass over the Arctic, meaning that this area has become the site of the concentration of early-warning and guidance systems. The main Canadian link to these systems is the Distance Early Warning (DEW) Line, a series of somewhat dated radar stations strung across the Canadian far north. They are part of a radar network from Alaska to Iceland designed to give early warning of a Soviet bomber attack. In addition to warning of attack, this network of stations is also capable of providing a communications network to transmit attack orders to U.S. strategic bombers at the outbreak of war.

Even though military planners now consider the Soviet bomber threat to be minimal, the DEW line is not considered to be an entirely reliable warning system since, in particular, low-flying Soviet aircraft could avoid detection. The U.S. has therefore stationed airborne radar systems, the Airborne Warning and Control System (AWACS), in Alaska and Iceland. The NORAD agreement provides for the AWACS to operate in Canadian airspace in emergency situations with Canadian government permission, and as such would detect intruders and guide Canadian and American fighter interceptors, whether armed with nuclear or conventional air-to-air missiles, to their targets.

Two other systems in which Canada also participates are central to nuclear combat and to providing targeting information to U.S. nuclear weapons systems. In any nuclear war-fighting scenarios, whether based upon launching a pre-emptive first strike or upon a protracted nuclear battle, a key American objective would be to destroy Soviet nuclear weapons submarines in an effort to limit the damage which the Soviet Union could inflict upon the U.S. mainland. The detection of Soviet submarines is essentially a two-stage process. The first stage is carried out by a series of stationary underwater listening devices which can detect submarines at a distance of up to 1,500 kilometres. These listening devices are located off the coast of Newfoundland and across the North Atlantic, but they are not capable of identifying the submarine, or giving its precise location. For this task, anti-submarine warfare (ASW) aircraft, including the Canadian long-range patrol aircraft, the Auroras, are maintained. The ASW aircraft are dispatched to the area in which the submarine has been detected and then, by means of underwater listening devices dropped from the aircraft, they identify and provide the precise location of the submarine to American killer submarines. The Auroras (CP-140) operate from bases at Greenwood, Nova Scotia and Commox, B.C.

An international network of radio transmitters, known as Loran-C, is used in sea navigation to calculate precisely the locations of ships and submarines. For a nuclear missile-carrying submarine such information is essential to plotting the course its missiles will have to follow in order to hit its target. As both sides move towards "counterforce" strategies that rely upon highly accurate weapons systems, the Loran-C navigational information becomes increasingly important to nuclear war fighting. Canada operates a station in the Loran-C network, at Cape Race, Newfoundland.

Canada also operates electronics eavesdropping facilities within the U.S. system, as well as facilities within the NORAD space detection tracking systems, both systems providing information on the locations and movements of land-, sea- and space-based systems of other nations.

Notably, all of these facilities would be targets in the early stages of any Soviet-American nuclear war. Add to these such additional targets as nuclear weapons components production facilities and refuelling stations for American strategic aircraft during an emergency, and it becomes clear that Canada is not only directly along the route of nuclear weapons but will also be the target for a significant number of those weapons (see Chapter 7 for a detailed discussion of the effects of such a war on Canada).

Canadian Components for Nuclear Weapons

As the direct custody of nuclear weapons by Canadian armed forces ends, another form of Canadian involvement with nuclear weapons has intensified. Canadian industrial participation in the manufacture of U.S. nuclear weapons systems is carried out under the aegis of the Canada-U.S. Defence Production Sharing Arrangements. Under those arrangements Canadian industry has access to the U.S. defence market for the supply of component parts to U.S.-designed and -built major weapons systems. Canadian industry has come to produce a wide range of components, and in many cases the parts themselves can be used either in military or civilian applications. Even though these items are tabulated as military sales when they are used in military equipment, from the point of view of Canadian government trade and defence policies, these transactions are treated as essentially commercial undertakings. The particular military or strategic functions of the major weapons system for which the Canadian component is manufactured is not part of the consideration in any sale. Canada has made the general decision to participate in the U.S. defence industry and beyond that no distinctions are made between various weapons systems. Accordingly, Canadian industry is free to participate in any military system produced by the United States, provided it can successfully compete with American suppliers for the business.

To help it compete more effectively, the federal government provides some special services and assistance to the Canadian defence industry. A crown corporation, the Canadian Commercial Corporation (CCC), operates under the authority of the minister of supply and services and serves as a contracting agency for foreign governments that wish to purchase defence-related or other supplies or services from Canadian industry on a government-to-government basis. The CCC receives requests from Canadian industry for the supply of the commodity and arranges the sale. The CCC enters into contracts, containing identical terms and conditions, with the Canadian firm and the foreign government for, respectively, the supply and sale of the goods or services concerned. The bulk of the contracts arranged by the CCC are for military sales to the U.S. Department of Defense (see Chapter 3 for the total Canadian defence-related sales to the U.S.).

Another attempt to improve the competitiveness of Canadian industry in the international market for military commodities is a federally-operated program of grants "to develop and sustain the technological capability of Canadian defence industry for the purpose of defence export sales or civil export sales arising from that capability." In fiscal year

1981-82, payments of $154,934,982 were made to Canadian industry under this Defence Industry Productivity (DIP) program.

Government promotion of Canadian participation in the supply of military commodities to the U.S. Defense Department also does not discriminate between nuclear and non-nuclear weapons or between offensive and defensive weapons, or even between stabilizing and destabilizing weapons. As a result, Canada participates in the production of components for nuclear weapons systems in every category, from tactical to intermediate to strategic.

The cruise missile has become firmly lodged in the Canadian consciousness and offers the most prominent example of Canadian industrial participation in U.S. nuclear weapons. The cruise is a pilotless jet aircraft that can carry either a nuclear or conventional warhead for a distance of about 2,500 kilometres, flying close enough to the ground to avoid radar detection, and land within fifty metres of its target (see Chapter 1 for the military/political implications of this weapon).

Litton Systems (Canada) Ltd. of Rexdale, Ontario, near Toronto, has been both a prominent recipient of DIP funds and the producer of navigational components for the U.S. nuclear-armed cruise missile. In the three fiscal years from April 1979 to March 1982 the company received a total of $43,435,142 in DIP funds. Of these grants, at least $26.4 million are directly related to the cruise missile production, and an additional interest-free loan has also been provided for the same purpose.

The contract is among the most publicized of Canadian participation in U.S. nuclear weapons systems. Under the agreement, Litton is one of two suppliers (the other is Litton's U.S. parent company) of the inertial guidance system for the missile. While the Canadian subsidiary was originally chosen as the second source supplier, in subsequent bidding it has won out over its parent to become the primary supplier, with the implication that it could supply more than half of the 11,000 systems expected to be ordered by the U.S. prime contractor for the cruise, McDonnell Douglas, over the next few years (although the U.S. air force has now said that deployment of this version of the cruise will be cut back in anticipation of a second generation of "stealth" cruise missiles — "stealth" referring to construction materials and electronic countermeasures designed to make radar detection much more difficult).

The federal government and the company have sought to characterize Canadian participation in the production of the cruise as being essentially a commercial activity. Accordingly, primary attention has been paid to the 1,400 jobs to be created at Litton itself and another 300 with secondary Canadian suppliers by the $1.2 billion in potential sales. Political and military justifications for the contract have been, as noted earlier, confined to statements declaring it to be consistent with the DPSA and with Canada's support for NATO.

Another potentially controversial Canadian industrial involvement with U.S. nuclear weapons systems, this time the MX intercontinental ballistic missile, cannot claim even that measure of political/military justification. A highly accurate missile that is intended to pose a threat to Soviet land-based missiles, the MX takes nuclear strategies another major step towards first-strike capabilities. Canadian officials, in fact, have privately expressed some doubts about the wisdom of deploying the MX, agreeing that the ability to threaten Soviet land-based missiles (a strategy relying on plans for a pre-emptive first strike) does not strengthen the American nuclear deterrent (a strategy relying upon the ability to retaliate after having absorbed a nuclear attack). In fact, as we have argued in Chapter 1, the deployment of missiles to threaten a first strike, far from deterring the Soviet Union, creates incentives for the Soviet Union itself to strike first.

Despite these reservations, however, the Defence Industry Productivity program has promised Boeing of Canada Ltd. in Winnipeg an interest-free loan of $120,000 if it wins a contract to supply components for the MX warhead to the U.S. prime contractor for the MX re-entry vehicles (warhead), Avco Systems of Wilmington, Mass. The initial contract would be worth $500,000, but could mean future contracts of many millions of dollars.

New Democrat MP, Terry Sargeant, who first raised the MX involvement in the House of Commons, says there is now evidence that a number of Canadian firms are lining up to get work on the MX, although the political difficulties the missile is having in the U.S. Congress have had an impact on Canadian plans for commercial exploitation of the new weapon. EBCO Industries of British Columbia, for example, had received a small contract to participate in a Boeing U.S. contract to develop a prototype transporter for the missile needed for earlier basing plans. The basing plan and associated contracts were cancelled, but the company is still optimistic that it will receive MX-related work once deployment is assured.

In 1981 the Defence Industry Productivity program awarded the company a major grant of $6.7 million to acquire precision machinery for aerospace manufacturing. The grant was part of the federal government's attempt to bring defence industry capabilities to Canada's West Coast. In announcing the grant, the Department of Industry, Trade and Commerce estimated that the new capability would add $70 million to the company's defence and aerospace exports over the ensuing five years.

Another Canadian company, Diemaster Tool Inc., currently has military-related contracts with Avco Systems, also supported by DIP funding, and also hopes to extend this work to include the MX missile.

Of particular political interest is the conflict of interest that support for the arms industry creates within government policy. On the one hand there is the government's active interest in controlling the proliferation of new generations of nuclear weapons systems, while on the other hand there is the government's active interest in promoting industrial participation in these same new weapons sytems. Of added significance is the fact that some of the DIP grants are, in a sense, speculative grants that rely for their full pay-off on repeat contracts and, consequently, on extensive deployment of the weapons system in question. In other words, the best return on the government's investment depends upon the greatest deployment of new systems (another way of saying an escalation of the arms race).

The cruise missile is, once again, the best example. To put it most simply, there is a conflict between efforts to limit deployment of the cruise in Europe and on B-52s and efforts to promote increased Litton sales to the U.S. At the same time that the Department of External Affairs was, in 1979, assessing Canada's attitude towards the deployment of cruise missiles in Europe, the Department of Industry, Trade and Commerce was negotiating with Litton Systems (Canada) to receive public funds in support of the company's bid to supply the guidance system for the cruise. As we have noted, a combination of loans and grants has placed close to $50 million of taxpayer money in the hands of Litton. The only way in which the Canadian government can hope to demonstrate substantial public benefits deriving from those public funds is if the cruise missile is widely deployed — in Europe and aboard U.S. B-52 bombers.

There is a similar contradiction in the government's attitude towards the MX missile. Public funds have already been committed to Canadian industry in support of MX-related work. The stakes are not yet as high as they have become in the case of the cruise, but once again there is a clear conflict between the objective of arms control and that of defence export promotion. And that conflict has become even more poignant now that the responsibilities for arms control and defence export promotion are in the same department (the 1982 reorganization of the Department of External Affairs made it responsible for export promotion, including defence exports).

What is clear is that any reservations Canadian policy-makers may have regarding the escalation of the arms race to new levels, to date those reservations have not been sufficient to prevent the promotion of involvement at each level.

Other examples of Canadian industrial participation in strategic and intermediate-range nuclear weapons are the production of components for U.S. nuclear submarines and for intermediate-range nuclear strike aircraft such as the F-111. Canadian nuclear involvement also extends to the tactical nuclear arsenal of the United States, specifically the Lance missile. The Lance missile has in recent years replaced, among others, the Honest John tactical missiles and has a range of about 110 kilometres. Hawker Siddeley Canada Inc. of Toronto supplied the lightweight, towed launcher for the Lance. The launcher can be delivered to battlefields via helicopters or dropped with parachutes from fixed-wing aircraft (the Lance missile is also launched from a self-propelled launcher, not supplied by Hawker Siddeley). It can carry conventional or nuclear warheads, including an enhanced radiation warhead (or neutron bomb). In the latter case, the U.S. has designed neutron warheads specifically for the Lance, but by early 1983 none had been deployed.

When the NORAD agreement was renewed in 1981 it was renamed the North American Aerospace Defence Agreement in recognition of the fact that outer space had become a prominent venue for the East-West military conflict. And when the Standing Committee on External Affairs and National Defence reported on its review of the NORAD agreement, it encouraged greater Canadian industrial involvement in space-based military hardware. Canada's participation in the American space shuttle program is perhaps the best example of new horizons in the militarization of space.

The space shuttle, and the Canadian remote manipulator arm which it carries, has long enjoyed the reputation of a civilian engineering marvel. This myth, however, has become more difficult to sustain since the most recent flight of the shuttle and its secret military cargo.

The military use of outer space aids nuclear war-fighting capacity in several ways — through more effective communications and control of air- and sea-based weapons, through more precise positioning and speed measurements of missiles for increased accuracy, and through more precise mapping of an adversary's terrain to enable programming of flight-paths for low-flying cruise missiles and for the next generation of manoeuvrable warheads on ICBMs. In war, either side would seek to destroy the other's space-based systems and the Soviet Union has argued that the manoeuvrability of the space shuttle makes it a potential killer satellite. The Soviets, having now begun tests of their own reusable space vehicles, have softened their opposition to the space shuttle, but its crucial role in developing space-war capabilities is not in doubt.

Under the Reagan administration the basic military role of the shuttle has become clear. Initial plans were for eleven of the first forty-four shuttle flights to be run by the military. Commercial flights have been substantially cut back however, so that now eleven of the first twenty-four flights will be under military control, with the United States air force counting on the space shuttle as the primary means by which to launch its military satellites into space. The Stockholm International Peace Research Institute has this to say of the military role of the space shuttle: "Among the measures planned [for the shuttle] are: transport of communications, reconnaissance and hunter-killer satellites into outer space as well as experiments on board the space shuttle aiming at destroying enemy satellites, among other means by using laser weapons and other radiation armaments. . . . It would also be possible to carry nuclear weapons into space on the space shuttle."

The Canadian remote manipulator arm is central to the effectiveness of the shuttle in space, permitting the dispatch of satellites from its cargo bay into orbit and the retrieval of others. It was designed and built by Spar Aerospace in Downsview, Ontario, under contract from the National Research Council with a $100 million grant from the Department of Communications. The first arm was presented as a gift to the U.S. — but at least three additional arms will be purchased by the U.S. National Aeronautics and Space Administration.

Canadian participation in the shuttle has refused to acknowledge the overtly military role of the project, even though the prime minister has expressed concern about the military-security implications of this arms race in space. Space weapons technology is rapidly outstripping the diplomatic effort to control it, and Canada has gone along for the ride, resting its case on the industrial benefits that may accrue to Canada from the project.

Incidentally, it is unlikely that the shuttle will make any worthwhile contribution to space-based technology designed to control and monitor the arms race, along the lines of the International Satellite Monitoring Agency (ISMA) under study by the United Nations (see Chapter 14). The Stockholm International Peace Research Institute says that for purposes of reconnaissance, "especially for day-to-day requirements of an ISMA, the space shuttle could be of limited value because of its short flight duration, its high orbital inclination, and difficulty with repetitive coverage of exact locations."

Training and Testing Nuclear Weapons Vehicles in Canada

As the major nuclear powers move inexorably towards first-strike and war-fighting scenarios, the reliability and the precision with which these systems operate become crucial — hence the testing of the systems and the training of personnel to operate them become more and more central to nuclear planning. No military authority, however powerful, could contemplate the use of nuclear weapons in attacks requiring high levels of accuracy without having undertaken extensive testing of the equipment and training of personnel beforehand. Over the years Canada has made its territory and facilities available to its allies for this purpose and now, in early 1983, plans to radically extend its commitment in this regard.

Nuclear-capable aircraft from the United States and several European allies have regularly trained in Canada. Goose Bay, Labrador has in particular been used, and continues to be used, by German and British air forces for training in low-level flying for nuclear-capable aircraft such as the German F-4 Phantom and the British Vulcan bomber. The Canadian nuclear-capable CF-101 interceptor aircraft are regularly used with similar aircraft from the U.S. and other allies in low-level air defence training out of Canadian Forces Base Cold Lake in Alberta.

In early 1983 the government announced a new "umbrella agreement" with the United States to provide for extensive U.S. testing of weapons systems in Canada. Referred to as "The Canada-U.S. Test and Evaluation Program," the agreement prohibits the entry of nuclear, biological or chemical warfare materials into Canada and specifically notes that any cruise missiles to be tested must be unarmed. The initial agreement is for five years and provides general guidelines for tests and evaluations including "projects related to weapons, weapons systems, stores and equipment, and electronic warfare systems and may include associated training and tactics development activities." The proposed tests of the cruise missile, if finally approved, are to take place at the 10,000 square kilometre Primrose Lake Air Weapons Range near Cold Lake, Alberta, northeast of Edmonton and straddling the Alberta-Saskatchewan border. The Canadian tests are to focus particularly on improving the guidance system of the missile.

The high level of accuracy attributed to the cruise missile is not easily achieved, but depends upon an extraordinary set of functions and calculations, the reliability of which cannot be assured without extensive testing. In the missile's TERCOM (terrain contour matching) guidance system, a radar altimeter reads the profile of consecutive strips of terrain along the flight path and compares the profile of each with a profile of the same strip of terrain which has been previously mapped and stored in the missile's computer. By comparing the two, the computer can calculate the degree to which the missile has drifted off course and thus make in-flight course corrections. It is important that the consecutive strips of terrain that are selected contain clearly distinguishable contour features to avoid ambiguous messages in correlating the radar's ground sitings and the data in the computer. Over long stretches of ice and snow such difficulties are more likely, which accounts for at least part of the need for more extensive testing in northern conditions — conditions which, in the words of a Pentagon official, "approximate what would be expected of the operational terrain of the Eurasian-Russian land mass."

Beyond that, the sheer complexity of the missile's guidance system requires extensive testing. Assuming several thousand missiles with at least 1,000 targets in the Soviet Union, detailed maps must be created of many thousands of strips of land, each with hundreds of identifiable features or "data points" which must be mapped and tabulated. This is said to produce over 100 million data points which must be fed into the preprogrammed TERCOM computer map for comparison with the actual terrain during flight. The potential for complications is substantial, but the margin of acceptable error for war-fighting strategies is minimal (given the declared need to strike within a few hundred feet of a target after more than 1,500 miles of flight).

Extensive testing of the cruise missile, therefore, is central to U.S. nuclear war-fighting capacity, and Canadian testing of it is not a demonstration of continued support for nuclear deterrence, as cruise supporters insist, but demonstrates instead support for a new, more dangerous, role for nuclear weapons.

On another front, test operations of considerable significance and interest have taken place for some time in a bay on Vancouver Island near Nanaimo. The Canadian Department of National Defence, however, is sufficiently modest about these underwater test facilities to omit any mention of them in its last annual report. The Canadian Forces Maritime Experimental and Test Range at Nanoose Bay is jointly operated by the Canadian armed forces and the U.S. navy and is devoted to the testing and development of underwater detection and warfare capabilities. The main part of the test range is a fifteen-mile stretch of the Strait of Georgia that varies in width from two to five miles and reaches a depth of 1,400 feet. The range is lined with a series of underwater tripods, each about forty feet high, which carry transmitters and listening devices. The U.S. navy tests torpedoes on the range, with the towers' listening equipment tracking the trajectory of the torpedo and transmitting the information back to the control room for interpretation. The torpedoes are tested to ensure that they meet specifications before being delivered to submarines of the U.S. navy. While the range has not been used primarily as a research site, new or modified pieces of equipment are regularly tested as well.

Under the Canada-U.S. agreement covering Nanoose Bay activities, Canada supplies the territory while the U.S. supplies the equipment. The facility is staffed by U.S. and Canadian armed forces personnel and by Canadian civilians. In 1976 the Canadian government confirmed that the United States "sleeping torpedo" was being tested at the range. The "sleeping torpedo" is capable of carrying a nuclear warhead and is designed to "sleep" on the ocean floor until it is triggered by the sound of an enemy submarine and propelled towards its target. More recently the Americans have used Beluga whales to retrieve spent torpedoes from the test range floor.

The U.S. torpedo tests at Nanoose Bay are part of a major Pentagon push during the past decade to enhance its anti-submarine warfare (ASW) capabilities. While a major focus of ASW activity is the protection of surface shipping lanes, the development of a capacity to seek out and destroy Soviet missile submarines represents a threat to Soviet second-strike forces and reinforces suspicions that the U.S. is pursuing a nuclear first-strike capacity.

Canada's own activity at the Nanoose Bay site fits into the same strategy. Canadian activity is focused on the testing of Canadian-built submarine-detection devices. The sonar buoys that are tested are small canisters which are dropped into the water by the Canadian Aurora long-range patrol aircraft and float at the surface. Upon impact, the buoys release a sensing device that transmits noises, including those of submarines, back to the aircraft. Other sonar units are suspended from helicopters and are retrievable.

The cruise missile, if Canada decides to test it on Canadian territory, joins these other Canadian contributions to the development of nuclear war-fighting capacity on the part of the United States. In 1977, a senior engineer at the Nanoose Bay test range offered this explanation of his role, which could stand as an epitaph to Canada's part in the preparation for World War III: "We are told what is to be tested, we do it and report back what we find. We don't even comment on efficiency or suggested modifications."

References

Clarkson, Stephen. *Canada and the Reagan Challenge: Crisis in the Canadian-American Relationship*. Toronto: James Lorimer & Co., 1982.

Diubaldo, R.J., and Scheinberg, S.J. "A Study of Canadian-American Defence Policy (1945-1975) — Northern Issues and Strategic Resources." Department of National Defence Operational Research and Analysis Establishment, extra-mural paper no. 6.

McLin, Jon B. *Canada's Changing Defense Policy, 1957-1963: The Problems of a Middle Power in Alliance.* Baltimore: The Johns Hopkins Press, 1967.

Standing Committee on External Affairs and National Defence. *NORAD* Report to the House, Dec. 19, 1980.

———. *Report on Security and Disarmament.* April 2, 1982.

Tucker, Michael. *Canadian Foreign Policy: Contemporary Issues and Themes.* Toronto: McGraw-Hill Ryerson, 1980.

6

Canada's Nuclear Industry and the Myth of the Peaceful Atom

Gordon Edwards

Through its dealings with other countries, Canada has played a major role in fostering the proliferation of nuclear weapons throughout the world. This chapter concerns itself with Canada's involvement as a *supplier* of nuclear reactors and uranium, leading to both "vertical proliferation" — the ever-accelerating competition for bigger, better, faster and smarter bombs among the existing nuclear powers — and "horizontal proliferation" — a more insidious process whereby dozens of national and subnational groups are slowly but surely acquiring a nuclear weapons capability. We shall also look at how the Canadian nuclear lobby has influenced the way Canadians view the proliferation problem.

Atoms for War: Uranium and Plutonium for Sale

Canada's involvement began at the very beginning. The World War II atomic bomb project was the largest secret operation in history. It involved elements of the military, government, industry and academia in Canada, Britain and the United States. At its height, it employed over 600,000 people, producing two of the most destructive weapons the world has ever known: the Hiroshima bomb, made from highly enriched uranium, and the Nagasaki bomb, made from plutonium. Building the bombs was relatively easy compared to the major technical difficulties involved in obtaining the two nuclear explosive materials. Canada and the U.K. helped the United States to overcome these obstacles.

Canada supplied uranium from Port Radium in the Northwest Territories, while Britain arranged for uranium to be shipped from the Belgian Congo. Some of it was processed directly into weapons-usable material at a top-secret enrichment facility covering several acres of land near Oak Ridge, Tennessee. The remainder was used to fuel nuclear reactors built at Hanford, Washington, in order to produce plutonium (which does not exist in nature). The Hanford reactors required an exceptionally pure form of graphite to moderate the nuclear reactions, for without a moderator, a plutonium production reactor simply cannot function.

Meanwhile, at the University of Montreal, research on a more efficient way to produce plutonium was carried on. The basic idea was to use heavy water instead of graphite as a moderator. It was expected, on theoretical grounds, that a reactor moderated by heavy water would produce two or three times as much plutonium as other kinds of reactors. The theory was proven correct after the war, when Canada's NRX reactor earned an international reputation as the world's best plutonium-producing reactor.

The work in Montreal was carefully supervised by British and French scientists, who had brought to Canada the world's only existing supply of heavy water, spirited out of Norway by a French diplomat to prevent it from falling into the hands of the Germans. Canada allowed the Americans to manufacture their own strategic supply of heavy water at a reconverted chemical plant in Trail, British Columbia. The Montreal laboratory also performed important chemical experiments involving plutonium.

By the end of the war, Canadian participation in the atom bomb project had become more expensive than all the other research activities of the Canadian government combined. A large organization had come into being under the direction of British scientists, and it was soon producing results. The dust had scarcely settled over Hiroshima and Nagasaki when, on 5 September 1945, the first Canadian nuclear reactor (called ZEEP) began producing plutonium for the continuing American bomb program. Nearby, construction of another, larger reactor for the same purpose (the NRX) was under way. Both reactors were located at Chalk River, 150 miles northwest of Ottawa, where bulldozers were preparing a huge nuclear site in accordance with a secret military decision taken in Washington, D.C. in 1944. Within weeks of the war's ending, however, both the Americans and the British were preparing to abandon the Canadian project in order to pursue their own military programs at home. For although the war was over, the nuclear arms race was just beginning.

On 6 September, one day after the ZEEP reactor started up, a cipher clerk in the office of the Soviet Military Attaché in Ottawa defected. Igor Gouzenko revealed the existence of an extensive Soviet spy network in Canada, whose mission included obtaining information about the atomic bomb. Incidents such as this heightened the mutual fear and distrust that have characterized the nuclear arms race ever since, even though the uncontrollable nature of this race was well understood from the outset.

On 15 November 1945, those countries involved in the original atom bomb project — the U.S., the U.K. and Canada — issued a Joint Declaration containing three prophetic insights:

(1)   nuclear weapons provide "a means of destruction hitherto unknown, against which there can be no adequate military defence";

(2)   "no system of safeguards will of itself provide an effective guarantee against the production of atomic weapons";

(3)   atom bombs are weapons "in the employment of which no single nation can, in fact, have a monopoly."

In other words, unless nuclear weapons are abolished, every country will sooner or later acquire them. At some stage, all-out nuclear war will likely result. To prevent this, the Joint Declaration urged the United Nations to find a way of "entirely eliminating the use of atomic energy for destructive purposes and promoting its use for industrial and humanitarian purposes."

But prejudices and preconceptions die hard. For millenia, military conquest has run like a bright red thread through human history. In the days following the Japanese atomic bombings, British Prime Minister Clement Atlee had observed that nuclear weapons would not be relinquished unless war itself was renounced. In his view, although people can easily understand that

> rivers as strategic frontiers have been obsolete since the advent of air power, it is infinitely harder for people to realize that even the modern conception of war is now completely out of date. The only course which seems to offer a reasonable hope of staving off imminent disaster for the world is joint action by the U.S.A., U.K. and Russia based upon stark reality. We should declare that this invention has made it essential to end wars.

There was, however, no basis for mutual trust. The USSR had not even been informed by its Western allies about the atomic program. The Soviets interpreted the bombing of Hiroshima and Nagasaki as an implied threat against themselves, which was partly true. The allies had apparently adopted Hitler's technique of terrorizing civilian populations from the air. Having used their dreadful weapon twice in a single week against an enemy which did not even have a nuclear research program, would they hesitate to use it again?

Meanwhile, fear of the Soviets replaced fear of Hitler as the driving force behind the American nuclear weapons program. The ambitious U.S. arms buildup was spurred by the realization that some day, someone might do to America what America had already done to Japan. Against such a projected threat, only one defence seemed possible: a counter-threat of massive retaliation which would inflict unacceptable damage on the enemy. In the meantime, any communist aggression could be met with nuclear bombardment if other measures failed.

Echoing America's determination to build a nuclear arsenal, the Soviets, the British and the French were equally determined to establish nuclear deterrent forces, as were the Chinese and many other nations. The profound insights contained in the Joint Declaration of 1945 were all but forgotten. The language of nuclear deterrence swiftly became the logic of nuclear proliferation.

In the ensuing Cold War atmosphere, the U.S. intensified its wartime policy of strict secrecy and non-cooperation with all other nations, including, in large measure, Canada and Britain. The U.S. Atomic Energy Act of 1946 placed a total embargo on the export of all nuclear-related materials and information, in a desperate attempt to retain the American monopoly on the atom bomb.

As it turned out, exclusive U.S. control was not to last long. Russia exploded its first atomic bomb in 1949, followed by the British in 1952. That same year, America detonated its first "hydrogen bomb" or "H-bomb," with an explosive force more than a thousand times greater than the Hiroshima bomb. The Soviets were only eight months behind the Americans with their own H-bomb, while France and China were hard at work to join the nuclear arms race.

But Canada chose a different course. Back in the autumn of 1945 Canada renounced any intention to build atomic bombs. Not long after, responsibility for the Chalk River complex was transferred to the civilian National Research Council, which funded the project until 1952. Canadian nuclear research, it was said, would be dedicated exclusively to bringing the peaceful applications of nuclear energy to commercial fruition. Nevertheless, for twenty years after World War II, Canada sold plutonium (from Chalk River) and uranium (from Ontario, Manitoba, Saskatchewan and the Mackenzie District) for use in the American and British nuclear weapons programs.

To a limited degree, revenues from plutonium sales helped to finance Canada's enormously expensive nuclear research program, including the construction of a second research reactor (called NRU) at Chalk River. Plutonium revenues also helped pay for repairs to the NRX reactor, which suffered a devastating accident in 1952, as well as a massive cleanup operation following severe contamination of the NRU reactor during another nuclear accident in 1958. However, it is fair to say that the government's motivation in selling plutonium was not primarily economic. A sense of loyalty, coupled with a desire to maintain close ties with the nuclear establishments in America and Britain, was the dominant consideration.

Meanwhile, stimulated by lucrative military contracts, Canadian uranium production boomed. It peaked in 1959, with twenty-three mines operating in five districts. Over 12,000 tonnes of uranium were exported in that year, valued at more than $300 million. Uranium ranked fourth among Canada's exports, after newsprint, wheat and lumber. It was almost all for bombs.

Many private fortunes were made in the uranium trade, but Canada as a whole derived little economic benefit from it. Indeed, as a result of Canada's participation in fuelling the nuclear arms buildup during the 1940s and 1950s, over 50 million tonnes of loose radioactive residues were dumped in huge tailings piles near Elliot Lake, Bancroft, Uranium City and Great Bear Lake. The cost of disposing of these long-lived toxic wastes is expected to run into the hundreds of millions of dollars. At some future time, Canadian taxpayers will be presented with the bill. Those who made the profits — and the bombs — are not legally liable.

We will return to the details of Canada's uranium trade later in this chapter. But first, we will examine the origin of the nuclear power industry and its subsequent role in the horizontal proliferation of nuclear weapons.

Atoms for Peace: The Non-Proliferation Treaty

On 8 December 1953, speaking to the UN General Assembly, President Eisenhower announced a new direction in U.S. nuclear policy. He proposed "to take this weapon out of the hands of the soldiers [and put it] into the hands of those who will know how to strip its military casing and adapt it to the arts of peace." A new international agency would be established, dedicated to "Atoms for Peace." In particular, nuclear power reactors would be developed "to provide abundant electrical energy to the power-starved areas" of the world.

Eisenhower's speech created an impression that the peaceful application of nuclear energy would be completely divorced from any possible military application. He even hinted that the nuclear powers would beat their swords into ploughshares, promising that the Atoms for Peace program would "diminish the potential destructive power of the world's atomic stockpiles." Taken at face value, it seemed that the new American initiative could fulfil both of the main objectives of the 1945 Joint Declaration by "entirely eliminating the use of atomic energy for destructive purposes and promoting its use for industrial and humanitarian purposes."

Canada enthusiastically supported Eisenhower's plan. Once adequately developed, nuclear power was expected to become an enormously profitable venture. Canada was fortunate to be in on the ground floor, it was thought. From a commercial point of view, the timing seemed perfect. Just one year earlier, in 1952, Ottawa had had the foresight to create a crown corporation, Atomic Energy of Canada Limited (AECL), to take over the Chalk River complex and to develop and market the peaceful applications of nuclear energy. Now, thanks to Eisenhower's Atoms for Peace concept, Canada's nuclear program might finally begin to pay for itself.

Between April 1955 and October 1956, Canada assisted in drafting the statute governing the International Atomic Energy Agency (IAEA). The IAEA non-proliferation objectives were carefully designed not to interfere with the activities of the nuclear salesmen. According to article 2 of the statute, "the Agency shall seek to accelerate and enlarge the contribution of atomic power to peace, health and prosperity throughout the world. It shall ensure, as far as it is able, that assistance provided by it is not used to further any military purposes." Nuclear regulation was clearly intended to take a back seat to promotional interests.

Over the next decade, the CANDU nuclear power system was developed at a cost of more than one billion dollars. Canada's nuclear electricity program began in earnest in 1954, when AECL and Ontario Hydro agreed to build a small nuclear power demonstration plant (the NPD reactor, with a 22 megawatt capacity) at Rolphton, Ontario. In 1959, three years before the demonstration plant was even completed, these same partners decided to proceed with a prototype CANDU power reactor (Douglas Point, 200 MW), ten times larger than the NPD reactor, located on the Bruce peninsula. Then, in 1964, without waiting for the Douglas Point plant to be finished, construction began on a huge nuclear generating station (Pickering "A") consisting of four even larger CANDU reactors (500 MW each) just 20 miles from downtown Toronto. In 1966, plans for the Gentilly-1 nuclear power plant in Quebec (250 MW) were set in motion. Only the Pickering plant, built by Ontario Hydro, was destined to become a commercial success. All the others, built by AECL, were subsequently plagued with poor performance records and serious design problems.

During this initial busy period, overseas contacts were also being established. In 1956, under the terms of the Colombo plan of foreign aid, Canada gave India an NRX-type research reactor (called CIRUS), worth almost $10 million. In 1959, Canadian Westinghouse contracted to supply a 125 MW power reactor to Pakistan (called KANUPP). In 1963, AECL offered to assist India in the construction of a 200 MW CANDU power reactor (called RAPP-l), modelled on the Douglas Point plant. A second unit (called RAPP-2) was sold to India in 1967. Of course, India and Pakistan gave solemn assurances that all these facilities would be used for peaceful purposes only. In exchange, Canada gave India and Pakistan loans of $33 million and $47 million respectively (the latter to be repaid over a fifty-year period with no interest charges, following a ten-year period of grace).

Around the time of the CIRUS and KANUPP agreements, the U.K. sold two power reactors — one to Japan and one to Italy— and France sold one to Spain. Canada also began selling uranium to West Germany, Switzerland, Japan, Sweden and Euratom (the European nuclear power consortium), all "for peaceful purposes only." However, although many countries acquired research reactors during this period, no further export sales of power reactors occurred until the late 1960s. On a global basis, the Atoms for Peace program was off to a rather slow start.

During these early years, one perplexing question kept recurring: How can "atoms for peace" be distinguished from "atoms for war"? Uranium has only two significant uses: atomic bombs and nuclear reactors. However, these two uses are not mutually exclusive. If the uranium which is used to power a reactor is not weapons-grade material to begin with, it will inevitably produce plutonium as a by-product. That plutonium can be recovered later and used to make atomic bombs.

During the 1940s, Britain and France had developed their basic expertise in plutonium recovery in Canada, beginning with the Montreal experiments and ending with the construction and operation of a pilot plutonium separation plant built at Chalk River. This pioneering work, which proved essential to both the British and the French atomic bomb programs, was difficult and dangerous. In order to extract plutonium from spent reactor fuel, everything must be done by remote control, because of the deadly radiation fields associated with the irradiated uranium as well as the extraordinary toxicity of the plutonium itself. The chemistry is further complicated by the presence of a great many radioactive substances unknown in nature. In 1950, during an experiment at Chalk River involving the extraction of plutonium, a chemical explosion injured six men, contaminating three of them and killing one.

Plutonium extraction on a large scale must be carried out in a special factory called a reprocessing plant, which resembles an oil refinery in appearance. Building on basic knowledge gained in Canada, Britain and France soon became the undisputed world leaders in plutonium reprocessing technology. In most instances, as we shall see, this has been the key technology in the horizontal proliferation of nuclear weapons. The only other route to atomic bombs is via uranium enrichment, which poses more difficult technical problems in general.

From the outset, the Atoms for Peace program was afflicted with an unfortunate ambiguity. Plutonium, the essential ingredient for "cheap atom bombs," was simultaneously portrayed as the nuclear fuel of the future. From the earliest days of the atomic age, it was recognized that uranium supplies would not outlast oil supplies if nuclear power were to provide a significant proportion of the world's energy needs. To keep the reactors running, plutonium would have to replace uranium as a reactor fuel. Indeed, a whole new generation of nuclear reactors called "breeder reactors" would be required to replenish the plutonium supply as needed. In accordance with this grandiose vision of the future, as Victor Gilinsky of the U.S. Nuclear Regulatory Commission has pointed out:

> a desire for plutonium has been kindled by almost universally held assumptions — our own included — that the use of plutonium is a natural, legitimate, desirable, and even indispensable result of the exploitation of nuclear power for the generation of electricity. The powerful grip of this assumption has complicated efforts to prevent this nuclear explosive material from becoming widely and freely available throughout the world.

In effect, by selling uranium and reactors overseas, Canada has helped to create plutonium repositories around the world. For any government wishing to build atomic bombs in the future, this is very convenient, for, at any time, the plutonium can be extracted from the spent nuclear fuel already on hand and used as a nuclear explosive. It can even be done under the guise of Atoms for Peace, ostensibly to gain experience in handling the "fuel of the future." Eisenhower's 1953 speech had skirted around this uncomfortable truth. He had assured the UN General Assembly that "our scientists will provide special safe conditions under which a bank of fissionable material can be made essentially immune to surprise seizure, [even without] a completely acceptable system of worldwide inspection and control." To this day, no one knows what he had in mind.

It was foreseen from the beginning that no system of international safeguards based solely upon auditing procedures, inspections and security measures could possibly prevent the diversion of plutonium from civilian reactors for military purposes. As early as March 1946, the U.S. Acheson-Lilienthal Committee concluded that

> the development of atomic energy for peaceful purposes and the development of atomic energy for bombs are, in much of their course, interchange-

able and interdependent. From this it follows that although nations may agree not to use in bombs the atomic energy developed within their borders, the only assurance that a conversion to destructive purposes would not be made, would be the pledged word and the good faith of the nation itself. This fact puts an enormous pressure upon national good faith.

We have concluded unanimously that there is no prospect for security against atomic warfare in a system of international agreements to outlaw such weapons controlled *only* by a system which relies on inspection and similar police-like methods.

The same conclusion had been succinctly stated in the 1945 Joint Declaration. By the 1950s, however, it had been unaccountably forgotten.

Meanwhile, the nuclear arms race was accelerating year by year. In 1957, Britain exploded its first H-bomb. Two years later, France joined the nuclear club by detonating an atomic bomb over the Sahara Desert. A worldwide public outcry over the health hazards of radioactive fallout led to a treaty in 1963 banning nuclear weapons tests in the atmosphere, in outer space and under water. However, in no way did the Limited Test Ban Treaty slow down the pace of the nuclear arms race. In the U.S. and the USSR, testing simply moved underground. France, refusing to sign the treaty, continued to explode its bombs in the atmosphere along with China, which detonated an atomic bomb in 1964 and an H-bomb in 1967. The Atoms for Peace program provided a convenient smokescreen to obscure what was really going on.

Other nations were also moving towards a nuclear weapons capability. In the early 1960s, ten years before India exploded its first atomic bomb, Indian scientists at Chalk River were asking Canadian scientists pointed questions about plutonium metallurgy — questions having no known civilian application. Also in the 1960s, India, Pakistan and Taiwan all made separate efforts to acquire their own reprocessing plants. Only India succeeded, with American assistance. Then, in 1964, in the greatest possible secrecy, India decided to build an atomic bomb. Knowledgeable observers in Canada, Pakistan, America and elsewhere had little difficulty in guessing the truth. Just a few years later, in a top-secret report prepared in 1968, the U.S. Central Intelligence Agency estimated that Israel had already developed its own atomic bomb.

By 1965, it had become obvious that assumptions made by the IAEA about the separation of civilian and military uses of nuclear power were simply not valid. The superpowers decided that something must be done to stop the bomb from spreading any further. Three years of negotiations took place before the Nuclear Non-Proliferation Treaty (NPT) was approved in 1968. Two more years elapsed before it came into force.

Built into the NPT is a sharp distinction between nuclear-weapon states and non-nuclear-weapon states. The distinction is frankly discriminatory, as the obligations imposed on each are quite different. Each non-nuclear-weapon state which is a party to the NPT has agreed to accept a system of full-scope safeguards policed by the IAEA. The safeguard measures (to be applied on all nuclear facilities, with exceptions) include elaborate accounting procedures and on-site inspections — exactly the kind of measures which were judged to be ineffective by the Acheson-Lilienthal Report of 1946. Moreover, nuclear-weapon states need not subject themselves to any such onerous requirements, according to the terms of the NPT. Thus the Soviets, who helped draft the NPT, have never allowed IAEA inspections of any of their own nuclear facilities.

The nuclear-weapon states signing the NPT agreed to provide "the fullest possible exchange of equipment, materials, and scientific and technological information for the peaceful uses of atomic energy," in exchange for promises from the non-nuclear-weapon states not to acquire atomic bombs or any other nuclear explosive devices. The nuclear-weapon states also undertook to negotiate in good faith a complete cessation of the nuclear arms race towards the ultimate goal of total disarmament — a pledge that has been honoured mainly in the breach.

Among the nuclear-weapon states, France and China flatly refused to sign the NPT. As an added inducement, nations that did sign were given the right to withdraw at any time on three months' notice. Even so, ten non-nuclear-weapon states with significant nuclear programs — Argentina, Brazil, Chile, India, Israel, Pakistan, South Africa, South Korea, Spain and Turkey — refused to sign. Despite these drawbacks, had the spirit of the NPT been rigorously upheld throughout the 1970s by all parties, it might have had a profound effect in restraining both vertical and horizontal proliferation. Without such a determined commitment, it was crippled from the start.

As subsequent events showed, vertical proliferation continued unabated while Canada and other nuclear vendors willingly engaged in nuclear trade with countries which had refused to sign the NPT. Major nuclear cooperation agreements involving Argentina, Brazil, South Africa, South Korea and Franco's Spain were soon entered into. The dictatorial and militaristic leanings of the ruling elites in these countries proved to be no impediment. In practical terms, their refusal to accept the NPT made little or no difference to their nuclear ambitions; they were still able to get what they wanted.

Soon, the international non-proliferation regime came to be regarded with cynicism. As in Hans Christian Andersen's classic tale of the Emperor's New Clothes, the splendid-sounding words cloaking the motives of the nuclear-weapon states and the reactor vendors appeared altogether transparent. Atoms for Peace was merely a slogan, not a genuine objective.

India, Pakistan and the Middle East

In October 1971, Prime Minister Trudeau of Canada warned Prime Minister Gandhi of India that the use of plutonium from the Canadian-supplied CIRUS, RAPP-1 or RAPP-2 reactors "for the development of a nuclear explosive device, would inevitably call on our part for a reassessment of our nuclear cooperation with India." Gandhi dismissed Trudeau's concern as "hypothetical."

On 18 May 1974, India's first atomic bomb was detonated in the Rajasthan desert. India later admitted that the plutonium for the bomb had been produced in the CIRUS reactor. Nevertheless, India insisted that the agreement with Canada had in no way been broken. The Indian government maintained that the bomb was a "peaceful nuclear explosive" and not a military weapon. It was also pointed out that the uranium fuel which bred the plutonium was not of Canadian origin.

France congratulated the Indian government on its accomplishment. Pakistan was the only Third World country to condemn those responsible for the test. The Americans, who had supplied heavy water for the CIRUS reactor and tutored Indian scientists in plutonium-handling techniques, were shocked and chagrined. Twenty years earlier, American scientists had created a fundamental ambiguity by introducing the foolish notion of a "peaceful nuclear explosive" which might be used to create harbours, dig canals and hollow out underground reservoirs of natural gas. Though the concept was subsequently discredited, the ambiguity remained and could now be exploited by any nation wishing to make its own "nuclear devices" — without calling them "bombs."

The Canadian government immediately suspended all nuclear cooperation with India. It was a relatively empty gesture, for the Canadians were not really needed in India any more. After RAPP-1 and RAPP-2, the Indians went on to build four more CANDU reactors without Canadian assistance. Towards the end of 1974, Canada responded further to the Indian explosion by announcing more stringent safeguards on all future sales of Canadian nuclear materials and equipment. Though well-intentioned, this approach unfortunately served to perpetuate the myth that truly effective safeguards agreements are possible. In effect, the Emperor was merely ordering a new set of clothes.

The Indian episode illustrates the uncanny accuracy of the insights contained in the 1945 Joint Declaration: there is no adequate defence, there is no effective control, and there is no possibility of monopoly. As long as nuclear weapons exist, they will surely spread like a contagious disease. Writing in *The Nation* in 1976, Richard Falk observed:

> Underlying the whole policy of the nuclear age is the fantastic notion that you can both promote a peaceful world and, at the same time, retain the domineering capacities that come from having nuclear weapons.
>
> In order to obscure the perverse logic, we have had to proliferate nuclear technology for so-called peaceful purposes; and that is where the Catch-22 factor comes in. To prevent the spread of nuclear capabilities, we've had to spread nuclear capabilities — because the problem of how to keep nuclear weapons exclusively for ourselves poses quite an impossible political puzzle. This immense process of deception and self-deception is implicit in the effort to have the benefits of nuclear force, but somehow deny them to others.
>
> And then we have the audacity to lecture the Indians on their temerity in exploding a single nuclear device, while in the same week that India exploded that device, the Soviet Union and the United States between them exploded seven far more destructive devices.

The Indian explosion also revealed something of great significance concerning the gap between the have and the have-not nations. Following hard on the heels of the OPEC oil embargo of 1973, the Indian action communicated a forceful message: the age of Western hegemony is drawing to a close. In 1978, the Cluff Lake Board of Inquiry into Uranium Mining in Saskatchewan reported that Canada had seriously underestimated

> the significance of the Indian achievement in the eyes of the Third World. India's action provided new incentives for other nations to go nuclear; revealed a new route via nuclear explosions for "peaceful purposes"; challenged the claim that nuclear explosives are only peaceful if done by a Nuclear-Weapon State; and successfully defied a system regarded by many of the Third World nations as one of superpower domination.

At the NPT Review Conference held in Geneva just one year after the Indian explosion, a new mood was apparent among the unaligned Third World countries, who clamoured for the superpowers to start living up to their own neglected NPT obligations. As William Epstein of Canada reported, the developing nations challenged the nuclear-weapon states " to end underground nuclear tests, to reduce nuclear arms, to pledge not to use or threaten to use nuclear weapons against Non-Nuclear-Weapon Parties to the Treaty, and to agree to rules for creating nuclear-free zones." However, "all of these major proposals were rejected by the superpowers and their NATO and Warsaw Pact allies." It is hardly surprising that the NPT came to be viewed as a combined East-West effort by nuclear bullies to prevent Third World countries from ever becoming equal.

Ali Bhutto, then prime minister of Pakistan, was especially determined not to knuckle under. Writing in 1979, he pointed out what must be obvious to most Arabs: "Israel and South Africa have full nuclear capability. The Christian, Jewish and Hindu civilizations have this capability. Only the Islamic civilization was without it." Throughout his political career, Bhutto was determined to make Pakistan a nuclear power. As early as 1967, when he was living in Paris, he had observed:

> All European strategy is based on the concept of total war. A war waged against Pakistan is capable of becoming a total war. Our plans should therefore include the nuclear deterrent. India is unlikely to concede nuclear monopoly to others. It appears that she is determined to proceed with her plans to detonate a nuclear bomb. Pakistan must therefore embark upon a similar program.

The decision to build the Islamic world's first atomic bomb was taken by Pakistan in January 1972, less than a month after Bhutto came to power. Since then, much of the necessary research has been financed through the efforts of Libyan dictator Colonel Qaddafi. Qaddafi had been trying to break into the nuclear club since 1968, when he first suspected that Israel had the bomb. His suspicions were not without foundation, for in December 1974, the president of Israel told a group of visiting science writers: "It has always been our intention to develop a nuclear potential. We now have that potential. If we should have need of such arms, we would have them in a short time — even a few days."

Pakistan had earlier acquired a source of plutonium in the form of the 125 MW KANUPP reactor from Canada, committed in 1959 with assurances that it would be used "for peaceful purposes only." The responsibility for safeguarding this nuclear power plant was transferred from AECL to the IAEA in 1969, three years before it went into commercial operation. Following the Indian atomic explosion, Canada tried to obtain binding assurances from Pakistan that plutonium produced in the KANUPP reactor would never be used as a nuclear explosive. By December 1975, it was evident that Pakistan would simply not agree to this condition; the Canadian government therefore terminated its program of nuclear cooperation with Pakistan. About the same time, Bhutto vowed that his country would "never surrender to any nuclear blackmail from India. The people of Pakistan are ready to offer any sacrifice, and even eat grass, to ensure nuclear parity with India."

Since 1973, Pakistan has been negotiating to purchase a large plutonium reprocessing plant from France. Despite Pakistan's reluctance, the plant would have to be subjected to IAEA safeguards or France would not sell. Pakistan finally agreed, but only after deciding to build a much smaller "pilot plant" for plutonium separation based on technical information and experience gleaned from the French project. The smaller plant would not be subject to IAEA inspections. According to a French telex dated 28 July 1975, Pakistan's nuclear chief Munir Khan boasted that, with such a pilot plant, "his country would be in a position to produce — using the irradiated natural uranium produced by their Canadian reactor — the few kilograms of plutonium necessary for an explosive device."

Although Ali Bhutto was overthrown by General Zia ul-Haq in April 1978, Pakistan's nuclear plans remained essentially unchanged. Two months later, France finally bowed to American pressure by cancelling the contract for the reprocessing plant. It was too late, however. Pakistan already had almost everything needed to complete the project alone. Both the large and the small plutonium separation facilities were expected to be operational in 1983.

The Indian explosion had ramifications throughout the Middle East. The Shah's Iran, an apprehensive neighbour of both India and Pakistan, promptly ordered several nuclear reactors. Iranian students were sent abroad to study nuclear physics and engineering. The equally militaristic Iraqi regime began shopping around for nuclear reactors as well. According to Yves Girard of the French Department of Energy (as reported in *The Islamic Bomb*), several CANDU salesmen who were in Baghdad in December 1974 were quick

> to point out the virtues of the CANDU reactor, hinting broadly at its excellence in producing the deadly substance [plutonium], and even more broadly at the possibilities of keeping safeguards to a minimum. What bothered Girard most was not that they had tried to sell the CANDU that way. It was their later hypocrisy in pointing to the French sale as a danger for nuclear proliferation, when actually they had desperately wanted the sale for themselves, and had indicated no concern whatsoever whether Iraq got the bomb or not.

In a general sense, hyprocrisy may be the crux of the proliferation problem. How can Canada expect other nations not to develop nuclear weapons, when it clearly accepts the right of the U.S., the U.K., the USSR, France and China to have them? Canada does not object in principle to nuclear weapons, it seems, but only cares whose finger is on the nuclear trigger.

Like all double standards, this one is odious. Herbert Scoville, who spent many years in the U.S. nuclear weapons business and in the CIA before joining the Arms Control and Disarmament Agency, portrays the nuclear arms race as

> symbolic of a perverted world, where the possession of nuclear weapons is taken as a sign that a country is important and should be listened to. Instead, I believe we must create an international atmosphere where the possession of nuclear weapons is a cause for embarrassment and shame, rather than for power and prestige.
>
> Unless we all work together to establish a climate in which nuclear weapons are not assigned political or military value, we may see mushroom clouds over Tel Aviv and Cairo, and lingering radiation casualties throughout the Middle East.
>
> But no one knows how to limit a nuclear war. It could escalate out of control. These horrors, multiplied many times over, could equally well be visited on Washington and New York, London and Belfast, Paris and Marseilles, Moscow and Leningrad.
>
> If the nuclear powers are seeking to halt the spread of nuclear weapons, they are certainly going about it the wrong way.

Taiwan, South Korea and Argentina

Canada's nuclear dealings with Taiwan, South Korea and Argentina, taking place later than those with India and Pakistan, revealed much about the nature of the international nuclear trade.

In 1969, Canada sold Taiwan an NRX-type research reactor very similar to the CIRUS reactor that was supplied to India in 1956. An agreement was signed whereby the reactor would not be used "to further any military purpose." Shortly afterwards, however, Canada recognized mainland China and severed diplomatic relations with Taiwan, an already-isolated country, obsessed with its own defence.

Supplying Taiwan with the means to make nuclear weapons, and then joining in its international abandonment, might be said to invite the spread of the atomic bomb. As former U.S. Department of Defense Director George Rathjens said in 1976: "If mainland China made a determined effort to take Taiwan, the Taiwan government could only effectively respond with nuclear weapons."

In fact, by 1974, Taiwan had actually built a small, clandestine facility for separating plutonium. It had also ordered a much larger reprocessing plant from France, similar to the one ordered by Pakistan. When the Americans got wind of this, they forced Taiwan to cancel the order and to dismantle the existing plutonium separation plant immediately, threatening to withdraw all military aid otherwise.

Canada's next export sale came in December 1973, when a contract was signed obligating AECL to supply a 600 MW CANDU reactor to Argentina (the EMBALSE reactor). The contract became effective in April 1974, just weeks before the Indian atomic explosion. Meanwhile, negotiations were under way with South Korea for the construction of another 600 MW CANDU (the WOLSUNG reactor), for which the contract was signed early in 1975. In retrospect, it is clear that both Argentina and South Korea were interested in acquiring nuclear arms.

Argentine dictator Juan Peron had boasted of his country's capacity to develop the atomic bomb as early as 1951, based on research done in Argentina by Ronald Richler, an ex-Nazi nuclear physicist. Of the thousands of German Nazis who fled to Argentina after the collapse of the Third Reich, many were destined to play key roles in the Argentine nuclear industry. To give one example, during World War II Walther Schnurr helped to develop Zyklon-B gas, which was used to exterminate millions in Nazi death camps. He fled Germany at the end of the war and settled in Argentina. Recalled to Germany in 1955, Schnurr subsequently negotiated the delivery to Argentina of a small plutonium separation facility in the 1960s, as well as a medium-sized reactor called ATUCHA-I (375 MW) which was started up in 1974. With these two German nuclear facilities, Argentina could in fact build an atomic bomb. In 1973, Schnurr was awarded the Mayo medal, Argentina's highest award for foreigners.

The additional purchase of a CANDU reactor would add significantly to Argentina's plutonium inventory. Because it is moderated with heavy water, the CANDU design produces more plutonium than any other power reactor on the international market. The CANDU reactor also has an efficient system of "on-line refuelling," by which spent fuel can be removed from the reactor by remote control at any time of the day or night, even while the reactor is operating at full power. No other commercial power reactor has a comparable capability. On-line refuelling makes it particularly difficult to safeguard a CANDU reactor; an inspector would have to be present 24 hours a day, 365 days a year, to ensure that all the spent fuel is accounted for at all times. Moreover, since the CANDU is fuelled with natural uranium, with which Argentina is well endowed, the Argentine regime would be free from any dependence on America, Europe or the USSR for supplies of enriched uranium. With the CANDU system, Argentina's nuclear fuel supply could never be cut off.

The Korean dictatorship of General Park Chung Hee had secretly decided in the early 1970s to build an atomic bomb. In 1972, discussions began with France for the purchase of a reprocessing plant, and the actual contract was signed early in 1975. As in the case of Pakistan and Taiwan, the military implications of this move were not lost on the Americans. On 8 March 1975, the French ambassador wired his government from Seoul: "The United States has no doubts that the Koreans have in mind putting to ulterior military ends what they can make use of, such as plutonium." In June 1975, General Park told the *Washington Post* that if the Americans were ever to weaken their support, South Korea would have to develop its own nuclear weapons. "We have the capacity to do it," he declared. That same month, *Newsweek* magazine reported that General Park had ordered the Korean Defence Development Agency to begin research on atomic weapons.

By December 1974, the political impact of India's explosion the previous spring began to be felt by the team of CANDU salesmen peddling their wares in Baghdad and Seoul, and by the Argentine officials about to sign an agreement to allow routine IAEA inspections of the EMBALSE reactor. Canada unveiled its new policy on nuclear safeguards: henceforth all items of Canadian origin, and all nuclear materials produced by or with Canadian-origin items, would have to be used exclusively for non-military and non-explosive purposes. In addition, prior consent would have to be obtained from Canada before any high-level enrichment, reprocessing or re-transfer of such nuclear materials would be permitted. IAEA safeguards (or equivalent) would have to be applied for the lifetime of the facilities or materials in question, and acceptable physical security measures would have to be employed to prevent theft or sabotage. Pending renegotiation of Canada's existing nuclear cooperation agreements, nuclear exports (including exports of uranium) would be allowed to proceed on a "business-as-usual" basis for one year. (This was later extended to two years.)

Throughout 1975, Canada worked to obtain bilateral agreements with Argentina and South Korea incorporating the conditions of the new policy, and agreements were finally concluded in January 1976. In South Korea's case, in view of that country's continuing efforts to obtain a plutonium reprocessing plant, the Korean regime was officially notified that Canada "would not be prepared, at this time, to agree to the reprocessing of nuclear material." Later, under intense pressure from the Americans, Korea (like Taiwan) was forced to abandon its efforts to purchase a reprocessing plant from France. However, rumours persisted that Korea was still intent on pursuing a nuclear weapons option, as documented in a

1978 U.S. congressional report. On the other hand, Argentina frankly and openly stated that a nuclear weapons option must be regarded as an Argentine prerogative. The Argentine regime refused to ratify the Treaty of Tlatelolco, which would keep Latin America free of nuclear arms. Under these circumstances, even the new Canadian safeguards agreements seemed but a flimsy defence against the proliferation of nuclear weapons.

The ineffectiveness of unenforced nuclear safeguards was recognized in the upper echelons of the federal government at this time. In October 1975, Joseph Stanford, director of the Legal Advisory Division of the Canadian Department of External Affairs, stated: "Safeguards by themselves cannot prevent the proliferation of nuclear weapons. All they can do is detect breaches of the safeguards." Speaking to an international gathering of lawyers in Washington, D.C., Stanford pointed out that even the most stringent safeguards were "not much good," because there was no international consensus "on what is to be done if the agreements are violated." Without such a consensus, any nation violating the non-proliferation objectives "could bargain one country off against the other." In that case, relaxation of the safeguards would inevitably "become a factor in commercial negotiations for nuclear reactor sales" — a prophetic statement, as subsequent events would show. At any rate, Stanford observed, safeguards without teeth are, by definition, not enforceable; they will never succeed in preventing the spread of nuclear weapons. Six months later, these sentiments were echoed by Sigvard Eklund, Director of the IAEA, in an address to the UN General Assembly.

At the same time, Canadian public opposition to nuclear power was growing by leaps and bounds. To begin with, the Indian atomic explosion in 1974 had shocked Canadians from coast to coast. The following year, evacuation of radioactively contaminated homes and schools in Port Hope, Ontario, made national news. Then, by the autumn of 1975, it became public knowledge that AECL was going to lose over $100 million on its Argentinian sale due to financial bungling. Around the same time, the Canadian Coalition for Nuclear Responsibility began publicly disputing the need for nuclear power as an energy source, arguing in favour of cheaper, safer, more suitable energy alternatives. The federal Liberal Party, at its policy convention in Ottawa in November 1975, unanimously adopted a resolution calling on its government leaders to launch a national public inquiry into nuclear power "in order to acquaint the people of Canada with the hazards and the benefits of nuclear technology." The government ignored this resolution and turned a deaf ear to the nuclear critics.

But the controversy would not die. In 1976, the Auditor-General's

Report revealed that on top of its $100 million loss, AECL had committed major financial indiscretions in connection with the Argentinian and Korean sales — including the payment of huge sums in unauthorized agents' fees. In the case of Argentina, AECL deposited $2.5 million in an anonymous Swiss bank account; the identity of the recipient was never discovered. In the case of Korea, Shoul Eisenberg of Tel Aviv received $18 million in unaccountable payments from AECL. Amidst charges of bribery, corruption and kick-backs, the House of Commons Public Accounts Committee launched an investigation. However, the committee was denied power of subpoena by the Liberal majority on the committee, AECL refused to present its books for inspection, and top AECL officials stonewalled the committee by refusing to answer questions. The committee reported that AECL witnesses were "reluctant," "uncooperative" and "evasive" in testifying. The committee also concluded that

> the successful concealment, by complex and sophisticated payment and banking procedures in foreign countries, of the identities of the ultimate recipients of the funds and the nature of services rendered, leads your Committee to suspect that some of the payments were indeed used for illegal or corrupt purposes.

It is sobering to reflect that IAEA inspectors have even fewer powers of inquiry than the House of Commons Public Accounts Committee has. If $20 million can disappear without being accounted for, then surely 20 pounds of plutonium — enough to make an atomic bomb — could also disappear without anyone being the wiser. (In the United States, the amount of plutonium which is officially acknowledged as missing — that is, "unaccounted for" — would be sufficient to make hundreds of atomic bombs.)

In June 1976, in the face of mounting public opposition, Prime Minister Trudeau publicly defended his government's determination to provide nuclear technology to countries like Argentina and South Korea. In a world "starved for energy," Trudeau insisted that Canada had a "moral obligation" to share its nuclear technology with Third World countries. "You've got to live dangerously if you want to live in the modern age," he said. "In a sense," he added, "we're relying on the signed word" to prevent misuse of nuclear technology. In a similar vein, Donald Macdonald, then minister of energy, told the House of Commons that Canada would have to "trust the motives" of her nuclear clients and rely on them "to honour their undertakings and obligations in good faith."

For all their emphasis on "moral obligations," both Trudeau and Macdonald avoided the most perplexing question: Are the military rulers in

Argentina and South Korea trustworthy? Under these brutally repressive regimes, political freedom is unknown. Human rights and civil liberties are trampled upon. Rigid class structures are maintained with an iron fist. Taiwan and South Korea both yielded to U.S. pressure and cancelled their orders for reprocessing plants, because they depended so heavily on American economic and military aid. But what could Canada do if either Argentina or South Korea decided to renege on the non-proliferation promises?

Just three months before Trudeau's speech, in March 1976, General Videla's junta seized power in Argentina by violently overthrowing the government of Isabel Peron. Since then, twenty thousand people from all walks of life have simply disappeared; most of them were never heard from again. Two-thirds of the "disappeared ones" were labour organizers, kidnapped and imprisoned by the army's security forces. Men, women and children have been tortured and murdered for obscure reasons. Writers and other members of the intelligentsia have been systematically incarcerated.

In South Korea, likewise, strong-arm methods have become a way of life. Strict censorship, illegal detentions, mass arrests and torture are not uncommon occurrences. General Park seized power in 1961 through a military coup. Throughout 1974, as CANDU salesmen were wooing Korean officials, the country was teetering on the brink of martial law. In May 1975, shortly after the contract was signed with AECL, General Park passed Emergency Law Number 9, which forbade any criticism of the government and prevented the reporting of any opinions not in accord with official government policy. Political gatherings, even in private homes, were outlawed, as were public demonstrations of any kind. Jail terms and death sentences were prescribed. The Emergency Law remained in force until 1979 — the year when General Park was shot through the head at a state dinner by his own chief of central intelligence.

In December 1976, in an effort to forestall further criticism, Canada unilaterally adopted the most stringent safeguards requirements in the world. The new policy went considerably beyond the 1974 requirements, but unfortunately, it was based on the crumbling foundation of the NPT. In future, nuclear cooperation would be authorized only with nations which had ratified the NPT, or which had made "an equally binding commitment to non-proliferation." In either case, full-scope safeguards on all nuclear activities would have to be applied.

Korea automatically satisfied the new Canadian requirements, having signed the NPT in 1975 with all the IAEA inspection and auditing procedures already accepted. However, Argentina stubbornly refused to conform. The Argentine generals accepted neither the non-proliferation objectives nor the full-scope safeguards demanded by Canada's new policy. Facilities built in Argentina without foreign assistance would not be subjected to the indignity of inspectors from outside the country. Since the construction of the EMBALSE reactor was well under way, Canada decided to abide by the 1974 policy in Argentina's case.

While Canada was stiffening her nuclear safeguards requirements, the U.S. was trying very hard to stop the sale of "sensitive technologies" — uranium enrichment and plutonium reprocessing plants — which could bring any country dangerously close to a nuclear weapons capability. If the atomic bomb becomes generally available, the American doctrine of nuclear deterrence based on "Mutually Assured Destruction" would become totally meaningless. As one U.S. official remarked, "in a few years' time we might wake up to find Washington, D.C. gone — and not even know who did it!"

As the result of a joint Canada-U.S. initiative to curb horizontal proliferation, the "Nuclear Suppliers' Group" (commonly known as the London Club) met for the first time in April 1975, with representatives from Canada, France, Great Britain, Japan, West Germany, the U.S. and the USSR. Meetings were held every few months. The list of participants gradually expanded to include fifteen industrialized nations, but with no representation from the Third World. Meanwhile, vertical proliferation continued unchecked. Despite six years of Strategic Arms Limitations Talks, the U.S. and the USSR produced only one meaningful agreement — the Anti-Ballistic Missile Treaty. In 1976, Herbert Scoville, director of the Arms Control Association, scornfully referred to the superpowers as "two nuclear alcoholics who take a pledge to stop drinking aperitifs and instead guzzle brandy into the wee hours."

Finally, in January 1978, the London Club published a "trigger list" of nuclear items which must not be sold without solemn assurances that they would be used solely for non-explosive purposes. The list included heavy water and reactor-grade graphite as well as plutonium and highly enriched uranium. However, the Canadians were not successful in having all nuclear suppliers require full-scope safeguards of their customers, and the Americans failed completely in their attempt to impose an outright ban on the export of enrichment and reprocessing facilities. France and West Germany, who were selling these technologies, were determined not to let the Americans tell them what to do.

Perhaps the most telling failure of the London Club lay in its inability or unwillingness to define a common course of action, to be followed by all, in the event of a violation of the "non-explosive use" clause. Thus the only assurance that a country would not misuse nuclear technology continued to be "national good faith." Safeguards without teeth, promulgated by nuclear powers showing no restraint in their own nuclear weapons programs, offered scant protection against horizontal proliferation.

The awkwardness of Canada's position was revealed in November 1978, when the *Washington Post* reported that Admiral Carlos Castro Madero of Argentina had clearly indicated his country's intention to build an atomic bomb. Madero's words were recorded on tape. When questioned on 21 November, Donald Jamieson, Canadian secretary of state for external affairs, told the House of Commons that Madero "may not be a formal spokesman for the [Argentine] Government. I think it can be said that the Government of Argentina has no intention of going into reprocessing." (At that time, Admiral Madero was Head of the Argentine Atomic Energy Authority.) Three weeks later, in response to further questioning, Jamieson confessed that "whether he is a spokesman for the Government of Argentina *per se*, and Argentina has endorsed his statements, we still have not officially determined." At any rate, Jamieson pointed out that Canada's 1974 safeguards policy forbids Argentina from using Canadian technology to make a bomb. "In the event of non-compliance," he declared, "Canada may suspend cooperation, and may request that Argentina immediately cease to use any Canadian supplies." Yet similar signals continued to come from Argentina without provoking any such response.

The Collapse of the CANDU Market

Throughout the turbulent 1970s, the CANDU salesmen never slackened their efforts. Prior to 1975, overtures were made by AECL to Mexico, Romania, Australia, Greece, Italy and Denmark, without any success. Each separate effort cost $1 million or more. In the latter half of the decade, Great Britain, Japan, China, Venezuela, Romania, Yugoslavia, Indonesia and Ireland (among others) were targets of CANDU marketing efforts. This ambitious sales push resulted in only one further sale of a single 600 MW CANDU reactor to Romania in 1978. Even that sale came under attack from Conservative MP Flora MacDonald who did not believe that Canada should be selling nuclear technology to Warsaw Pact nations.

By the end of 1978, the future was beginning to look bleak for the Canadian nuclear industry. Domestic markets for CANDU reactors had evaporated. Electrical growth rates had been dropping steadily since 1973, and most provincial utilities were beginning to experience large surpluses of electrical capacity. A similar phenomenon was occurring all over North America and Western Europe. Yet a report commissioned by the Canadian Nuclear Association (CNA) indicated that two sales per year would be needed to keep the CANDU industry alive. Where would these orders come from?

The American light-water reactor had already captured the European market, while Japan and Great Britain were more interested in developing their own reactor systems than importing Canadian technology. Not a single reactor vendor had yet turned a profit anywhere in the world, yet the competition was extraordinarily keen. Only Third World countries were seen as potential customers for CANDU reactors, but the obstacles were formidable. It soon became apparent that nuclear power is not a suitable energy source for most developing countries, for a variety of reasons.

To begin with, only a handful of Third World countries have electrical grids large enough to accommodate a nuclear power plant. Even then, in many cases the majority of people live in areas where there are no electrical services. Amulya Reddy of India's Bangor Institute has observed that "most Third World countries are in fact dual societies with small, affluent, largely urban-based elites (10-20 per cent of the population) and large masses of poverty-stricken people, most of whom live in rural areas. When electricity is introduced into rural regions, it rarely penetrates beyond the richer farmers of agribusiness who are close to major distribution grids. So the development impact of nuclear power transfer, for the majority of rural poor, will not be great." Even in the cities, few are rich enough to afford electricity.

In most cases, then, nuclear power actually concentrates more economic and political power in the hands of those who already have too much. David Rogers, a Canadian nuclear physicist, wrote that, for this reason, nuclear programs generally increase "the degree of undemocratic social control exerted in developing countries." At a 1979 conference at the Massachusetts Institute of Technology hosted by the World Council of Churches, delegates from over fifty developing nations signed a declaration asserting that the only Third World governments wanting nuclear power were dictatorial regimes with ulterior motives: "The motivation for importing reactors in these states derives from military-political considerations and aspirations for prestige." The declaration was read out to the assembly in support of a resolution calling for a global moratorium on nuclear power plants, which passed by a wide margin.

These observations are valid even in the more technically advanced Third World countries. Dr. Miguel Ussher, a special assistant to the president of Argentina, appeared on a panel in Knoxville, Tennessee in

November 1981 to discuss the role of nuclear power in developing nations. He said:

> ... if we consider the amount of money invested, [nuclear power] is the most costly electricity ever made. But from other points of view it has been entirely convenient. Militarily and strategically, it's not exactly the same.
>
> For example, since we [Argentina] have 70 years reserve of gas, we could cover the country with gas turbines and that would solve all the problems. We know that perfectly, and it would cost less. But this is a different matter. We have to deal with the problem under the conditions that *really* exist. Brazil is in the same case.

When asked if this meant that Argentina wanted nuclear technology in order to have a nuclear weapons option, Dr. Ussher said "Right."

Once a developing nation decides that it wants nuclear power, the biggest practical obstacle is lack of capital. Romania is a case in point. Despite a billion-dollar line of credit advanced by the federal government's Export Development Corporation in 1979 to help finance the CANDU sale, Romania had still not ordered a single CANDU component three years later. During the intervening years, tortuous trade negotiations took place. In order to earn enough foreign currency to pay for the CANDU, Romania wanted Canada to buy (or find buyers for) Romanian farm machinery and textiles. In June 1981, to keep the negotiations alive, Romanian officials initialled an agreement to purchase a second CANDU — but still no orders were placed for the first. In the spring of 1982 the Export Development Corporation finally withdrew the Romanian line of credit.

None of these bleak realities jibed with the magnificent vision of a nuclear-powered planet that had been conjured up earlier by nuclear enthusiasts. For example, in 1974, AECL vice-president A.J. Mooradian had stated that, thanks to nuclear power, "For the first time in human history, mankind can look forward to a world civilization of 10 or 20 billions, well-clothed, well-housed, well-fed, living in peace and harmony for thousands of generations." Four years later without domestic or export markets, the CANDU manufacturing industry was facing inevitable collapse. While the full ramifications were not to be felt for several more years, the handwriting was on the wall as early as 1978.

And so it was a lean and hungry sales team that returned to Argentina in 1978-79 to try to sell a second CANDU reactor. Admiral Madero, head of the Argentine Atomic Energy Authority, offered the Canadians a lukewarm reception. Lengthy delays and serious cost overruns had plagued the EMBALSE reactor, and there had been the irksome negotiations necessitated by Canada's evolving safeguards requirements. The Argentinians were not pleased.

By April 1979, however, AECL had come up with an offer which (it was hoped) Argentina could scarcely refuse. For $1 billion, Argentina could acquire not only a second 600 MW CANDU reactor, complete with a five-year supply of heavy water and uranium fuel, but also an NRX-type research reactor, a heavy-water manufacturing plant, a CANDU fuel fabrication plant, uranium exploration and exploitation technology, and a licensing arrangement which would allow Argentina to build and sell its own CANDU reactor in future — in short, everything needed to make Argentina self-sufficient in CANDU technology. Meanwhile, a German and Swiss consortium offered a very similar package at a much heftier price of $1.5 billion. Moreover, the European deal involved a 600 MW heavy-water reactor which had not yet been designed, whereas the Pickering reactors in Ontario had already proven themselves to be the best electricity-producing reactors in the world. The Canadians were jubilant. It seemed the contract was in the bag.

In the summer of 1979, longshoremen and other workers in Saint John, New Brunswick, refused to load a shipment of heavy water bound for the EMBALSE reactor. They demanded the release of sixteen trade unionists who had been imprisoned without charges in Argentina. The action was organized by the No CANDU for Argentina Committee, and had the full backing of the Canadian Labour Congress, representing 2.5 million Canadian workers. A few days after the boycott, six of the trade unionists were released from Argentine prisons. In October of that year, speaking at the United Nations, External Affairs Minister Flora MacDonald denounced the atrocious human rights record of the Argentine regime. Within days, the Argentinians announced that they were accepting the more expensive German-Swiss deal over the AECL offer.

Disappointed and angry, AECL spokesmen lashed out at the Canadian government for its vacillations on nuclear safeguards, and at Flora MacDonald for her ill-timed remarks. "Canada's standards are too tough," lamented Ray Burge, chief of public relations for AECL. Ross Campbell, chairman of AECL, bitterly criticized Ottawa's "waffling" on nuclear safeguards, saying that AECL's position internationally had been "thoroughly undermined." He also referred to Flora MacDonald's remarks as a "gratuitous offence by Canada." "The ripples from this will be far greater than we've estimated," said Mr. Campbell, warning that the CANDU system was in danger of becoming extinct. Liberal external affairs critic Allan MacEachen took up the refrain in the House of Commons, blaming the loss of the sale on "imprudent remarks at a critical time. It was a very ham-handed way to deal with a very important international negotiation involving billions of dollars."

However, it seems that if anyone deserved such sharp-tongued criticism, it was the German government. In April 1980, the Canadian embassy in Bonn publicly expressed disappointment that "non-proliferation safeguard requirements did become an element of the competition" for the Argentine sale, despite a previous commitment from West Germany to accept Canada's position on the need for full-scope safeguards as a non-negotiable condition of the sale. Just before the contract was awarded, the German-Swiss consortium apparently broke this agreement with Canada by dropping the requirement for full-scope safeguards. At the time, a confidential memorandum circulated within the German cabinet warned Chancellor Schmidt that there would probably be hostile reactions from Ottawa and Washington. Nevertheless, combined Canadian-American pressure exerted in the spring of 1980 was unable to prevent the sale on non-proliferation grounds. Thanks to the Germans and the Swiss, Argentina would soon be able to build a complete nuclear fuel cycle of its own, free from any kind of international safeguards.

The heavy water boycott may have been taken as a warning by Argentina to tread cautiously with Canada. Still, the Canadian reactor being built in Cordoba province was vitally important. "If the Cordoba plan fails," declared Mario Bancora, director of the Argentine utility Thermomission, "then I feel all our atomic program will be affected. We need this desperately to achieve our future Argentine atomic program." With this in mind, Admiral Madero went to Ottawa in April 1980 to placate the Canadians and to ensure that the EMBALSE reactor would be finished without any hitches. The Canadians were relieved to learn that they would not be losing any more than the $130 million they already knew they would lose on the project. They were also encouraged to think that Argentina might order more CANDU reactors later on if Canada was not too demanding.

In July, Ian Adams published an article in *Today* magazine entitled "Nazi A-Bomb," telling the story of Argentina's nuclear ambitions. Referring to Madero's visit to Ottawa, Adams wrote:

> Of course there was no press conference. The Liberal ministers, willing to shake hands with fascists in private, were not about to let themselves be photographed doing so. Some two weeks later, on May 16, General Videla and President Joao Figueiredo of Brazil signed a nuclear accord and weapons development treaty. The dream of the generals — engineered by former German Nazis, fuelled by the CANDU reactor, and subsidized in part by the Canadian taxpayer — moved one step closer to reality.

On 1 May 1980, immediately after Admiral Madero's visit to Ottawa, Prime Minister Trudeau declared to the House of Commons that only urgent action would salvage the CANDU industry. "The time schedule for keeping our industry viable is very, very short," he said. "We are now in danger of seeing the Canadian industry become obsolete and lose its chance to sell in other countries unless we make some quick decisions on some basic questions." Trudeau revealed that an in-depth review of the nuclear industry would be undertaken by the Department of Energy, but he rejected opposition demands for a public inquiry. While there was "no intention" of preventing the Canadian public from expressing its views, Trudeau maintained that "we cannot wait for a long inquiry to decide whether we stay in the game or get out of the game."

The nuclear review was carried out by an interdepartmental committee of government officials, with assistance and advice from AECL, Eldorado Nuclear Limited, the Atomic Energy Control Board, and the Canadian Nuclear Association — all organizations which are dedicated to the promotion of nuclear technology. However, there was no opportunity for groups critical of nuclear power to make their views known effectively. Despite a written mandate from sixty-five organizations across Canada, which was communicated personally to Marc Lalonde, then minister of energy, the Canadian Coalition for Nuclear Responsibility was prevented from even making a presentation to the minister or to the review committee.

A draft version of the committee's final report was leaked to the Ottawa press in June 1981. The review committee noted that it was doubtful "whether the nuclear industry in Canada will survive the 1980s." With no domestic demand for CANDU reactors, "virtually all firms in the industry could be out of business by the mid-to-late 1980s." The committee observed that export sales were hampered by safeguards requirements and financial constraints, as well as soft markets and fierce competition. Significant relaxation of safeguards could open up the possibility of "nuclear cooperation with a number of countries: South Africa, the Middle East and Taiwan," not to mention the "U.S. military program," but only at great political cost. The report urged Ottawa to offer "concessional financing" in relation to potential CANDU sales — in effect, large "implicit subsidies" to the nuclear industry, to be paid for by the taxpayer. Meeting the terms being offered by competitors such as France and Germany "may involve subsidies equivalent to 25% to 30% of the cost of a reactor sale." Since the federal government had already invested more than $3 billion in the Canadian nuclear industry, Ottawa mandarins argued that Canada could not afford to let the nuclear industry collapse.

Two months earlier, in April, the federal government "forgave" $825 million in loans owed by AECL's Heavy Water Division. The draft report made it clear that were was no "plausible scenario in which the output of all Canada's heavy water plants will be required. The stark alternatives are to accumulate costly inventories or to shut plants down. Even with the most optimistic sales scenario, [heavy water] inventories could total 15 reactor loads by 1990 at a cost of about $2 billion." The only alternative market for heavy water, according to the report, was the U.S. nuclear weapons program.

Lorne Gray, who had been president of AECL during the signing of the Korean and Argentinian contracts, and who had been reprimanded by the House of Commons Public Accounts Committee for mismanagement and evasion, addressed the Annual Meeting of the Canadian Nuclear Association on 9 June 1981. He ridiculed Canadian efforts to restrain the proliferation of nuclear weapons, portraying Canadian officials as quixotic knights wearing blinkers, out of touch with reality. On 15 July 1981, James Donnelly, then president of AECL, told the House of Commons Committee on Latin American Relations that Argentina already had everything it needed to make atomic bombs, so selling it a second CANDU reactor would make no difference in terms of proliferation. He said it would be "poor sales tactics" for him to discuss the stability of the military government in Argentina or the likelihood of its seeking nuclear weapons. In fact, he admitted, "the consideration as to the political regime of the country with which we are trading has not been an uppermost consideration" to AECL.

Senior cabinet members intensified their efforts to sell CANDU reactors abroad. During the summer, Energy Minister Marc Lalonde's parliamentary secretary, Roy McLaren, went to Romania to try to sell more CANDU reactors. In September, Prime Minister Trudeau went to South Korea with the same objective in mind. Since the murder of General Park in 1979, political repression had not been lifted in Korea. Martial law had remained in force throughout 1979 and 1980. In May 1980, violent clashes with Korean police and paratroopers had resulted in 1,200 civilian deaths and countless arrests. Only government-controlled trade unions were allowed to exist, so that "cheap labour" practices could be perpetuated. However, human rights issues were not even mentioned by Prime Minister Trudeau for fear of jeopardizing the sale of a CANDU reactor.

Meanwhile, in October, AECL had submitted a bid for four CANDU reactors to be built in Mexico. Competitive bids were also submitted, in sealed envelopes, from France, Germany, Sweden and the U.S. Mexico, however, did not like Canada's safeguards requirements, particularly the clause requiring "prior consent" from the Canadian government before any high-level enrichment or reprocessing could be carried out. Accordingly, the Department of External Affairs had for some time been searching for a more "non-intrusive" arrangement which would not prove so irksome to potential customers. In a paper prepared by External Affairs in the spring, it was pointed that that "the Canadian Government is not opposed to reprocessing and plutonium use or to high enrichment *per se*, but does wish to satisfy itself that effective measures to minimize the risk will be developed and applied."

In January 1982, the Canadian cabinet approved a financing package in support of the Mexican bid. Canada offered to pay 100 per cent of the capital costs of the project, to be repaid at a very attractive interest rate — less than 8 per cent. This was at a time when the Canadian government would have to borrow on the international money markets at a rate of about 16 per cent. Trudeau visited Mexico to promote the deal. A few days later, Marc Lalonde was signing a nuclear cooperation agreement with Egypt. The nuclear industry was still hoping for a miraculous recovery, but its hopes were dashed in May, when Mexico returned all the bids unopened. The Mexican government had decided that it could scarcely afford to invest in nuclear reactors that it did not need.

Despite these setbacks, the Trudeau cabinet continued to act as if recovery of the CANDU industry was just around the corner. The problem of proliferation of nuclear weapons was publicly downplayed.

In the spring of 1982, when Argentina invaded the Falkland Islands, there was the added dilemma that Argentina had provoked a war with a Canadian ally, the U.K. At the time of the invasion, 3,000 CANDU fuel bundles were being manufactured in Moncton, New Brunswick, for the EMBALSE reactor. The Trudeau cabinet met to consider whether to discontinue nuclear cooperation with Argentina. Should Canada withdraw all AECL and Ontario Hydro personnel from Argentina, who were now putting the finishing touches on the reactor? Should the fuel bundles be delivered as promised?

In April, a secret cabinet briefing document was leaked to Margaret Munro at the Ottawa *Citizen*. The document reveals that

> Argentina continues to show no inclination to accept Canadian policy requirements. In fact, Admiral Madero has in recent statements been unequivocal in rejecting the NPT and full-scope safeguards, while reaffirming his country's desire to retain a nuclear explosives option. Argentina is well on the way to developing an indigenous fuel cycle that is completely free of safeguards. Fuel fabrication, heavy water production and reprocessing facilities are all nearing completion.

The choice, according to the document, was to "continue with business as usual, suspend cooperation, or terminate the relationship." If either of the latter two options were chosen, then with EMBALSE "added to RAPP and KANUPP, Canada's reputation as a reliable reactor supplier might be irretrievably damaged." The cabinet therefore opted for a "business as usual" policy.

The Saint John longshoremen announced that they would refuse to load the fuel bundles. If necessary, they would go to jail rather than comply. The Canadian Labour Congress again supported the longshoremen, and hundreds of letters and telegrams of support were received from across Canada. The brutal reality of the Argentine regime was now more evident than ever. Thousands of Canadians joined in expressing opposition to the shipment of uranium fuel to Argentina — fuel that could be used to breed plutonium for bombs. To avoid trouble, with cabinet approval, the fuel bundles were secretly trucked to Mirabel airport in Quebec and airlifted to Argentina.

The future of the CANDU industry is not looking good. Ontario Hydro, with 50 per cent overcapacity above peak demand and a $14 billion debt, has begun to cut back on the Darlington nuclear station (already under construction). Quebec and New Brunswick are the only other provinces with CANDU reactors operating, and, in both cases, those plants are entirely surplus to provincial needs for electricity. Hydro-Québec announced in December 1981 that it would make no further nuclear investments until at least 1990. In the fall of 1982, AECL recommended that its two heavy water plants in Cape Breton be closed, and hundreds of nuclear scientists from AECL's Mississauga research centre have been laid off. Those countries which have opted for CANDU technology are in dire financial straits, and it is questionable whether they will ever be able to pay for the reactors they have ordered. Of course, the problem of raising additional capital for waste disposal and decommissioning — two enormously expensive undertakings which yield no return on investment — will become a monumental problem for the future. Canada accepts no obligations for these future expenses.

It is to Canada's role as a supplier of nuclear fuel that we now return.

Canada and the Uranium Cartel: The South African Bomb

As we saw earlier, the Canadian uranium industry started out as part of the American war machine. In 1942, Ottawa expropriated a privately-owned

radium company and turned it into a crown corporation now known as
Eldorado Nuclear Limited. Its original job was to mine and refine uranium
for atomic bombs. In the ten years following World War II, Canada sold
uranium only to the U.S. and the U.K., for their nuclear weapons programs. After 1956, however, no new defence contracts were signed, since
both countries had developed alternative sources of supply — Colorado,
Portugal, Australia and South Africa. Without the lucrative military
markets, Canadian uranium production declined rapidly: by 1965, production had fallen below 3,000 tonnes per year (down from 12,000 in 1959),
and only three mines (out of twenty-three) remained in operation. By that
time, Elliot Lake was in danger of becoming a ghost town, and there had
been virtually no uranium exploration in Canada for almost a decade.

The practice of selling Canadian uranium for use in nuclear weapons
was officially terminated in 1965, when Prime Minister Pearson told the
House of Commons that henceforth any uranium exported from Canada
"is to be used for peaceful purposes only." Under the circumstances,
Pearson's words simply reflected the status quo. However, selling uranium
for peaceful purposes turned out to be exceedingly difficult, partly because
of American protectionist policies which were soon to emerge.

From 1964 to 1967, over sixty electricity-generating reactors were
ordered in the United States. It was the first major commercial break-
through for the nuclear power industry anywhere, precipitating a blizzard
of reactor orders from overseas. The American light-water reactor system
very quickly dominated the world market. Uranium exploration resumed
in Canada in 1966, in anticipation of a rapidly expanding demand for
nuclear fuel. However, U.S. markets were effectively closed to foreign
suppliers of uranium because of policies adopted in Washington, and the
expected economic recovery did not occur. World uranium prices dropped
to an all-time low of about $4 per pound. In a desperate attempt to keep the
Canadian uranium industry alive, Ottawa paid for the stockpiling of more
than $100 million worth of uranium during the late 1960s. By 1971, when
all diplomatic efforts had failed, the Trudeau cabinet decided to embark on
a different course of action.

In April 1972, with the blessing of the Canadian government, an international uranium price-fixing cartel was established in Paris. The purpose of
the cartel was secretly to manipulate world uranium prices using a phony
bidding system. Hidden quotas were established by representatives from
Canada, France, Australia, South Africa and Rio Tinto Zinc (RTZ), the
giant British mining conglomerate that, through its holdings in South
Africa, Namibia, Canada and Australia, accounts for about a quarter of
both the world's present uranium production and its estimated reserves
(excluding the USSR and China). At an Ottawa meeting on 28 May 1972,

Jack Austin — then deputy minister of energy under Donald Macdonald, now a Liberal senator and cabinet member — intimated that the cartel might be judged illegal under Canadian anti-combines legislation. Nevertheless, by June, the cartel had formal government approval.

The Canadian government's role in the cartel was questionable not only from the point of view of Canadian law, but also from the broader perspective of international morality. In effect, for purely commercial motives, Canada was turning a blind eye to South Africa's brutal apartheid policies and its determination to develop a nuclear weapons capability. Canada was also acting in defiance of the International Court of Justice, which had ruled in 1971 that South Africa's occupation of the territory of Namibia was illegal and that UN members were to "refrain from any dealings with South Africa that would imply recognition of, or the legality of, such presence." Since most of South Africa's uranium is mined in Namibia at RTZ's Rossing mine, Canada was directly contravening the court's ruling by conspiring with South Africa and RTZ to fix world uranium prices. Indeed, when Energy Minister Donald Macdonald was asked in 1981 why RTZ had been involved in the cartel discussions as an equal partner, he replied that the participation of RTZ was essential because of the Namibian uranium it controls.

Beyond the narrow question of legality is the ethical reality of the RTZ operation in Namibia. *The Plunder of Namibian Uranium*, a booklet published by the United Nations in 1982, describes Namibian uranium as being

> mined by virtual slave labour under brutal and unsafe working conditions, transported in secrecy to foreign countries, processed in unpublicized locations, marked with false labels and shipping orders, owned by a tangle of multinational corporations whose activities are only partially disclosed, and used in part to build the nuclear power of an outlaw nation....

Nevertheless, from a business point of view, Canada's collaboration with RTZ and South Africa was a great success. In just four years — from 1972 to 1976 — the world price of uranium rocketed to $40 per pound. By the end of 1974, the uranium market had improved so much that the cartel was disbanded. However, great secrecy was maintained for several more years in order to circumvent anti-trust laws in various countries.

In 1974, around the time when the Canadian government was scolding India for failing to live up to the spirit of the safeguards agreement associated with the CIRUS reactor, the UN Council on Namibia issued a decree ordering that

> no person or entity, whether a body corporate or unincorporated, may search for, prospect for, explore for, take, extract, mine, process, refine, use,

sell, export or distribute any natural resource, whether animal or mineral, situated or found to be situated within the territorial limits of Namibia.

The Canadian government has completley ignored this decree. The practice of refining Namibian uranium at Eldorado's federally-owned facility in Port Hope, Ontario, was already well established by 1974, and has continued uninterrupted into the 1980s. RTZ's Canadian subsidiary, Rio Algom, actually owns 10 per cent of the Rossing mine, and Falconbridge Nickel — a Canadian subsidiary of Superior Oil of Texas — has been exploring for uranium in Namibia since the mid-1970s. The Canadian government does not consider itself legally or morally bound to obey the UN Council's decree, or the UN General Assembly's 1981 resolution, which requests that Canada and the other countries involved in the cartel "take measures to prohibit their state-owned corporations, together with their subsidiaries, from all dealings in Namibian uranium."

When news of the cartel finally surfaced in 1976, one result was that Westinghouse Electrical Corporation launched a lawsuit against the cartel. To prevent secret cabinet documents from being released, the Trudeau government responded with an Order-in-Council making it a criminal offence, punishable by five years in jail and/or a $10,000 fine, for any Canadian citizen to discuss details of the uranium cartel in public. This law has never been repealed, but it was amended in 1977 to apply only to civil servants, government officials and members of the Canadian nuclear industry.

Other repercussions were not long in coming. Ontario Hydro contracts signed in 1977 guaranteed the Elliot Lake producers, Rio Algom and Denison Mines, over $2 billion in profits for a thirty-year supply of uranium at cartel-inspired prices of about $35 per pound (by 1982, the spot price for uranium was under $20 and still going down). A four-year investigation into the entire affair, launched by Solicitor-General Warren Allmand, was completed in May 1981. Although the report has never been made public, six uranium firms were subsequently charged with conspiracy to engage in illegal price-fixing activities, and two senior government officials — John Runnals and Gordon McNabb — were named as unindicted co-conspirators. No charges were laid against these men, since they were technically only carrying out the directives of Energy Minister Donald Macdonald and a few of his cabinet colleagues (the combines law dictates that agents of the crown are exempt from prosecution if their actions are in accordance with this mandate).

Ontario was not the only province to be affected by the cartel. Following the remarkable rise in the price of uranium, there was a sudden boom in

uranium-prospecting activities across Canada. Every province and territory was subjected to intense exploration: holes were drilled, lakes drained,
ground bulldozed and rock formations blasted. Logistical and financial
support was lavishly provided by the federal and provincial governments,
beginning with a $50 million Uranium Reconnaissance Program launched
by Ottawa in 1974. Over a hundred multinational corporations became
involved. For the most part, these were controlled by British, American
and Dutch oil companies, or by electrical utilities in France, Germany,
Spain, Italy and Japan.

As we saw in Chapter 5, many of the companies involved have nuclear
weapons connections. In Saskatchewan, for example, the Cluff Lake mine
is jointly owned by the provincial government and by Amok, an aptly-
named French company. One of Amok's parent companies is le Commissariat de l'Energie Atomique, a corporation wholly owned by the French
government, which is in charge of that country's nuclear weapons program. The entire output of the rich Cluff Lake deposit is destined for
France and Germany. These two countries are among the worst offenders
in terms of the horizontal proliferation of nuclear weapons, because of
their willingness to sell plutonium reprocessing equipment to regimes in
Pakistan, Taiwan, Korea and South America.

In March 1978, the Cluff Lake Board of Inquiry absolved itself from all
moral responsibility for approving the exploitation of Saskatchewan's
uranium resources by French and German transnational corporations.
"Because 'wars begin in the minds of men'," reads the Final Report,

> all people ought to work to create the political will for world disarmament,
> the real answer to the problem of proliferation. The withholding of uranium
> from Saskatchewan from world markets is an action which for all practical
> purposes is irrelevant to the formulation of that political will for world
> disarmament.

In the same report, Saskatchewan's uranium reserves were estimated to
be "about 30% of the known Canadian reserves, which in turn represent
between 10% and 13% of the known total world reserves." Thus Saskatchewan alone controls between 3 and 4 per cent of the world's uranium.
The export of this dangerous material was justified by Saskatchewan's
NDP government on the grounds that it was to be used "for peaceful
purposes only." Premier Allan Blakeney, writing in 1978, sidestepped the
proliferation problem with familiar "atoms for peace" arguments:

> ... for many Third World countries, the only energy available for industrial
> development is nuclear energy. To refuse them energy is to condemn them to

a future of subsistence living. I do not believe that we, in energy-rich Canada, have the right to make that choice for other people.

This attitude, so prevalent in official circles at both the federal and provincial levels, was not noticeably ruffled when, on 22 September 1979, a nuclear explosion reportedly took place in the South Atlantic, in a region near the Prince Edward Islands. A bright flash of light, followed by a longer flash, was detected by a U.S. satellite high over the Indian Ocean. Peculiarities in the upper atmosphere at that site make it difficult to detect an atomic test with certainity, but many scientists are agreed that a nuclear weapon was exploded and that South Africa did it. (The Cluff Lake Board of Inquiry heard evidence from competent witnesses in 1977 that South Africa had made preparations for a nuclear test, but aborted it after international diplomatic pressure was brought to bear. The incident was offered as an indication to the board that international safeguards to prevent the horizontal proliferation of nuclear weapons can be made to work.)

As it happens, South Africa's most important ally in the nuclear field has been the U.S., which not only supplied the apartheid regime with its first research reactor, but also gave it access to classified information which the Americans would not even share with the Canadians or the British. In a less conspicuous fashion, Canada has also assisted the South African regime by trading with it and conspiring with it in violation of national and international law.

The Canadian nuclear safeguards policy depends entirely upon the pledged word of the recipient that the spirit and the letter of the law will be respected. As the story of the uranium cartel shows, the Canadian government has proved to be quite adept at twisting the law to suit its own purpose, ignoring important moral considerations in the process. Is there any reason to suppose that other governments will not be equally willing to do so?

Canada's Uranium Abroad: The Ambiguous Atom

Canada is one of the world's largest suppliers and processors of uranium. It was second only to the United States as of 1982, though Australia may surpass Canada by 1985.

As mentioned previously, since 1965 Canada has insisted that its uranium is not to be used for military purposes. Nevertheless, by continuing to sell uranium to countries with nuclear weapons programs — the United States, Britain and France — Canada is undoubtedly helping them to make bombs. As Ernie Regehr points out in Chapter 5, even if Canadian uranium were being used in these countries only to fuel electricity-producing reactors, still, that frees up more uranium to be used in bombs. In addition, as we will see, some Canadian uranium does find its way into weapons. Directly or indirectly, therefore, Canada is helping to sustain three nuclear weapons programs — and, perhaps more importantly, to justify those programs by lending them a veneer of respectability. As Bill Harding of Regina wrote in 1981:

> The claim that this particular pound of uranium will be the one used for producing weapons is a monstrous fantasy designed to get concerned citizens debating that very question, the way we might debate the question of how many angels can dance on the head of a pin. What difference does it make where the uranium comes from, if the country it goes to is making nuclear weapons?

Following the Indian nuclear explosion, Canada's 1974 policy dictated that no uranium of Canadian origin might be highly enriched or reprocessed without the prior consent of the Canadian government. Despite two years of intense negotiations, neither Japan nor the European Economic Community (EEC) would submit to the "prior consent" clause. Accordingly, all shipments of Canadian uranium bound for Japan or the EEC were halted in January 1977. Within months, Japan agreed to accept Canada's terms, and regular nuclear trade was restored. However, the EEC — comprised of two nuclear-weapon states and seven non-nuclear-weapon states — proved to be a much more difficult customer.

Uranium shipments to the EEC were resumed in July 1977, but only under the conditions of an interim agreement. Except on a strictly temporary basis, the Europeans were not willing to concede Canada's right to consultation prior to the reprocessing of nuclear fuel of Canadian origin. Negotiations dragged on for two more years. Finally, in September 1980, the Canadian government signed an agreement with the EEC which was seen by many as a simple act of capitulation. Canada agreed to waive the requirements for consultation on a case-by-case basis. Moreover, although France stubbornly refused to sign the NPT or to accept full-scope safeguards, the Canadian government judged that the conditions of its 1976 safeguards policy were met well enough when France arranged for IAEA safeguards on its civilian (but not its military) nuclear facilities.

As this episode shows, Canada has never actually tried or intended to *stop* selling uranium. In fact, the Canadian government has gone to great lengths to *continue* selling uranium, subject to "acceptable" safeguards. The definition of "acceptable," however, seems to depend on circumstances. In particular, it depends on whether or not the customer will stop buying.

Speaking at the United Nations in 1978, Prime Minister Trudeau advocated a "strategy of suffocation" for halting the nuclear arms race by choking off the "vital oxygen" which feeds it. He was referring only to those materials which are defined as "strategic nuclear materials" by the IAEA — namely, highly enriched uranium and plutonium, neither of which is presently sold (as such) by Canada. But the surest way to strangle the nuclear arms race is to stop the trade in uranium, for without uranium there could be no nuclear weapons of any description. Cutting off access to weapons-grade uranium and plutonium, without suppressing the raw material from which they are both derived, is rather like pulling a weed without removing the root.

What is weapons-grade uranium? A brief explanation follows. Natural uranium is a blend of two types: uranium-235 and uranium-238. Only the first of these can be used directly as a nuclear explosive, and it is rare: less than 1 per cent of the natural uranium blend. Since this concentration of uranium-235 is too low to allow an atomic explosion to occur, natural uranium is not a strategic material. In an enrichment plant, however, the concentration of uranium-235 is significantly increased by separating out the unwanted uranium-238 — a sophisticated and difficult operation, for the two types of uranium are chemically identical. At present, only countries having large nuclear weapons programs have uranium enrichment plants, each occupying a huge tract of land and requiring as much energy as a large city. The weapons-grade uranium produced by these plants is typically enriched to more than 90 per cent uranium-235, although a bomb could be made with uranium of only moderate enrichment — 20 per cent uranium-235 would suffice.

The Canadian CANDU reactor, moderated by heavy water, uses natural uranium directly as fuel. However, the American light-water reactor requires low-enriched fuel (about 3 per cent uranium-235). It follows that if Canadian uranium were used only in CANDU reactors, no enrichment would be required at all. But such is not the case. Eighty-five per cent of the uranium mined in Canada is sold abroad, mostly for use in light-water reactors. A sizable portion of that (between 5 and 40 per cent, depending on the year) goes to the USSR for enrichment, while almost all the rest goes to enrichment plants in the U.S., France and Britain. These enrichment plants are primarily military facilities with civilian spin-offs, but the military and civilian aspects are in no way separated except by bookkeeping methods. Natural uranium from several different countries is used as a feedstock. When it has been enriched to the 3 per cent level, the correct amount is siphoned off and forwarded to Canadian customers in various countries. However, most of it continues to be enriched until it becomes weapons-grade material. Thus the peaceful nuclear power program "piggybacks" on the weapons program, by using military enrichment facilities to produce civilian fuel.

To produce one pound of fuel for a light-water reactor requires more than five pounds of natural uranium as feedstock. Consequently, over 80 per cent of all uranium exported by Canada is discarded as "depleted uranium" — mostly uranium-238, with very little uranium-235. This cast-off uranium is not explicitly mentioned in any of the nuclear safeguards agreements, nor are stocks of depleted uranium (usually stored at the enrichment plant) ever inspected by the IAEA. Although depleted uranium is not categorized as a strategic nuclear material, it is an essential ingredient in the construction of H-bombs. For this reason, when the USSR enriches Canadian uranium for use in Finnish, Swedish, Spanish or East German reactors, Canada requires that the depleted uranium be forwarded to the customer along with the enriched fuel. However, the Americans, the British and the French are trusted not to use the leftovers from the enrichment of Canadian uranium for military purposes. (In actual fact, there is only one stockpile of depleted uranium at any enrichment plant, which is drawn upon for military uses as needed. Canadian depleted uranium has no independent existence, except in terms of bookkeeping: so many tonnes are simply "designated" as Canadian.)

Although depleted uranium is not by itself directly usable as a nuclear explosive, nevertheless, it is responsible for 50 per cent of the explosive power in an H-bomb. An H-bomb is a three-stage nuclear weapon: it is a "fission-fusion-fission" bomb. First a small plutonium bomb (called the "trigger") is detonated. This ignites an enormously powerful nuclear fusion reaction, involving isotopes of hydrogen (hence the "H" in "H-bomb"). The energy of the fusion reaction causes fission to occur in a surrounding blanket of depleted uranium, which accounts for about half of the force of the explosion. So, for a nuclear-weapon state, depleted uranium *is* a nuclear explosive; but for a non-nuclear-weapon state, it is *not*. Consequently, depleted uranium is not regarded as a strategic material by the IAEA, whose job it is to impede new countries from acquiring nuclear weapons without interfering with the mass production of H-bombs by the existing nuclear powers.

Depleted uranium is also used in military reactors to breed plutonium for nuclear weapons. (Inside the reactor, some of the uranium-238 is converted into plutonium which can subsequently be separated out by reprocessing.) Slugs of depleted uranium could be used in a CANDU reactor for the same purpose. By inserting depleted uranium into a few selected fuel channels when no inspector is around, and then removing them again — using the CANDU system of on-line refuelling — a large stockpile of weapons-grade plutonium could be accumulated without fear of detection.

In fact, this trick has already been attempted in a different context, and there is a Canadian connection to the story. When Israeli jets levelled Iraq's OSIRAK reactor near Baghdad in 1981, Prime Minister Menachem Begin justified his action on the grounds that the Iraqis were intending to produce plutonium for bombs by a method similar to the one just described. This allegation was supported by an IAEA inspector, who had resigned his job in order to provide public testimony to that effect.

Just about a year before the Israeli bombing raid, Eldorado Nuclear Limited was engaged in a bizarre transaction set up by the West Germans. After chemically refining some depleted uranium from Britain, Eldorado sent the material to a firm in the U.S. to be fabricated into metal rods and then returned to Port Hope, Ontario. American officials became extremely curious and began asking questions. What on earth did Eldorado want with depleted uranium? It soon emerged that the ultimate destination for the material was Iraq. The deal was hastily squelched.

In sum, for a material that is classified as "non-strategic," depleted uranium is remarkably useful to those in the nuclear weapons business; yet Canada has done little to control its disposition. As one official from the Department of External Affairs commented: "There's so much of the stuff around that it's hardly worth worrying about."

Meanwhile, newer methods of enriching uranium are being developed, such as the "nozzle process" (developed by West Germany and South Africa, and assumed to be the means by which the latter was able to arrange the 1979 test explosion in the South Atlantic), which require less land and less energy than the existing "gaseous diffusion" plants, but they are still very demanding technologies. In recent years, Pakistan — still determined to acquire nuclear weapons — has been trying to build an ultracentrifuge uranium enrichment facility. Pakistani agents have been shopping for crucial components in several countries. In 1980, three Canadian men of Middle Eastern origin were arrested in Montreal by the RCMP for smuggling strategically important information and electronic equipment to Pakistan, related to the ultracentrifuge project. For security reasons, their trial had to be held in secret.

The latest concept in uranium enrichment is "laser separation," which may eventually make it possible to enrich uranium to weapons-grade material in a basement or garage, at a reasonable cost, in a relatively short time, using only modest amounts of energy. If this technique succeeds, natural uranium — like plutonium — may have to be regarded as strategic nuclear material. Overnight, Canadian uranium facilities could become top-security installations requiring paramilitary police surveillance. As the Flowers Report, published by the British Government in 1976, has pointed out:

> The construction of a crude nuclear weapon by an illicit group is credible. We are not convinced that the Government has fully appreciated the implications of this possibility. Given existing or planned security measures, the risks from illicit activities at the present level of nuclear development are small; the concern is with the future.

At present, weapons-grade uranium and plutonium are imported into Canada in small quantities for use in research facilities at Chalk River and elsewhere. Precise transportation routes are kept secret, communities along the way are not notified, and even the provincial police are left uninformed. Nuclear authorities feel that the less people know about the shipments, the better. When plutonium is flown into Mirabel or Toronto airports from Europe, even the Atomic Energy Control Board (AECB) does not know what plane it will be on until the last moment. Stringent security also applies to shipments of highly enriched uranium, travelling by truck from Tennessee to Chalk River, since each shipment contains enough weapons-grade uranium for one or two atomic bombs. Indeed, in the late 1970s, the U.S. briefly suspended such shipments because of overly lax Canadian security measures.

After the weapons-grade uranium has been irradiated, the spent fuel is returned to the United States so that the unused portion can be recycled in the American bomb program. Successive bans on the transit of this dangerous material by the St. Lawrence Bridge Authority, the Governor of Michigan and the Governor of Vermont, have made the routes more circuitous, but the traffic has continued. According to the Canada-U.S. Agreement on the Civil Uses of Atomic Energy, no Canadian-supplied nuclear materials are supposed to be used for weapons purposes. However, officials in the Department of External Affairs have argued that the weapons-grade uranium in question was American property to begin with; the Americans are merely taking back what was theirs already, and if they wish to make bombs with it, that is their business, not Canada's.

It is a dangerous kind of argument to use, for Canada does not give Third World countries the same latitude. As it happens, the 23,000 CANDU fuel bundles that were flown to Argentina in July 1982 were fabricated from Argentinian uranium, since Canadian safeguards policies prevented the sale of domestic uranium. Might not Argentina feel justified in using those fuel bundles for military purposes, since it was Argentinian uranium in the first place? Legally, the situation is not comparable to the Canada-U.S. situation, but in terms of practical politics, it may be.

Since 1975, public opposition to uranium mining in Canada has been growing, not just because of the proliferation question, but for reasons of public and occupational health, environmental pollution, waste disposal, Native rights and socio-economic impact. In Saskatchewan, all the major churches came out against the government's plan to exploit the province's uranium resources for export purposes. Nevertheless, the government of Premier Blakeney went ahead with the Cluff Lake, Rabbit Lake and Key Lake mines. In British Columbia, the B.C. Medical Association and the West Coast Environmental Law Association joined with churches, unions, fruitgrowers, anti-nuclear activists and Native people to oppose uranium mining. This unprecedented coalition exerted such political pressure that the government of William Bennett declared a seven-year moratorium on uranium mining and exploration in the province, without even waiting for the results of a Royal Commission of Inquiry which was under way at the time. Eldorado's plans to build two new uranium refineries at Warman, Saskatchewan and Port Granby, Ontario, were soundly defeated by the overwhelming opposition of local residents. Following a public inquiry in Labrador, the government of Newfoundland prohibited uranium mining in that province. Public inquiries have also taken place in Ontario, Nova Scotia and the Northwest Territories, as a result of widespread public concern.

Yet public dissent against uranium mining — and against the export of Canadian nuclear technology — is clearly still in its early stages. Canadian citizens do not yet have the resources or the contacts with decision-makers that might compare with those enjoyed by the Canadian nuclear lobby, which has become entrenched over the last forty years.

The Nuclear Lobby in Canada: Towards a Plutonium Economy

The Atoms for Peace program was based on a carefully cultivated myth, promulgated by a powerful international lobby. Nuclear power was portrayed as safe, clean, cheap and abundant — a miraculous energy source of infinite potential, having little or nothing to do with atomic bombs. Due to its strategic origins, every aspect of the nuclear industry was shrouded in extraordinary secrecy. In addition, the mysterious world of nuclear science seemed incomprehensible to the uninitiated. Government policies were largely based on the uncontradicted advice of the nuclear technologists who had dedicated their lives to making nuclear power a success.

The power base of the Canadian nuclear lobby originates in the upper echelons of AECL and Eldorado. Most of the key figures in the Atomic Energy Control Board (AECB) come from these two crown corporations, as do most of the top Canadian government advisors on nuclear policy. In 1970, the Canadian Senate Committee on Science Policy declared that it was "startled to learn that most of the members of the AECB prove to be senior representatives of the very agencies" which the AECB is supposed to control. This tightly-knit power base is supplemented by the nuclear divisions within Ontario Hydro, Hydro Québec and New Brunswick Electric, together with the Canadian Nuclear Association (CNA), comprised of nuclear manufacturers and financial backers. Movies, slide shows, comic books, brochures, museum displays, educational kits for schools, full-page ads, even a glossy magazine called *Ascent*, all are used by the nuclear lobby to promote a near-utopian vision of a nuclear-powered world. As one CNA comic book (still in circulation in 1983) glowingly reports: "In time it is possible that nuclear power will lead to temperature-controlled, germ-free cities and a better life for all mankind."

Within the U.S. industry-regulatory structure there has been some awakening to the fallacies of Atoms for Peace. David Lilienthal, the first chairman of the U.S. Atomic Energy Commission, confided in 1970:

> The basic cause I think was a conviction, and one that I shared fully and tried to inculcate in others, that somehow or other the discovery that had produced so terrible a weapon *had* to have an important peaceful use. We were grimly determined to prove that this discovery was not just a weapon.

By 1976, however, Dr. Lilienthal had concluded that Atoms for Peace was in fact a dangerous exercise in self-deception:

> Once a bright hope shared by all mankind, including myself, the rash proliferation of nuclear power plants is now one of the ugliest clouds hanging over America. Proliferation of capabilities to produce nuclear weapons of mass destruction is reaching terrifying proportions. If a greater number of countries come to have an arsenal of nuclear weapons, then I'm glad I'm not a young man, and I'm sorry for my grandchildren.

But in Canada, even after the Indian nuclear explosion, the Canadian nuclear lobby expressed no concern whatsoever about the proliferation aspects of the nuclear trade. Lorne Gray, president of AECL during the signing of the Korean and Argentine contracts, told a graduating class at Carleton University in November 1975:

If we don't help the developing world with their energy resource problems, the odd nuclear explosion will be a minor event to the international conflicts that will arise.

A few months later, on 30 March 1976, Ian MacKay of AECL testified to the Prince Edward Island Legislature as follows:

Now first of all, what is nuclear power? Well, it's just a method of generating electricity using uranium as fuel instead of oil. It has practically no technology in common with nuclear bombs. This, of course, is undramatic, and any possible relationship with bombs is much more news than claiming no relationship; so you can't blame the press for reporting on that sort of thing. Now the used fuel contains plutonium, which is about a quarter of one percent of the used fuel, and this is potentially useful in the future. Right now it is not useful. It is not useful for making bombs. I would like to emphasize that.

This kind of assertion has been discredited many times, perhaps most forcefully just two days before MacKay's address, when Dr. Bernard Feld, in charge of the explosive mechanism for the Nagasaki bomb during the World War II Atomic Bomb Project, had this to say on British television:

Plutonium is the stuff out of which atomic bombs are made. And the amount of plutonium in the world is increasing year by year as nuclear power spreads. Within the next ten years nuclear power plants will be producing around 100 tons of plutonium a year, enough for 10,000 atom bombs, each with the same power as the one that destroyed Nagasaki.... This terrifying possibility will become an inevitability if the major industrialized nations persist in their current grossly irresponsible policies. Nuclear reactors, plutonium reprocessing plants, uranium enrichment facilities and the technologies needed to operate them are today being sold to any country with sufficient cash or oil to buy them.

Yet Ian MacKay's remarkable explanation that plutonium "is not useful for making bombs," broadcast live throughout the Maritimes, has never been set straight by AECL or by the Canadian government, despite repeated requests to three successive Liberal energy ministers to do so.

The nuclear lobby in Canada has defended its position by arguing that "reactor-grade plutonium," produced by a nuclear power plant, is not the same thing as "weapons-grade plutonium." Ross Campbell, chairman of Atomic Energy of Canada Limited, told the House of Commons Standing Committee on National Resources and Public Works on 14 December 1977:

As far as quality goes, neither light-water reactors nor the CANDU produce plutonium of a grade that would make a high-energy release weapon. You could in theory make a weapon from it but it is quite likely to go off in the face of the man who tries.

Campbell's statement was incorrect and misleading. Nevertheless, members of the committee were baffled, and hence unable to deal with the weapons issue in a realistic way. Frank Maine, one of the few MPs on the committee with any technical training, lashed out angrily at nuclear critics for muddying the waters by suggesting a link between nuclear power reactors and nuclear weapons which, he felt, had no basis in fact.

But like Ian MacKay, Ross Campbell was no expert. He was a career diplomat who had become a CANDU salesman. Where did he get his information? Since AECL had never built an atomic bomb, the organization had no experts in nuclear weapons. Among those who are experts in the field, there is a broad consensus that there is no magical dividing line between "reactor-grade" and "weapons-grade" plutonium. In July 1976, *Science* magazine reported that Carson Mark, one of the few Canadian nuclear scientists with extensive bomb-making experience in the U.S. military program, "is on record as saying that nuclear weapons can be made without insuperable difficulty from 'essentially any grade of reactor-produced plutonium.'" In November of the same year, Victor Gilinsky of the U.S. Nuclear Regulatory Commission was even more explicit;

> There is an old notion, recently revived in certain quarters, that so-called "reactor-grade" plutonium is not suitable to the manufacture of nuclear weapons. The floating of this idea is perhaps a natural move by those who want to exclude plutonium from strict controls. The obvious intention here is to create the impression that there is nothing to fear from separated plutonium derived from commercial power plants. This is not true.
>
> As far as reactor-grade plutonium is concerned, the fact is that it is possible to use this material for nuclear warheads at all levels of technical sophistication. Even simple designs, albeit with some uncertainties in yield, can serve as effective, highly powerful weapons — reliably in the kiloton range.

Despite the added "uncertainty in yield," Albert Wohlstetter, author of a major study on proliferation for the U.S. Arms Control and Disarmament Agency, has pointed out that if the Nagasaki bomb had been made of reactor-grade plutonium, it still would have devastated the city. In fact, the U.S. has since detonated an atomic bomb made from reactor-grade plutonium to demonstrate the feasibility of using this material as a nuclear explosive.

As it happens, the CANDU is an exceptionally versatile reactor. It can produce weapons-grade plutonium as well as reactor-grade plutonium, without interfering with the normal operation of the plant. Early in 1977, a major U.S. nuclear policy review — the Ford-Mitre Report — singled out Canadian reactors as being particularly suited to meet clandestine military needs, noting that the CANDU

> can be operated without undue economic penalty at low fuel irradiation to produce plutonium with a low concentration of plutonium-240, which is more suitable for reliable weapons. It is in operation or under construction in Argentina and India as well as Canada.

Victor Gilinsky was right when he intimated that the nuclear lobbyists did not want to see tough international restrictions imposed on plutonium reprocessing, because they were eager to get into the act themselves. Even in Canada, they estimated that, with a large nuclear program, uranium supplies would become inadequate early in the twenty-first century. In February 1977, AECL hosted a secret briefing where top civil servants were told that Canada should immediately begin planning for the separation of plutonium from spent CANDU fuel. Ross Campbell opened the day-long seminar on a note of urgency: "We are already late in starting to bring this new energy source on stream in the critical last decade of this century, when real shortage of energy will appear." AECL president John Foster closed the seminar with this thought:

> Admittedly, a positive decision takes a certain amount of guts, because authorities all over the world are proceeding with understandable caution in the face of the bad name undeservedly attached to plutonium. But plutonium is an extremely useful substance and we will be dealing in it.

AECL was proposing that, in addition to the $2.2 billion in subsidies that the federal government had already provided to develop the CANDU system, another $2.2 billion should now be invested in an experimental "Fuel Cycle Centre." At the Centre, all the spent fuel from CANDU reactors would be reprocessed and plutonium would be fabricated into new fuel for reactors, while the rest of the radioactive garbage would be solidified and buried in underground storage chambers excavated out of hard rock.

The prospect of plutonium becoming the nuclear fuel of the future has alarmed more than one observer of the nuclear industry. As Dr. Bernard Feld puts it:

> So within the next ten years, there will be hundreds of tons of plutonium

wandering around the world. It will be as easy as pie for a determined group to get hold of the twenty or so pounds needed for a Nagasaki-type bomb. And making a crude version of one of these bombs, once you've got the plutonium is not all that difficult. Even a crudely-made bomb, much less efficient that the Nagasaki bomb, would be powerful enough to level whole areas of a city and to cause thousands or tens of thousands of immediate fatalities, not to speak of the further thousands condemned to slower death by lung or bone cancer from plutonium inhalation.

The Canadian government forbade AECL to proceed with its plans for reprocessing until the results were in from the Carter administration's International Nuclear Fuel Cycle Evaluation, set up in the fall of 1977 to see if there is any way that nuclear fuel could be reprocessed without producing weapons-usable materials. The answer, delivered in 1980, is "no." Since then, the nuclear lobby in Canada and elsewhere has nevertheless been pushing hard to get commercial reprocessing facilities committed.

Canadian nuclear lobbyists often refer to the "thorium cycle" as an alternative to the "plutonium economy." By itself, thorium — which is more plentiful than uranium — cannot be used to build an atomic bomb or to fuel a nuclear reactor. However, when thorium is placed inside a nuclear reactor, it "breeds" a new substance called uranium-233, which does not exist in nature. If the thorium is then reprocessed, the uranium-233 can be separated from the rest of the radioactive garbage and used as a reactor fuel. But uranium-233 is also an excellent weapons-grade material, in many respects superior to plutonium. Thus the thorium cycle in no way avoids the security problems associated with a plutonium economy. In January 1982, AECL announced plans to build a laboratory at Varennes, Quebec, to produce uranium-233 as an "artificial substitute" for natural uranium. (In technical terms, the AECL thorium cycle involves a "near-breeder" rather than a "breeder" concept.)

The new enthusiasm for the plutonium economy and the thorium cycle shows that, as before, any attempt to change the priorities of Canada's nuclear industry will run up against the wall of technological complexity that has given it a certain degree of immunity from lay scrutiny. But there is a larger obstacle: because of huge investments of public money and extensive public ownership, the goals of the nuclear lobby are inextricably intertwined with those of governments at various levels. It sometimes seems that the nuclear industry is a force unto itself, operating with impunity. On one of the rare occasions when AECL was held publicly accountable, during the investigations into financial wrongdoing by the House of Commons Public Accounts Committee, unsettling revelations came to light. In its final report, tabled on 27 February 1978, the committee concluded:

> Some witnesses of AECL management were reluctant and uncooperative in testifying, and in the case of the chief witness, J. Lorne Gray, evasive as well.
>
> Mr. Gray, then President of AECL, on his own initiative, committed the Crown corporation, and therefore the Government and the people of Canada, to immense expenditures of public funds for agents' fees. Furthermore, Mr. Gray did not know what services were being performed by the agents nor who ultimately received the payments. In the case of the Argentine sale, he stated that he did not even want to know the agent's identity.
>
> Mr. Ross Campbell, Chairman of the AECL, not only failed to put the agreement [with sales agent Shoul Eisenberg] on a better footing, but also appointed Eisenberg as exclusive agent for the sale of a second [CANDU] unit to South Korea without specifying the charges to be made for these services.
>
> AECL management did not follow acceptable business practices ... nor did it have due regard for the high standard of business ethics which Crown corporations should observe.
>
> The senior management of AECL, including the Secretary, the Treasurer, and the Internal Auditor, did not properly discharge their responsblities as officers.

Following the publication of the committee's report, John Foster was fired from his position as president of AECL for financial mismanagement. Nevertheless, a few years later, Lorne Gray and John Foster were elected to serve terms as executive director and president respectively of the CNA, during which time they assailed the government's non-proliferation efforts and called for a relaxation of Canadian safeguards to help promote overseas sales.

Conclusion

Over the years, in Albert Wohlstetter's words, Canada has been "spreading the bomb without quite breaking the rules." By accepting the double standard implicit in the Non-Proliferation Treaty, which assumes that some nations are entitled to have nuclear weapons while others are not, the Canadian government has blinded itself to the true magnitude of the challenge facing humanity, which is to eradicate these weapons from the face of the earth. Sister Rosalie Bertell of Toronto has suggested that Canada withdraw from the NPT on the grounds that the superpowers have already violated it. This could be a very constructive step on Canada's part, for the NPT could then be tested in the International Court of Justice. Unless one of the parties to the treaty alleges that its provisions have been breached, the International Court has no jurisdiction to intervene.

Canada is too small to be a world power in terms of military might, but not too small to be a world leader for peace and disarmament. It is time to recognize that nuclear disarmament is an essential prerequisite for any peaceful application of nuclear power on a large scale. Canada could withhold its uranium and its reactors from world markets while bending all its diplomatic efforts to halt the nuclear arms race, and to reverse it. During the fall of 1982, in 118 municipal elections held across Canada, 76.5 per cent voted in favour of phased, multilateral disarmament. If the government in Ottawa wishes to represent the people of Canada, these are the kind of policies it should be pursuing.

In so doing, Canada would acknowledge the wisdom of the Flowers Report from Britain, which concluded that horizontal proliferation and vertical proliferation are inextricably linked. Preventing horizontal proliferation

> would be possible only in an atmosphere of general disarmament, and the prospects for this are receding rather than improving. It has been argued that the possession of these weapons by the USA and the USSR has been a powerful force for mutual toleration, but however true this is it would be folly to suppose that proliferation would necessarily lead to a similar balance and restraint in relations between other nations. Indeed, we see no reason to trust in the stability of any nation of any political persuasion for centuries ahead. The proliferation problem is very serious and it will not go away by refusing to acknowledge it.

References

Atomic Energy of Canada Limited. "Nuclear Fuel Cycle Seminar." Ottawa, 1977. (Available from Canadian Coalition for Nuclear Responsibility, C.P. 236, Snowdon P.O., Montreal H3X 3T4.)

Canada. *Nuclear Policy Review Background Papers.* Ottawa: Department of Energy, Mines and Resources, 1981.

Dunn, Lewis A. *Controlling the Bomb.* New Haven: Yale University Press, 1982.

Duric, Sheila, and Edwards, Rob. *Fuelling the Nuclear Arms Race.* London: Pluto Press, 1982.

Flowers, Sir Brian. *Nuclear Power and the Environment.* London: H.M. Stationery Office, 1976.

170 Canada and the Nuclear Arms Race

Harding, Bill. *Uranium Mining in Northern Saskatchewan: Correspondence with the Premier*. Regina: Regina Group for a Non-Nuclear Society, 1979.

Inter-Church Uranium Committee. *Atoms for War and Peace: The Saskatchewan Connection*. Saskatoon, 1981.

Lovins, Amory B., and Lovins, L. Hunter. *Energy/War: Breaking the Nuclear Link*. San Francisco: Friends of the Earth, 1981.

Markey, Ed. *Nuclear Peril: The Politics of Proliferation*. Boston: Ballinger, 1982.

Moss, Norman. *The Politics of Uranium*. London: Andre Deutsch, 1981.

Nuclear Energy Policy Study Group. *Nuclear Power: Issues and Choices* (Ford-Mitre Report). Boston: Ballinger, 1977.

Nuclear Free Press, c/o OPIRG, Trent University, Peterborough, Ontario.

Robertson, A. *Preventing Nuclear Weapons Proliferation: A Positive Factor for Peace*. Ottawa: AECL, 1982.

Saskatchewan. *Final Report of the Cluff Lake Board of Inquiry*. Regina, 1978.

United Nations. *The Plunder of Namibian Uranium*. New York, 1982.

Weissman, Steve, and Krosney, Herbert. *The Islamic Bomb*. New York: Times Books/Quadrangle, 1981.

Wohlstetter, Albert, et. al. *Swords From Ploughshares*. Chicago: University of Chicago Press, 1979.

7

What Would Happen to Canada in a
Nuclear War?

Don G. Bates, Donald P. Briskin, Lisa Cotton,
Maureen McDonald, Linda Panaro
and Alasdair Polson

Information is readily available on the possible effects of a nuclear attack on the United States,[1] but there has been practically nothing in circulation about Canada. Is there anything known? Can we make some educated guesses? What *would* happen to Canada in a nuclear war?

Canadians who have given no thought to this question probably have a vague foreboding that the answer is not very comforting. They may have a disquieting sense of Canada's geographical position, knowing that a satellite's-eye view from the North Pole shows Canada squarely placed between the United States and the Soviet Union. Canada has been called "the ham in the sandwich," and, according to a plain-talking taxi driver, "the minced ham," in the event of a nuclear war.

There are a couple of reasons for these fears. One is a concern about the heavy traffic of intercontinental ballistic missiles (ICBMs) flying overhead, as the two superpowers unleash their nuclear weapons at each other over the North Pole. Here the worry is that Canadians could be the innocent victims of missiles that were inaccurate, malfunctioning, or perhaps shot down by some defensive measure. (This last worry is groundless because at present there is no defence against ICBMs.) It does nothing to allay fears of this sort to learn that it has never been possible to flight-test these missiles across the magnetic north pole and no one knows for sure how such a path would affect their guidance systems.[2]

Because there is no unclassified information (and probably no secret knowledge either), of the reliability of missiles flying over our heads in actual war conditions, the influence of this factor on Canada's fate in a nuclear war is purely conjectural. In any event, its significance pales beside the impact of far more serious events that we can be reasonably sure would take place.

The other effect of Canada's proximity to the United States would be the likelihood of large clouds of radioactive debris drifting across the border to contaminate our land and cities with fallout.

To make an assessment of this possibility and anything else that would likely happen, it is necessary to construct a map of North America that locates the targets that have most relevance to Canada and, from this, to make some estimate of the damage that would be done. Over the course of the summer of 1982, a task force of the McGill Study Group for Peace and Disarmament, composed of four medical students,[3] a post doctoral fellow in biology, a media consultant of the university, and the chairman of the study group,[4] set out to construct such a map and, from it, to work out the possible consequences.

Arriving at a Scenario

Almost at the outset it became apparent to us that much guesswork is involved and that many arbitrary decisions have to be made in creating such a scenario. Because of this, it is relatively easy to bias the outcome in the direction of making things look much worse or much better than would otherwise be the case. Wherever possible, therefore, we sought to use official documents and to apply official estimates of the most likely events that would be involved. Whenever we felt we had good reason to depart from such official sources, however, we did not hesitate to do so. Both the fact of such departures and the reasons for them are given in the account that follows.

Likely targets for a nuclear attack on the United States are described in readily available literature. They include missile silos, Strategic Air Command (SAC) bomber bases and nuclear submarine pens, other major military centres, energy sources such as oil refineries, nuclear reactors and other thermal and hydroelectric power generators, and, finally, cities because of their industries, their governmental and other vital social and economic institutions, and their populations.

Even if there was no concomitant attack on Canada, and even if none of the explosions on U.S. targets gave rise to radioactive fallout north of the border, Canada would undergo a total transformation. One can only guess the outcome — the massive invasion by injured and destitute humanity; the loss of our most important trading partner (and possibly our other major markets in an equally devastated Europe); and the disappearance of our national security in a world of totally changed power relationships. But we cannot assume that Canada itself would not be attacked, and we certainly cannot expect to escape radioactive fallout in an intercontinental nuclear war.

To get a clearer impression of what this fallout on Canada might be like, it was necessary for the task force to choose for their target map those sites from which radioactive fallout could land on Canadian soil in significant amounts. To do this we had to know a lot more about fallout.

Radioactivity is an unavoidable part of nuclear explosions because nuclear weapons depend upon fission, or atom-splitting, as the major source for the energy released at the time of detonation. Most of that energy, about half, is released in the form of a blast, like dynamite. Another third, typically, is released as heat. But the final 15 per cent is discharged as nuclear radiation. It is this part that gives rise to radioactive fallout.

The radioactive particles that rise up into the air, and fall to the ground later, come from two sources. Some come from the materials used in the original bomb, materials that were radioactive before the explosion as well as others that become so when the detonation occurs. The other source is dust particles and debris on the ground directly under the explosion, which are made radioactive by the intense radiation that reaches them from the fireball at the time of detonation. As the massive rush of air rises rapidly into the sky, it takes with it, and mixes together, these two sources of radioactive particles.

What happens next depends on how close to the ground the original detonation takes place. If, for example, the target is a city and the intention is to spread devastation as widely as possible across the surface of the earth, the detonation would be triggered high up in the air. In this case the radioactive particles come largely from the explosion itself, since ground dirt is less affected by the radiation, no crater is formed, and little dirt is sucked up into the rising fireball. Furthermore, what does go up goes up very high into the atmosphere.

For all of these reasons, radioactive fallout from an airburst does not start descending to the ground in the hours following the explosion. In fact, most of the particles are lodged high in the stratosphere, above the weather layer of the earth's atmosphere, where they circle the earth for weeks, months, or even years and only gradually fall to the ground on a worldwide basis. For obvious reasons this is called "global" fallout. Its relevance for Canada will be considered later.

By contrast, a detonation near or on the ground causes a crater and brings the maximum amount of energy to bear on a target that may be "hardened," such as the underground silo of an ICBM. In this case, a great deal of dirt is made radioactive, and this dirt is then sucked up in the cloud and mixed with the debris of the weapon itself. Furthermore, the cloud does not rise so high.

For these reasons, the heavy particles of radioactive dust fall to earth over the first few hours after the explosion. Because the cloud is blown by the wind, it scatters this dust in a cigar-shaped pattern on the ground, downwind from the blast. The most intensely radioactive part of the "plume," as this pattern is sometimes called, will be closest to ground zero, the amount of radioactive fallout diminishing as the cloud moves farther away from the target site. How much radioactivity will result in a given place will depend on the size of the explosion, i.e., how much radioactivity was released to begin with, and the speed of the wind which causes the cloud to spread its dust thickly or thinly over a shorter or longer distance.

Thus, in identifying a U.S. target of relevance to Canada, it is necessary to know the size of the warhead that would likely be used on it, whether an air or ground burst would be employed, and the direction and speed of the wind at the time of the explosion. Since all of these could vary considerably, a great deal of conjecture must go into the criteria used to single out a U.S. target that has implications for Canada.

Fortunately, several authoritative sources have described the sorts of targets likely to receive a ground burst — SAC and submarine bases, major military installations, and, above all, missile silos. These same sources also indicate the size of warhead that would likely be used.

There is also a widely used convention for wind speed, namely, 15 mph (24 km/h). Moreover, although in actual fact the wind direction could change, even several times, over the course of the time the fallout is occurring, it is also a convention to assume that the wind holds steady in a particular direction at the same velocity for the entire time. Upon these stable, if arbitrary, conventions, plumes of "local" fallout, as it is called, can be calculated: their length and width, and the amount of radioactivity that will be present on the ground at various distances from the target area.

In order to identify the targets we were interested in, we had to make the additional assumption that the wind could blow straight north and we also decided that, for a plume of radioactive fallout to qualify as being important for Canada, significant levels of radioactivity would have to cover Canadian soil for at least 100 miles inside the border. To simplify matters, we temporarily supposed every target to be subject to a one-megaton weapon. Since the plume from a ground burst of one of these produces significant levels of radioactive contamination for at least 450 miles, it was decided to mark on our map all U.S. targets within 350 miles of Canada. This area was therefore demarcated with a grey boundary-line running through the United States parallel to our border (Figure 1, p. 179). In addition, targets outside this area were also plotted if their plumes could reach Canada because of special circumstances to be explained later in the chapter.

Of course not all the targets chosen for our map would, in fact, suffer ground bursts, or warrant warheads of one megaton. And the wind would not likely, in most cases, blow due north. But we chose to include all targets in this 350-mile border area because, theoretically at least, nuclear explosions on them *could* have an effect on Canadians and this is what we wanted to show. In the map of plumes that we subsequently constructed on the basis of our target map, however, such unlikely events were not presumed to have occurred and our results are not therefore biased by them.

On the contrary, both in choosing targets, and later in deciding on those that would likely suffer ground bursts, we tried to keep our estimates on the conservative side. For example, the United States Federal Emergency Management Agency suggests that all U.S. cities of 50,000 or more might be attacked. An international study, however, restricts itself to cities of 100,000 and above.[5] We chose the more conservative estimate of this latter study, but, unlike it, considered these cities to be subjected to air bursts which would not produce plumes of local fallout. In another conservative decision, we made no allowance for the approximately 150 nuclear warheads that are stored at each SAC bomber base,[6] although, if a substantial portion of them were around when the base was attacked, the ground burst of 300 kilotons (see Table 1)[7] would yield a very much larger and longer plume.

In the case of nuclear reactors, we did not include any with an output of less than one gigawatt (1,000 megawatts), nor did we include any research reactors, of which there are many in the United States within 350 miles of the Canadian border. We did, however, assume that reactors of one gigawatt or more would be subjected to ground bursts since, besides destroying the reactor, such detonation would assure much more intense, widespread and long-lasting radioactive contamination. On the other hand, for simplicity's sake, all U.S. reactors of more than one gigawatt were assumed to be only one gigawatt in size. Nor was any account taken of the nuclear wastes that frequently reside in large quantities at a reactor site. Underestimates like these mean that the actual doses of radioactivity that might be released by a nuclear explosion on a reactor complex could be several times greater than we have calculated.[8]

On such criteria as these, then, a basic map of U.S. targets that could be relevant to Canada was constructed so that, on the basis of our calculations, a second map of the radioactive plumes that would result could be developed. But before making such a plume map to show the potential fallout on Canada, it seemed sensible to address the other question still outstanding: Would Canada itself suffer a direct nuclear attack? After all, if the answer is "yes," we would have to take into account the immediate effects of blast and fire that would directly affect Canadian targets as well as the fallout plumes from ground bursts that took place on our own homeground. These are effects that would mostly precede any damage done by fallout from south of the border and exceed its effects many times over.

In building our scenario we decided that Canada would itself be attacked, and indeed extensively. There were several minor reasons for this decision, and one major and particularly persuasive one.

The minor reasons were as follows. First, a nuclear war that had become intercontinental would quite likely follow upon hostilities in Europe between the NATO and Warsaw Pact countries. Canada is a part of the North Atlantic Treaty Organization (NATO) and would likely be already a declared enemy of the Soviet Union, before the ICBM's started flying. Second, Canada is a partner in the North American Aerospace Defence Command (NORAD) with the United States whereby the two countries have jointly agreed to integrate their efforts at defence against a nuclear attack. Third, Canada similarly has Defence Production Sharing Arrangements with its southern neighbour whereby Canadian industry is involved in the production of components for nuclear and conventional arms used by the U.S. The military strategists in Moscow could be excused if they were to see Canada as a significant part of the larger enemy whom they would be confronting.

But there is a more basic reason that has little to do with Canada's foreign policy — either now or whatever it might become in the future. Again it comes down to our geography. An all-out nuclear war would not be, as in past wars, an effort at the invasion and occupation of one superpower by the other. It would be, rather, a war of annihilation. Any significant margin of survival after an exchange of nuclear weapons could easily constitute "victory," however hollow and short-lived such survival might be.

In these circumstances it is difficult to believe that military planners in the Soviet Union would try their utmost to destroy the United States while leaving on its northern border an intact ribbon of land that is rich in natural resources, energy (already being exported to the United States in large quantities), agriculture and industrial development which could give the American survivors a margin that could make the difference between such a "victory" and total annihilation.

In view of these considerations, it seemed reasonable to us to conclude that Canada could not escape a direct attack aimed at much the same targets as those that had been identified for the United States. As a result, to the targets south of the border, we added comparable sites in Canada — military, energy and population.

In taking this step, we departed from a scenario that is reputed to have been produced by Canada's Department of National Defence (DND) as a guide for the civil defence preparations of Emergency Planning Canada (EPC).[9]

According to conversations with individuals in the latter agency, DND thought that Canada would be attacked but that these attacks would be limited to major population areas like Montreal, Toronto and Winnipeg, to some both populous and militarily significant cities such as the Vancouver-Victoria area, Halifax and Ottawa, to some smaller but militarily significant cities like North Bay and Saint John, and to some cities of presumably great industrial significance like Edmonton and Windsor. However, we were able to find no precise rationale for the choice of these cities, and the exclusion of others such as Oshawa, Hamilton and Sarnia. It may be that the DND was trying only to suggest examples, rather than to create a scenario for Canada as a whole.[10]

A spokesman for EPC explained further that, apart from this list of ten cities, DND does not think that other types of targets would be attacked. Apparently it is surmised that the Soviet Union would not regard Canada's military targets as significant, while it would want to spare Canadian energy resources for its own exploitation once Canada had come under its control.

These explanations did not appear to us to be very satisfactory; but, as far as EPC publications are concerned, the list of ten cities is the only official statement we have been able to obtain as to likely targets in Canada.

We saw no reason, however, to change our views that military installations, energy resources and population centres in Canada should be regarded as probable targets if the Soviet Union was to deny the United States access to Canadian resources. As a result, these were duly entered on our target map. The one concession made to the DND scenario was that cities of 100,000 population or more, that were neither on the DND list nor significant for energy or military reasons, were not put on our map. In addition, the subject of nuclear reactors was again treated conservatively in that only the very large reactors at Bruce and Pickering in southern Ontario were included. These were calculated as being two gigawatts each, although they are both somewhat larger and in the process of becoming larger still.

Finally, airports that appeared to be large enough to land the SAC B-52 bombers were included as military targets to be struck by 300-kiloton bombs, as applied to the SAC bases in the United States. But, unlike those targets, the Canadian civilian airports were judged subject to air bursts because they do not have "hardened" installations.

The reason for including these civilian airports is that, in a crisis, B-52 bombers could be deployed to them. In the Cuban missile crisis, for example, these bombers were dispersed to civilian airports in the United States. It has been suggested that permission to land them on Canadian runways was requested, although, if this is so, there is no evidence that such permission was ever granted.[11] Soviet strategists could hardly count on Canada's non-involvement again in the face of a general nuclear war.[12]

With these considerations, our target map was now complete (Figure 1). But because a direct attack on Canada seemed to be a likely part of a nuclear strike on North America, it became necessary to consider first the acute, immediate impact on targets in our own country. Only then could the significance of the radioactive fallout, which would subsequently blanket many of the areas already suffering from this initial devastation, be properly assessed.

The amount of nuclear explosives that might be dropped on Canada was calculated by counting the Canadian targets, using the size of bomb for each that official documents regard as likely (Table 1). For Canadian targets alone this amounts to anywhere from 20 to 40 megatons. Just *one*

TABLE 1
Amounts and Types of Nuclear Warheads that Could be Used on Various Targets*

Target	Size of Warhead (Megatons)	Air Burst	Ground Burst
Hydroelectric stations	0.01	√	
Thermal energy plants	0.01	√	
Airfields	0.3	√	√
		(Canadian)	(SAC)
Oil refineries	1	√	
Cities	1 or more	√	
Nuclear reactors			
(1 or more gigawatts)	1		√
ICBM silos	1 per silo		√
Submarine bases	1		√
Special military	1		√

*Used in determining ground burst targets, plume size, and, in the case of Canadian targets, the range of total megatonnage.

Sources: Compiled from information in "Reference Scenario: How a Nuclear War Might Be Fought," *Ambio, A Journal of the Human Environment* 11 (1982): 94-99, and Emergency Planning Canada, *Planning Guidance in Relation to a Nuclear Attack on North America in the 1980s*, document EPC 2/81.

North American Targets of Potential Relevance to Canada

Military Targets
● ICBM silos (with number of missiles)
▲ SAC bomber bases
■ Submarine bases
◆ Canadian military targets

Energy Targets
△ Nuclear reactors
□ Oil refineries
○ Thermal power plants
◇ Hydroelectric plants

Population Targets
□ Cities ≥ 1,000,000
□ Cities ≥ 100,000
□ Cities < 1,000,000

▨ Boundary within which nuclear explosions in U.S. could affect Canada

Pentagon

★ Norad

0 100   500   1,000 miles

megaton is equivalent in explosive power to one million tons of TNT and is seventy times more powerful than the bomb dropped on Hiroshima. Five megatons is more than all of the explosives used in the Second World War. Twenty megatons, if translated into the equivalent amount of TNT and placed on a freight train, would require a train that would reach from Halifax to Vancouver. Hence the explosive force unleashed on Canada in an all-out nuclear war could, in equivalent amount of TNT, fill a train that would stretch across the country and back again! Yet this destructive force represents less than 1 per cent of the Soviet Union's intercontinental nuclear arsenal and could easily be spared by them for use on Canadian targets.[13]

The Immediate Effects

Combined Canadian casualties for the First and Second World Wars and the Korean War, amounted to the deaths of just over 100,000 Canadian soldiers. If a one-megaton nuclear warhead exploded over a major Canadian city, six times that many people would be killed instantly. Based on our scenario, half of the population of 24 million would be affected immediately, at least six to eight million of these being killed or seriously injured. Most of the latter would die over the next few days, often because of the lack of medical facilities, which would have been largely destroyed. It is impossible to say how many would be added to this number over the next few weeks and months from the cumulative effects of radioactive poisoning, famine, epidemics and violence resulting from social disorder. However, it is hard to believe that more than a third of Canada's present population would still be living at the end of one year.

The immediate effects[14] are best imagined by thinking of the consequences of a one-megaton explosion detonated about two miles above a large Canadian city. Unlike chemical explosives, a thermonuclear weapon has three important effects — blast, thermal and nuclear radiation. These occur almost simultaneously, but, for simplicity's sake, are usually described separately.

Out of the bright fireball, in which the temperature and pressure are the same as those at the centre of the sun, a blast front or concussion wave moves out in a widening circle at supersonic speed, followed by high winds. Within a two-mile radius of ground zero nothing can withstand this blast or the 500 mph winds that follow. Even at four miles, only the skeletons of buildings with steel-beam construction would remain, the following winds still having twice the velocity of a hurricane. Out to eight miles from the centre, large commercial buildings would be heavily damaged and all homes destroyed. Up to twelve miles the concussion would be great enough to shatter glass, and send the splinters flying off at over 100 mph. Out at this distance, damage to homes would be significant but they would probably continue to provide shelter.

Even before this blast front, however, there would be a heat wave radiating out from the fireball at the speed of light, spontaneously igniting everything inflammable within a three- to five-mile radius. Ten miles away this thermal radiation is still severe enough to cause second-degree burns to exposed skin. At thirty miles, a person who happened to focus his gaze at the spot just as the detonation occurred would suffer retinal burns and possibly blindness.

In a typical explosion, about half of the energy is released as blast and another third as thermal radiation. The remainder, roughly 15 per cent, is in the form of nuclear radiation. But those who would have been exposed to this immediate radiation would not have survived the blast and heat. The rest of the radiation occurs as fallout, which will be discussed later.

Mortality within the two-mile radius is essentially 100 per cent and almost entirely instantaneous. Even out to four miles it is 50 per cent, another 40 per cent being seriously injured. At eight miles, half would be dead or injured and at twelves miles a quarter of the population would be injured, some seriously, by flying glass and debris.

People can withstand concussion much better than rigid buildings, but, in a city, this fact has little relevance. Death and injury occur not so much from the blow itself as from the fact that it turns people and debris into projectiles that hurl into stationary objects and into each other. Multiple fractures, puncture wounds, and the smashing of skulls, limbs and internal organs make the list of possible injuries endless. But the special horror of nuclear war, so far as immediate effects are concerned, is flesh-cooking heat.

In the central area, total devastation is combined with incineration. Nothing is left. Beyond this perimeter of annihilation, whatever injury survivors may or may not have sustained from the physical blow, the great likelihood is that they are seriously burned. Third-degree burns, even to protected skin, can occur within three miles and, to explosed flesh, within five.

Burns can also occur secondarily. In Hiroshima, the hundreds of fires started by thermal radiation coalesced within twenty minutes into a raging inferno or fire storm. This is a giant self-feeding bonfire in which the updraft sucks powerful surface winds towards its centre, thereby fanning the flames of the ever-widening perimeter. Temperatures can reach 800° Celsius (almost 1500° Fahrenheit). Anyone in the area, even if in a shelter, is either incinerated by the intense heat, asphyxiated by the lack of oxygen (which is consumed by the flames), or suffocated by the lethal doses of carbon dioxide that are given off.

An alternative result of many small fires is a conflagration in which a wall of flame, fanned by prevailing winds, marches in one direction on a wide front. Under certain conditions, either sort of fire, fire storm or conflagration, could lead to a destructive force that would kill more people than the initial effects of the bomb. But the likelihood of either of these events is disputed. With bigger bombs, there is a lag between the preceding heat wave and ensuing concussion and winds. Possibly fires started by the thermal pulse would be snuffed out by the following blast. Moreover, it may be that the density of inflammable materials in modern cities is not sufficient to generate or sustain such mammoth fires. Since only a nuclear explosion over a modern city could resolve the debate, it is hoped that the controversy remains academic.

But the number of severely burned survivors would, in any event, be very large. At Hiroshima it is estimated that half of the early deaths resulted from burns. So far as immediate effects upon people are concerned, it is this high proportion of severe burn cases that distinguishes injuries from a thermonuclear attack from those of other kinds of warfare.

In the first twenty-four hours, then, the immediate effects of a one-megaton bomb would be to leave a circle of destruction twenty-five miles in diameter in which an inner core, fifteen miles wide, would be more or less totally destroyed. At least a third of the population would be dead, another third seriously injured, many of these dying in the days ahead, in part because of a total lack of medical assistance.

But in the case of larger Canadian cities, Montreal for example, urban dwellers would not get off so lightly. The EPC planning document postulates an attack from two to five megatons on Montreal, an assumption in keeping with our own estimates based on population and the presence of the east end refineries, industry and two international airports. Almost certainly the whole of Montreal Island and much surrounding countryside would simply be obliterated. But this is only the beginning.

Fallout

Even the relatively healthy survivors in the target areas would face serious obstacles in the destruction of their economic and industrial base, the fundamental disruption of the social fabric, and the burden of the dead and suffering injured. But before they had lived through the first twenty-four hours of this nightmare, they would be subjected to radioactive fallout.

To assess the extent of this factor, we constructed, as has been said, a plume map incorporating fallout patterns arising both from ground bursts on U.S. targets and those occasioned by similar targets in Canada. But, in order to do this, one additional assumption has to be made — the direction of the wind.

In actual fact, the direction of the wind in any given place can vary considerably over a twenty-four-hour period, indeed even from hour to hour. For example, within hours of the beginning of the Three Mile Island nuclear reactor accident, the escaping radioactive emissions were being wafted due north across eastern Ontario and the Montreal region. Only after a day or two did they follow the more easterly path that one would expect from prevailing west winds. Even so, from hour to hour, they circled through almost 360 degrees.[15] Indeed, to say that the "prevailing" winds are from the west, for example, may be to reflect actual conditions that prevail a mere 15 per cent of the time. For the other 85 per cent, winds are coming from other directions around all points of the compass, but, for each of these directions, less than the "prevailing" 15 per cent.

Again an arbitary decision had to be made and it was decided that the plumes should be laid down along the lines of wind directions which are said to be typical for North America in the summer months. Under actual local weather conditions, some parts of Canada might be more fortunate than this wind pattern would suggest, but it is just as likely that other parts would be worse off than we have predicted. It was felt, therefore, that for the country as a whole, the extent of radioactive contamination might not be too different from what is postulated in our particular scenario.

One other decision had to be made. The plumes can be calculated a number of different ways, depending on what it is that one wants to illustrate. Because civil defence planners characteristically talk in terms of sheltering people for two weeks, we decided to mark off areas of contamination that would represent the two-week dose of radiation that a person would accumulate if, during that time, he or she had had no shelter from its effects (plume lengths for this period are given in Table 2).

Within each plume we further designated three areas where the accumulated two-week dose of an unprotected person would be 450 rems, 100 rems and 10 rems (Figure 2). Rems are units of the biological effects resulting from radiation, and the three levels indicated in each plume represent dosages with important practical significance.

In a population of healthy individuals, a dose of 450 rems within a two-week period would cause sickness in all and death to many. In the conditions existing after a nuclear attack the mortality rate could be anything from 50 to 90 per cent. Only special sheltering for the two-week

TABLE 2
Length of Radioactive Fallout Plumes from Ground Bursts of Various Sizes on Various Targets

Size of Warhead	Length of Plume (in miles)		
	450 rems*	100 rems*	10 rems*
300 kilotons	42	100	262
1 megaton	80	175	440
1 megaton on 1 gigawatt nuclear reactor	150	320	620
1 megaton on 2 gigawatt nuclear reactor	220	405	720
17 megatons on one ICBM silo field	290	480	800
150 megatons on one ICBM silo field	560	740	1,020
200 megatons on one ICBM silo field	630	860	1,200

*Accumulated two-week dose if unprotected.

Sources: Steve Fetter and Kosta Tsipis, *Catastrophic Nuclear Radiation Releases*, Program in Science and Technology for International Security, Report no. 5, 2nd printing (Cambridge, Mass.: MIT Department of Physics, Sept. 1980), and S. Glasstone and P. Dolan, eds, *Effects of Nuclear Weapons*, 3rd ed. (Government Printing Office, Washington: U.S. Departments of Defense and Energy, 1977).

period would prevent this. In the area out to 100 rems, most exposed persons would suffer some symptoms of radiation sickness and some of these would die, particularly the aged and infirm as well as many of the injured. Hence sheltering within this area would also be necessary, at least for a good part of the time.

Finally, the zone marked off by an accumulated dose of 10 rems indicates territory in which the unsheltered person would receive, in two weeks, twice the yearly dose regarded as safe for high-risk occupations such as uranium miners. In a nuclear war such doses would have to be risked and normal indoor living would probably reduce this level further. The purpose for showing this on our plume map, therefore, is not so much for the immediate dangers posed to inhabitants but rather to demonstrate the geographic extent of radioactive contamination with long-lasting substances like strontium-90, caesium-137 and plutonium 239. In this outer zone, these contaminants would be spread too thinly on the ground to cause an immediate threat, but they would linger for years and, through inhalation

FIGURE 2
"Local" Fallout
(accumulated two-week dose in rems)

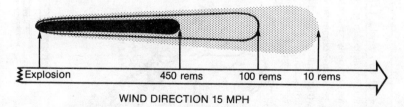

WIND DIRECTION 15 MPH

or ingestion, become concentrated in the bodies of the local people to the point where long-term radiation effects, such as cancer, could result.[16]

Again our diagrammatic representation gives a conservative impression of what would take place. Actual deposition of the fallout would be affected by weather and terrain, making an erratic pattern of "hot"spots where radiation would be many times higher than calculations would predict, and other areas where dose rates would be lower than expected. Only the constant use of special detection equipment would alert people to the actual levels of radiation from place to place.

The conventions used to depict these plumes are conservative in other respects. For instance, the various two-week accumulated doses given for each area would only apply to the outer margins of these zones. In the black zone, for example, doses of *at least* 450 rems could be expected out to the edge of that zone. As one moves back towards ground zero, in any of the zones, the dose is higher than the 450, 100 or 10 rems designated for the zone as a whole. And again, no effort has been made to depict the additive effect of overlapping plumes where doses would be roughly the sum of the two zones overlapped. Thus, the overlapping of two 100-rem zones would create another area close to the 200-rem level where a substantial death-rate from radiation could be expected.

Finally, while the rate of radioactivity declines rapidly, and in most areas would have reached levels safe enough, after two weeks, for people to return to outdoor activity, the whole of these areas could remain contaminated for a long time in the sense of giving rise to inhaled or ingested concentrations of radioactivity that could cause trouble for the inhabitants over the long term. Moreover, areas close to ground zero would have persisting, high levels of radiation that could make them uninhabitable for months or even years. This is particularly true for the area contaminated by fallout from a nuclear warhead exploding on a nuclear reactor. For example, in the case of a one-megaton bomb falling on a one-gigawatt

FIGURE 3
Radioactive Fallout Plumes

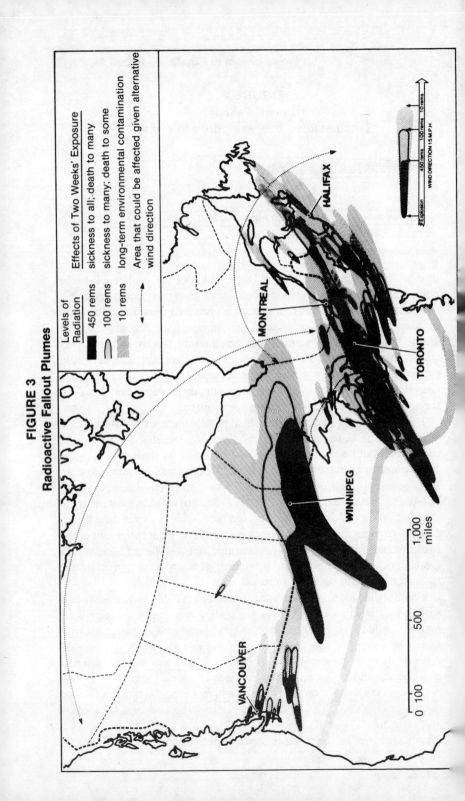

Levels of
Radiation
450 rems
100 rems
10 rems

Effects of Two Weeks' Exposure
sickness to all; death to many
sickness to many; death to some
long-term environmental contamination
Area that could be affected given alternative
wind direction

VANCOUVER

WINNIPEG

TORONTO

MONTREAL

HALIFAX

0 100   500   1,000
miles

Explosion   450 rems 15 M.P.H.   100 rems   10 rems

WIND DIRECTION 15 M.P.H.

reactor, an area of 680 square miles would have a level of radioactivity so high and long-lasting as to make it still uninhabitable after one year.[17]

It will be appreciated, on the basis of all of these considerations, that the plume map we finally designed (Figure 3) is highly hypothetical. However, in view of the fact that we attempted to construct a realistic but conservative estimate of the effects, we believe that the map reflects, within broad limits, some idea of the magnitude of the impact of the fallout on Canada from a nuclear attack on North America. Almost certainly, if the scenario is faulty, it is that it falls short of what would actually happen and reflects a *minimum* estimate of the effects.

A special feature of this map deserves comment: the plumes arising from strikes on missile silo fields in the United States. On the target map (Figure 1), numbers beside the various fields indicate the number of ICBMs in each. It is considered likely that each silo in each field would be hit with a ground burst of one megaton, at the very least. This is the situation we have depicted, but, of course, it results in very large plumes arising from fields that have been struck by 150 to 200 megatons, some of the plumes reaching Canada from sources more than 350 miles below our border. It has even been suggested that each silo would also be subjected to a second megaton, detonated in the air. This would add to both the amount of radioactivity and its dispersal, but we have no idea how much and have not contemplated this possibility. Nor did we make allowance for the consequences of the ICBM's own warhead being vaporized in the explosion.

In trying to imagine the consequences of this local fallout, it must be remembered that the affected areas largely *are* Canada, i.e., they are the centres of population, industry and agriculture which constitute the viable part of our national territory. Vast tracts of land that would likely remain unaffected are also uninhabited. Even so, faint arcs sketched around the tips of some of the major plumes indicate how these or any of the plumes could be rotated by changes in wind direction. They are a reminder that practically no inhabited place in Canada can be deemed safe from the contamination of local fallout.

In the Windsor, Ontario to Quebec City axis, almost 55 per cent of all Canadians live on 2 per cent of the nation's land.[18] A combination of urban centres, many nuclear reactors in both the United States and Ontario, and several other targets, make it clear that this area would be devastated far beyond anything that has ever happened in any war, or any natural disaster, anywhere in the world in the history of mankind.

It must also be kept in mind that only ground bursts give rise to the plumes that have been drawn on the second map. Yet all of the air bursts, such as those over most of the cities, would already have wreaked their havoc, leaving behind no mark to be made on the map of local fallout patterns.

Would the air bursts cause any radioactive dust to fall on Canada? Does their "global" fallout that descends from the stratosphere weeks and months later have any special relevance for us? A rough calculation suggests that it does.

On the basis of measurements made of the global fallout from atmospheric tests of nuclear explosives, it is clear that, within a week to ten days, such stratospheric debris travels completely around the world, from west to east, more or less within the latitudes into which it was first injected.[19] Some, but much less, dispersion of the dust occurs in the north-south axis. In the atmospheric tests done before the Limited Test Ban Treaty of 1963, for example, the peak regions of deposition of strontium-90 were between 30° and 50° North latitude, reflecting the fact that the majority of the tests occurred in the northern hemisphere.[20]

In an all-out nuclear war, injections of radioactive debris into the stratosphere would occur within the latitudes that mark the regions of the major targets. North American targets include, it is true, a great many points in the United States that are well south of Canadian latitudes. On the other hand, almost all targets throughout the whole of non-Mediterranean Europe, and the vast majority in the Soviet Union, are situated between 40° and 60° North latitude. For all intents and purposes these are the latitudes of Canada as far as its population, industry, agriculture and even most of its natural resources are concerned. The likelihood is very great, therefore, that for a year or two after the war, surviving Canadians would continue to be exposed to the chronic deposition of radioactive substances almost anywhere in the country.

It is not unreasonable to suggest, then, that after a nuclear war, as a result of local or global fallout, or both, the entire surviving Canadian population would sooner or later find itself in areas where there was a risk of exposure to harmful doses of radioactivity.

The contemplation of our place in the northern latitudes brings one final thought to mind. Little is known about the long-term ecological effects of a nuclear holocaust on the northern hemisphere where it would likely take place. Several studies suggest that, through the depletion of the ozone layer, the creation of stratospheric dust or water crystal clouds, or other such disturbances, weather patterns in our part of the world might be profoundly disturbed. Canada is a land of bountiful resources but the carrying capacity of the land is limited. We live in a northern clime with a short growing season. A drop of just one degree Celsius in our annual mean temperature could seriously jeopardize the cultivation of wheat in much of western Canada.[21] It is not impossible to believe that Canada, more than countries in southern parts of the northern hemisphere, might no longer be able to support more than a marginal existence.

Care has been taken, throughout this account, to make clear the many points at which guesswork has been necessary. Much more careful analysis by experts with more than our meagre financial resources might refine and revise the details of this work. But this would only be to the purpose if it changed the above conclusions in the direction of a significantly better outcome. We believe, however, that we have consistently understated the effects and that a more extensive investigation would make the outcome look worse, probably much worse.

On the basis of our analysis, it seems reasonable to conclude that, in an all-out nuclear war, the short-term impact on Canada would be every bit as great as it would be on the United States. And, in the long run, it might even be a good deal worse.

Notes

[1] The standard source is *The Effects of Nuclear War* (Washington, D.C.: Office of Technology Assessment, Congress of the United States, 1979).

[2] Eliot Marshall, "A Question of Accuracy," *Science* 213 (1981): 1230-31.

[3] Maureen McDonald, Alasdair Polson, Linda Panaro and Lisa Cotton.

[4] Donald P. Briskin, Christopher Schon, and Don Bates, respectively.

[5] "Reference Scenario: How a Nuclear War Might Be Fought," *Ambio, A Journal of the Human Environment*, Royal Swedish Academy of Sciences, 11 (1982): 94-99.

[6] Center for Defense Information, Washington, D.C., verbal communication.

[7] "Reference Scenario: How a Nuclear War Might Be Fought."

[8] Steven A. Fetter and Kosta Tsipis, "Catastrophic Releases of Radioactivity," *Scientific American*, April 1981, p. 47. For an explanation of why there is an increasing likelihood that reactors would be targets in a nuclear war, see Bennett Ramberg, *Destruction of Nuclear Energy Facilities in War: The Problem and the Implications* (Lexington, Mass.: D.C. Heath, 1980), especially p. 63f.

[9] Emergency Planning Canada, *Planning Guidance in Relation to a Nuclear Attack on North America in the 1980's*, document EPC 2/81. In a letter to Don Bates, dated 30 November 1982, Dr. G.R. Lindsey, chief of the Operational Research and Analysis Establishment (ORAE) of the Department of National Defence said that personnel of ORAE had done some work "in the early stages of the preparation of EPC 2/81."

[10] Again, in his letter, Dr. Lindsey said that "the target list eventually published in that document [i.e., EPC 2/81] did not come from us." And later, "I cannot give you the thinking behind the scenario adopted in EPC 2/81, as we were not

involved in devising it." Either the scenario came from elsewhere in DND or our informant in EPC was mistaken. Dr. Lindsey went on to say, "I have heard defense planners debating the various types of attack.... They usually conclude that no differentiation would be made between USA and Canada, with the USSR considering them as a single entity from the military and economic point of view." Hence, there seems to be a general consensus that Canada would be attacked, and support for our view that the attack would be similar to that directed against the United States. But of course, as Dr. Lindsey emphasizes, "no man knows what is going to happen," and the selection of targets and rationale for those targets is, finally, speculative.

11 Jon B. McLin, *Canada's Changing Defense Policy, 1957-1963: The Problem of a Middle Power in Alliance* (Baltimore: The Johns Hopkins Press, 1967), p. 157f.
12 That large Canadian civilian airports would be prime targets was suggested to us by the Center for Defense Information, Washington, D.C.
13 Estimates of the number of megatons of nuclear explosives in the strategic arms of the Soviet Union vary somewhat. The lowest we have seen is 4,123 megatons, given by *Ambio* (cited above) on the basis of figures in the Stockholm International Peace Research Institute Yearbook for 1982.
14 For an overview see D.G. Bates, "The Medical and Ecological Effects of Nuclear War," *The McGill Law Journal* 28:3 (in press), which includes references to the basic literature on this subject. The following paragraphs on immediate effects are largely taken from that article.
15 Thomas Pawlick, "The Silent Toll," *Harrowsmith Magazine*, June 1980, figures on p. 37.
16 Of the many sources available on this subject, we were particularly helped by Joseph Rotblat, *Nuclear Radiation in Warfare*, Stockholm International Peace Research Institute (London: Taylor and Francis, 1981).
17 Fetter and Tsipis, "Catastrophic Releases of Radioactivity," p. 45.
18 Wendy Simpson-Lewis, et al., *Canada's Special Resource Lands: A National Perspective of Selected Land Uses* (Ottawa: Land Directorate, Environment Canada, 1979), p. 192 and Map 1.
19 Lester Machta and Kosta Telegadas, "Radioiodine levels in the U.S. Public Health Service pasteurized milk network from 1963-1968 and their relationship to possible sources," *Health Physics* 19 (1970): 469-85.
20 *Long-term Worldwide Effects of Multiple Nuclear-Weapons Detonations*, a committee report to the National Academy of Sciences (Washington, D.C., 1975), pp. 25-38 and especially Figure 1.7.
21 Edward Goldsmith, "The Future of an Affluent Society: The Case of Canada," a report commissioned by the Advanced Concepts Centre of Environment Canada published in *The Ecologist, Journal of the Post Industrial Age*, Wadebridge, Cornwall, U.K., 7 (1977): 160-94; see especially p. 168f.

We are grateful for the helpful suggestions of G.R. Lindsey, of the Department of National Defence, Ottawa, and Joseph Romm of the Department of Physics at the Massachusetts Institute of Technology, Cambridge, who both read this chapter in draft form. They are, however, in no way responsible for the final result.

PART III

The Failure of Policy

8

No More Holocausts: The Ethical Challenge

David MacDonald

> What I want is love, not sacrifice, knowledge of God, not holocausts.   Hosea 6:6

The summer of 1945 is poignantly remembered with relief as the occasion when the suffering and sacrifice of World War II came dramatically to an end. It was the week before my ninth birthday that I learned the war was finally over. Only days before, on the morning of August 6, we had awakened to the news of an explosive device of incredible proportions that had eliminated almost the entire population of a Japanese city. Prior to that date, the name Hiroshima was virtually unknown to us all. Then, it heralded the arrival of peace. Yet ever since, it has served as a constant reminder of the nightmare of agony and destructive force that the atomic age unleashed.

In a more innocent world, war and its aftermath seemed both explainable and containable, even supportable. But Hiroshima was carnal knowledge to our innocence. It "nuked" every safe assumption held about war. Our moral and intellectual landscape turned into an after-the-atom-bomb wasteland of hollow concept and construct, devoid of life and meaning. Since the fateful summer of 1945 we have considered, discussed and debated without truly confronting the essence of our moral dilemma: What is our responsibility to this new and cataclysmic force?

Thousands of books have been written, conferences held, speeches made, resolutions passed, all to put into some manageable system an invention which has defied its maker. We are the corporate Doctor Frankenstein of the twentieth century, desperate to control the monster that threatens us all. Numerous scenarios have been created to attempt to convince us that we had achieved this end. In the late 1940s and early 1950s, it was common practice to talk about "atoms for peace." This has even included nuclear explosions in the name of human progress, such as the Indian nuclear device assisted by Canadian technology. In fact, hundreds of atomic explosions have been rationalized by the major nuclear powers as primarily peaceful or scientific.

This "benign monster" perspective had many adherents as our imaginations were encouraged to contemplate the enormous benefit that would shortly derive from the peaceful uses of nuclear power. Atomic electrical generators in the 1950s and 1960s were proud testimony and justification for the development of nuclear technology. The wonder of medical isotopes was equally acclaimed while scientists in every discipline raced to find the newest applications of radiation technology.

While our scientific curiosity and technical achievements carried us forward, our moral and ethical capacity lagged. In 1945 and shortly thereafter, it was almost unanimously believed that we would develop some sensible international systems for the control of this new technology. We could not have imagined the incredible nuclearization of our planet in the succeeding forty years.

We realize with the irony of despair how both East and West have built up nuclear weaponry in the name of peace, equality and freedom. To have lived with this incredible contradition is to condemn our ethical fantasy. To wonder at its assumptions is to invite profound and painful questions as to our beliefs, our morality and, ultimately, our right to stewardship of Earth. We have allowed a system to be based on active preparation to destroy all life on this planet, not to mention humanity. How can we claim to stand as the defenders of basic human values and freedom if we participate in a system whose ultimate defence is to blow the world to smithereens? Our record is totally irrational, morally bankrupt, and unbelievably dangerous.

As is so often the case, it is not the discoveries themselves but their economic and political development that have been anti-human. Our task is to rediscover reality, to renew and create the ethical and social forms that will allow us to use our understanding of the universe to enhance life, not destroy it. It was Brazilian bishop, Dom Helder Camara, at the second UN Special Session on Disarmament, who addressed this most clearly: "Time is running out. The West must acknowledge the materialistic foundations of capitalism, and stop posing as the defender of Christian civilization. The East must recognize its own imperialism and suppression of liberty, especially religious liberty and the rights of workers."

At issue in the 1980s is our hiatus of the conscience. The basic questions of value which either would not or could not be raised from the

1940s through the 1970s, relentlessly haunt every man and woman of the 1980s.

What we are faced with are questions of power. What is our responsibility, for example, to our descendants? How do we develop systems that do not increase the likelihood that nuclear weapons and technology will either instantly destroy life or gradually diminish its quality as we know it on this planet? Those who would argue that nuclear capacity is simply an extension of earlier forms of technological activity simply do not understand its finality.

What has brought all this home are the reports of American strategies to fight and win a limited nuclear war. Many are shocked and stunned by this speculation. But it "worked" in World War II. And that remains a fact of life for the nuclear powers. Ask the Elysée, Whitehall, the Pentagon, the Kremlin, New Delhi, Peking. The bomb is a peace deterrent, or in other words, we owe it our survival (a piece of doublethink George Orwell would have appreciated). While it may not have been a point of articulation or rhetoric for previous American administrations, or for that matter, Soviet ones, it is clear that the Reagan administration today is sufficiently uninhibited and paranoid to express this view directly.

We may be appalled at the naiveté and dangerousness of this belief. But we should not think that it is new or inconsistent with nuclear deterrence theories. Rather it makes the case that once you have accepted a system that makes possible the use of nuclear weapons, they may be used in dealing with any event.

At the United Nations Special Session Philip Potter, General Secretary of the World Council of Churches, said, "New weapons and new strategies have introduced new elements to deterrence. It has fuelled the arms race at various levels. The concept of deterrence is politically unacceptable and morally indefensible."

In the past, the dilemmas posed by new weapons technologies were easier to resolve. Following World War I, we created an international convention that outlawed the use of poison gas in international warfare. It was convenient for us to do so because we could create other, more serviceable weapons, to give us national security.

But our situation with nuclear weapons is unique. We are rapidly discovering that not just modern weapons but war itself is obsolete — not only politically but also morally unacceptable. How do we deal with this new phenomenon?

Our challenge is to create an expectation. One which believes that the assumed right of nations to unleash violence on one another or their own citizens is not acceptable. Just as individuals in modern society cannot at will inflict violence on one another without public penalty and chastisement, so societies, corporations, institutions or nations must not continue to be allowed to wage violence at will on one another.

This century has so far seen only feeble steps in that direction. Despite a legacy of two world wars and well over one hundred and fifty regional and civil conflicts, neither the League of Nations nor the United Nations has so far helped us to confront reality. Even during the recent outpouring of desire for peace, we have been witnesses to nations arbitrarily waging war: Great Britain, Argentina, Israel, South Africa, Libya, the Soviet Union, Indonesia, and the list goes on and on. Thus one challenge of disarmament is the very nature of the present political system of nation-states. The relation of power to military institutions and spending must surely be challenged.

The century-old concept of the purpose of the nation-state was to ensure domestic order and collective security. The very nature of that order and security is now threatened by the reality of nations which possess a power and potential that threatens not only their own citizens but human beings and their environment on a worldwide basis.

Awareness is growing that we have not been successful in earlier peace movements because this political system has made nation-states supreme and their ability to wage war unquestioned. This failure leaves untouched not only the right assumed by governments to wage war against human beings — externally or internally, as in the case of Guatemala, El Salvador, Ethiopia, the Philippines, etc. — but also their rights to torture, to impose War Measures Acts, to muzzle dissent, to rape the environment, to sterilize populations, to divert resources into armaments.

A recent phone-in on CBC "Cross-Country Checkup" identified this new factor motivating the peace movement — a fundamental concern with the need to participate in basic political questions. "People want the right to say whether we should go on building more bombs or threatening to use them."

There is in our time a coming together of basic questions of value with political reality. The nuclear bomb, in other words, has triggered an ethical explosion. Our will or foresight to renew our thought and institutions to serve us in this new age, is contingent upon our fundamental understanding of morality — post Hiroshima — and mortality. Without consensus on the moral inacceptability of nuclear, indeed all forms of, violence, we will not have the will to create a future free from the threat of global annihilation.

Not since the movement for the abolition of slavery in the early part of the nineteenth century have we been faced with such a fundamental shift in basic values or patterns of life. While we may neither fully understand nor accept the full dimensions of the present anti-nuclear movement, it is increasingly clear that a whole series of forces are joining to halt the madness of the nuclear weapons race.

Beyond that there will be a continuing pressure to deal with other forms of unrestricted violence between nations which we have traditionally called "war." This new abolitionist movement is, in effect, a movement to end war as an accepted form of behaviour between nation-states. And ultimately, it will be the very notions of nation-states and sovereignty, of political territory and military power, that are called into question.

One of the principal difficulties in coming to terms with the nuclear issue is the degree to which technology has infiltrated our sense of society and of ourselves. As Alan Geyer suggests in his book, *The Idea of Disarmament*:

> Technology has become the ever more powerful engine of our material existence in most societies in recent decades: its institutional patterns dominate styles of life, work, communication, transportation, knowledge, health, leisure, government — and especially schemes for national security and international aggrandizement. So thoroughly are all our institutions in North America and Europe, including even the churches, committed to relentlessly accelerating modes of technology that our very beliefs and values are increasingly expressed in technological symbols.

Labour-saving, life-saving, time-saving ... all that we attribute to "technology the good," is the underpinning of the arms race. Technology is so pervasive, from hospital to kitchen, from office to logging camp, that we easily apply the same mentality to war of bigger, faster, better, kill more, destroy more, in an ever-widening spiral.

Either we abandon technology, or we renounce war, but our moral sanity is stretched dangerously thin to countenance both within the same society. The discussion of the nuclear threat in the 1980s is not based on a narrow anxiety or concern. It is rather increasingly seen in the larger context of the uses of technology itself, the reality of political power, the effective functioning of our economic system, and even the importance of new developments such as those in communications and information technology.

The challenge for the latter part of the 1980s is to develop not only new political institutions which provide real security and de-escalation of the nuclear confrontations, but also a moral framework that allows humanity to work out serious political, social and economic norms of disapproval consistent with the knowledge unleashed in that first explosion in 1945.

We will need the creative skills of theologians, scientists and artists alike if we are to develop from the ground up, so to speak, a society which can benefit from the incredible success of science without destroying itself in the process. If a new context for technology and war is to be sustained and ultimately successful, our point of departure will be new forms of participation in all political systems coupled with real limitations on national power. New international or transnational ways for people to make decisions and share responsibility must be found.

We have some initial moves in that direction. In Western Europe, the development of a European Parliament with direct elections which transcends national borders is a hopeful sign. The recent Law of the Sea Treaty has the elements of sharing power and resources on a global scale for the two-thirds of the earth's surface that is covered by the oceans. Agencies of the United Nations, if they become more directly accountable to us, the people of the world, hold the same promise.

But these are only beginnings. We will all have to work very hard to put roots down in long-term political action for transformation of the rule of the nation-state. At the same time we must struggle with our personal liberation of the mind from the tyranny of technological modes. And ultimately, the abolition of war itself is inseparable from the equitable sharing of resources so that the horrendous and growing disparities between rich and poor, between economic slave and perpetrator, can be effectively addressed. Only that kind of agenda and set of goals will address the roots of nuclear madness in our profoundly immoral system.

9

The Liberal Leadership and Nuclear Weapons

Walter Gordon

Except for the Diefenbaker years from 1957 to 1963 and the Clark interregnum of 1979, the nuclear arms race has been addressed in Canada by a Liberal federal government. The way in which two men in particular have viewed the nuclear question has done much to shape Canadian policy: Lester Pearson, minister of state for external affairs during the 1950s, and then prime minister from 1963 to 1967, and Pierre Trudeau, prime minister from 1968 to 1979, and again from 1980 on.

In this short memoir, Walter Gordon, finance minister in the Pearson government, shows how Pearson and Trudeau have in similar ways changed their positions on Canada's role with regard to nuclear weapons, and how the issue, one among many on Parliament Hill, took on a greater importance for one powerful Liberal insider — Gordon himself.

E.R. & S.R.

The Canadian military establishment was drastically reduced at the end of World War II. But in 1949, following the formation of NATO, it was decided that the Department of National Defence should be reorganized and Canadian military capacity strengthened as quickly as possible. The fear was that the Soviets might be tempted to overrun Western Europe; if they had attempted to do so at that time there was nothing to stop them.

The Hon. Brooke Claxton, the minister of national defence, asked me to assist him in the reorganization of the department. In the course of doing so, it was necessary for me to have a number of confidential discussions with the military authorities in the United Kingdom and the United States respecting the potential threat to Europe and what Canada's defence role should be. This was my first experience in the field of Canada's defence policy and of course it was before the days of nuclear arsenals.

A decade later the situation was very different. I was chairman of the Policy Committee at the convention of the Liberal Party in January 1961, when John Diefenbaker was in the middle of his first term and proceeding to acquire nuclear capability for Canada's forces both at home and in Europe. The delegates, in discussing defence policy in the nuclear age, approved a formal resolution which read in part as follows:

> Canadian defence policy must be based on the fundamental truth that in the nuclear age, the only protection is the establishment and maintenance of a creative peace.... The main lines of Liberal policy would be:
>
> Any extension of the possession of nuclear weapons under national control will greatly increase the danger of accidental outbreak of nuclear war and also the difficulty of achieving disarmament. Membership in the nuclear club therefore should not be extended beyond the four countries which now possess such weapons [U.S., USSR, U.K. and France]. The objective should be not the extension of ownership of such weapons but their abolition before they destroy the world.
>
> Canada cannot deny nuclear weapons to other nations and at the same time arm her own forces with them. A new Liberal government therefore should not acquire, manufacture or use such weapons either under separate Canadian control or under joint U.S.-Canadian control...
>
> Under a new Liberal government Canada will withdraw from NORAD insofar as its present interceptor role is concerned...
>
> We would stop using our defence resources on interceptor fighter squadrons or on Bomarc missiles....

Then suddenly two years later, in January 1963, Lester Pearson, the leader of the Liberal Party, unilaterally reversed this position. During an election campaign he stated that under the NATO and NORAD treaties Canada was committed to use "tactical" nuclear warheads, and that if a Liberal government was elected, it would honour these commitments.

I was one of those who did not agree with Mr. Pearson's decision, which was made without consulting any of his senior colleagues. But by that time an election was in the offing. I had become chairman of the Liberal Party's National Campaign Committee and was a member of Parliament. In view of these responsibilities, rightly or wrongly, I decided to stay on.

Some people thought Mr. Pearson's change of heart was an astute move in political terms, but this was not so. The opinion polls at the time made it clear the public was primarily concerned with bread and butter issues. It was not much interested in defence policy.

In fact, the change in policy probably resulted in the Liberal Party's failure to obtain an overall majority in the election three months later. I say this because Jean Marchand, Gérard Pelletier and Pierre Trudeau, all of whom had agreed to stand as Liberal candidates in the next election, withdrew from the party over Mr. Pearson's reversal of policy on nuclear weapons. With them and their close supporters the Liberals almost certainly would have won an overall majority. As it turned out, they were able to form a minority government following the election of April 1963.

Mr. Trudeau was especially critical of Mr. Pearson's turnabout, writing in the April 1963 issue of *Cité libre* as follows:

> No importance was attached to the fact that such a policy [the acceptance of nuclear arms] had been repudiated by the party congress and banished from its program; nor to the fact that the chief had acted without consulting the national council of the Liberal Federation or its executive committee; nor to the fact that the leader had forgotten to discuss it with the parliamentary caucus or even with his principal advisers. The 'Pope' had spoken. It was up to the faithful to believe.

Mr. Trudeau went on to document the long-standing official opposition of Mr. Pearson and the Liberal Party to nuclear arms and suggested that the switch was made under American pressure.

> Fate had it that the final thrust came from the Pentagon and obliged Mr. Pearson to betray his party's platform as well as the ideal with which he had always identified himself. Power presented itself to Mr. Pearson; he had nothing to lose except honour. He lost it. And his whole party lost it with him.

I do not recall any broadly-based discussion in cabinet about defence or foreign policy during the five years that Mr. Pearson was prime minister. The only exception was the acceptance of nuclear warheads under American control for Canadian troops in Europe and for the Bomarc missiles based in Canada. That the question of nuclear arms should arise only once was probably due to Mr. Pearson's pre-eminence in defence and foreign policies.

In February or March 1968, the NORAD agreement was due to come up for renewal. I informed Mr. Pearson that if there was to be renewal, I would insist upon a public debate and if this was not agreed to, would be forced to resign from the cabinet over the issue. At the time, I did not think there was any question as important as the threat of nuclear annihilation. This is still my opinion. Apart from that, I have always been opposed to the NORAD agreement because it is really a bit of a fake. It implies that Canada really has something to say about the defence of North America. If there was an attack from the Soviet Union, the decision to retaliate would be made by the Americans. I cannot believe they would bother too much about the reaction of Canada.

Mr. Pearson knew that I planned to resign anyway over another matter. Accordingly, the question of renewing NORAD was not raised until after I had left the cabinet.

Since then, many people, myself included, have become even more disturbed by the nuclear threat and the failure to achieve disarmament, particularly under conditions where the Soviets have the capability to retaliate in kind. More recently, there has been the Soviet buildup in nuclear weaponry, intervention in Afghanistan, and the fear, whether justified or not, that their forces might invade Poland as they did Hungary in 1956 and Czechoslovakia in 1968.

Since 1981, these anxieties have been added to by the tremendous buildup in armament planned by the Reagan administration in the United States — and by the bellicose statements of U.S. leaders. In this kind of atmosphere, there is increasing risk of nuclear confrontation occurring between the superpowers either by intention or by accident.

With this in mind, along with seventy-seven prominent Canadians, I signed a statement headed "Canadian Foreign Policy in the 1980s" initiated by Andrew Brewin, for many years a member of Parliament and NDP spokesman on foreign policy and defence. He sent this statement to the prime minister on 15 October 1981. Among other things, it proposed "declaring Canada to be a nuclear weapon free zone."

Mr. Trudeau replied in a long letter dated 27 December 1981 in which he stated: "There is a great deal in what you and your associates have said with which I am personally very sympathetic." He went on to review Canadian foreign policy at some length. However, on the key point of declaring Canada a nuclear-weapon-free zone, he stated: ". . . support for multilateral disarmament has been a key element in our policy. It is also the reason why we believe that declaring Canada to be a nuclear weapon free zone would not add to, and could well detract from our own security and that of our Allies." This is a far cry from the position taken by Mr. Trudeau in early 1963 over Mr. Pearson's unilateral reversal of the Liberal Party's nuclear policy. I agreed with Mr. Trudeau's position then, although his bitter denunciation of Mr. Pearson personally went too far. I find it difficult to understand, however, his diametrically opposite opinion on the same subject today.

In the United States, authorities as different as George Kennan and Henry Kissinger have urged that American nuclear strategy be reconsidered because long-range nuclear missiles developed by the Soviet Union have rendered the United States and Canada impossible to defend.

In this situation of being defenceless many Canadians feel helpless about their doing anything constructive. Many are extremely nervous about the reintroduction of Cold War rhetoric and postures in Washington and the apparent inability of the two superpowers to get together on any meaningful proposals for disarmament. Canadians are aware of course of the reservations of Europeans respecting U.S. policies and attitudes, and of the suggestions that the territories of the North European countries should be declared a nuclear-free zone.

In these circumstances Canada could declare itself a nuclear-free zone and state that it will eschew the manufacture, use or possession of all nuclear weapons. At the same time, Canada could take the initiative in urging other middle powers to join in proscribing the use of all nuclear weapons. Critics of such a move will point out that such action would not guarantee our safety, if nuclear weapons were passing over our territory in both directions. Even if the superpowers agreed to respect our neutrality there could be no guarantee against accidents or fallout.

And while the Soviets might welcome such a declaration on our part, the Americans would almost certainly oppose it. The Americans are of course our allies and our friends. Moreover, despite some current squabbles over economic matters, Canadians and Americans have many intimate ties. We want these relationships to be continued.

This means that most Canadians, and almost certainly the Canadian government, would be reluctant to take a stance that would mean taking an independent line from that of the U.S. But if enough of us were seriously fearful of the possibility of a nuclear holocaust, should we not consider any rational action that might reduce the probability of this happening?

10

"Suffocation" of the Arms Race: Federal Policy 1978-82

Pauline Jewett

"The most unpardonable failure," Pierre Trudeau told the second United Nations Special Session on Disarmament (UNSSOD) on 18 June 1982, "would be to kill, by inaction, the hope in people's hearts. For, in the face of the demented threat of a resumption of the nuclear arms race, to kill hope in the possibility of disarmament is, in a very real sense, to risk killing life itself." These are challenging words spoken by the man who had challenged the United Nations four years earlier to suffocate the nuclear arms race. Yet from the time of Pierre Trudeau's speech at the first United Nations Special Session on Disarmament in 1978 to the fall of 1982, Canada moved sharply backwards in nuclear arms control and disarmament policies and actions. This movement has been punctuated only occasionally by the prime minister's increasingly hollow rhetoric.

In order to examine the recent record of the Trudeau government on the nuclear arms race, one must look at the proposals made, and the hopes implied, in the prime minister's "Strategy of Suffocation" speech, delivered at the United Nations on 26 May 1978.

Canada, the prime minister proclaimed, stands as an example to the world in its choice not to build its own nuclear weapons, in its demand that its troops in NATO have no nuclear role, and in its decision to rid itself of the last foreign nuclear weapons based on its soil since the early 1960s. "We were thus not only the first country in the world with the capacity to produce nuclear weapons that chose not to do so, we are also the first nuclear armed country to have chosen to divest itself of nuclear weapons," Trudeau declared of these unilateral defence and foreign policy decisions.

Trudeau then made a very strong commitment on behalf of Canada

---

This chapter was prepared with the generous help of my research assistant, Steve Lee.

to nuclear arms control and disarmament measures. "It has been an assumption of our policy that countries like Canada can do something to slow down the arms race . . . we must impart a fresh momentum to the lagging process of disarmament. The time for doing so could not be more opportune."

"What particularly concerns me," the prime minister continued, "is the technological impulse that continues to lie behind the development of strategic nuclear weaponry. It is, after all, in the laboratories that the nuclear arms race begins."

The prime minister then made his dramatic proposal. "The conclusion I have reached is that the best way of arresting the dynamic of the nuclear arms race may be by a strategy of suffocation, by depriving the arms race of the oxygen on which it feeds." An attack on the technological impulse that lies behind the development of strategic nuclear weaponry could bring a halt to the nuclear arms race in the laboratory, said Trudeau. Such a strategy of suffocation could be achieved by a combination of four elements:

- a comprehensive test ban to impede the further development of nuclear explosive devices;
- an agreement to stop the flight-testing of all new strategic delivery vehicles, to complement the ban on the testing of warheads;
- an agreement to prohibit all production of fissionable material for weapons purposes;
- and an agreement to limit and then progressively to reduce military spending on new strategic nuclear weapons systems.

Such a strategy of suffocation, the prime minister urged, "is not merely declaratory . . . it will have a real and progressive impact on the development of new strategic weapons systems."

In this speech Pierre Trudeau raised hope in both Canada and the international community that Canada *would* do something to slow down the arms race and impart a fresh momentum to disarmament, that Canada *could* do something, that the time *was* opportune and that Canada would play its full part. The prime minister's speech was a clear signal that Canada was prepared to facilitate, promote and initiate new international agreements, that Canada was prepared to build on its own previous unilateral nuclear arms decisions, that the Canadian government was prepared to undertake research, analysis and public education. The speech was a signal of hope. Five years later that hope lay dead.

The two Liberal governments since 1978 have not only failed to promote the strategy of suffocation either at home or abroad, they have actively pursued policies that directly undermine and even contradict that strategy. These include:

- increased military spending, on the F-18A fighter-interceptor for example;
- increased government financial support for nuclear arms components production;
- government efforts to secure new nuclear arms manufacturing contracts;
- continuing plans to export nuclear fuel and technology to Argentina, South Korea and any other potential buyer (see Chapter 6);
- Canadian participation in "operational" nuclear war plans and exercises;
- uncritical renewal of the NORAD agreement, potentially tying Canada into the militarization of space;
- Canada's support for and failure to raise concerns about the NATO decision to deploy cruise and Pershing missiles in Western Europe;
- Trudeau's refusal to comment on or criticize increased nuclear spending and the development/deployment of new nuclear weapons such as the neutron bomb;
- the enthusiastically-welcomed visits of nuclear-armed warships to Canadian ports;
- and — the most direct contradiction — secret negotiations to flight-test the U.S. air-launched cruise missile over Canadian territory.

Before looking in detail at some of these regressive policies and decisions, some comment should be made about the government's claims of positive action.

Canada's continuing scientific contribution to verification efforts through seismic expertise can be applauded. Canada's continuing participation at specialized arms control talks should be noted. The minister of national defence in a form letter used to respond to disarmament inquiries,[1] says that Canada is "actively engaged" in Mutual and Balanced Force Reduction Talks, the Conference on Security and Co-operation in Europe (CSCE) and "various United Nations activities in this field." The minister does not sound convincing and the facts are even less so. Canada has done little more than seat-warm at such councils, and has even occasionally, as in the case of CSCE-Madrid in 1980, played the hawk.[2]

After Trudeau's 1978 suffocation speech, the Liberal government did establish the position of disarmament advisor at the Department of External Affairs. This position was later upgraded to ambassador rank. While its creation is admirable in intent, this office bears no comparison in size or resources to even one of the specialized strategic or arms advisory divisions of the Department of National Defence (DND), or even its public relations division. The ambassador for disarmament's total budget was $150,000 a year until 1982 when it was increased to $288,000. DND spent $300,000 on its own magazines in 1980.

The political support for the ambassador for disarmament has been as glaringly lacking as the financial support. One of Canada's most distinguished figures in the field, Bill Epstein, says the government has shown "a progressive lack of interest" in the office, and moved nuclear disarmament "not just to the back burner but right off the stove."[3]

Epstein, former director of disarmament at the UN, is a member of the ambassador's Consultative Group on Disarmament and Arms Control Affairs, a group touted by the minister of national defence in his form letter. Yet lack of consultation with this group and failure to consider suggestions and proposals from distinguished non-government representatives who make up the group have put it in open revolt with the Department of External Affairs and the Liberal government.

The government's list of positive moves is short. Even Canada's participation in verification efforts would carry greater weight if the Liberals had not refused to commit Canada to active participation in the establishment of an international satellite monitoring agency advocated by France (see Chapter 14). Much longer is the list of the government's failures to take initiatives to promote suffocation, initiatives that were surely implied by the prime minister's speech at the UN.

The Missed Opportunities

The basis of the Trudeau speech was that technological change was fuelling the nuclear arms race and that technological developments had to be suffocated in the laboratory. The nuclear freeze concept, which enjoys widespread and growing public support in the United States, is based on an identical conclusion, namely that technological advances in nuclear arms must cease, at least until negotiations between the nuclear superpowers have caught up to arms developments. The prime minister himself, when asked in the House of Commons on 14 June 1982 if he supported a nuclear freeze, did admit that "the policy of suffocation... is a freeze."[4]

Yet the prime minister and his ministers have emphatically refused, when presented with the opportunity, to declare support for a balanced and verifiable nuclear weapons freeze. The same government that takes pride in the unilateral decisions to renounce the idea of nuclear weapons on Canadian soil denounces those who call for a nuclear freeze by *both* superpowers as "unilateralists."[5]

If the Canadian government really believed in the strategy of suffocation it would not only be supporting a global freeze, it would be taking the lead in promoting such a concept. But Canada has failed to promote even Trudeau's own strategy in places where such advocacy could have had some effect. Canada has participated in nuclear arms control talks in Geneva, permanent United Nations Disarmament Committee efforts, all important NATO discussions and plans, and integrated North American defence efforts with the United States. Yet the strategy of suffocation and its crucial elements were not seen or heard at conference tables, were not heard in NATO councils, were not heard in Washington when SALT II ran into difficulty. The prime minister and his government failed even to give directions to the civil service to elaborate further the strategy of suffocation. No in-house studies were done by government departments, no attempts were made to initiate independent Canadian research or analysis of defence and nuclear arms related questions.

The Rearmament of Europe

The abandonment of the strategy became particularly obvious when, on 12 December 1979, despite grave concerns by some of Canada's closest allies in Europe, the NATO ministers decided to proceed with the nuclear rearmament of Western Europe. Norway had long made it clear that it would not harbour nuclear weapons. The Netherlands, Belgium and Denmark expressed misgivings about the planned deployment of a new generation of missiles. British public opinion has been deeply divided, with the Labour Party now clearly committed to unilateral nuclear disarmament for Britain and opposed to the nuclear rearming of the Royal Navy's nuclear submarines. Yet Canada supported without question the deployment of land-based cruise and Pershing II missiles in the back gardens of Western Europe. Although a Conservative government was in power in Ottawa at the time of the NATO decision, a Liberal government had prepared the way for support and a Liberal government, re-elected in 1980, was soon carrying it out — with Conservative support.

The balance of forces in Europe, NATO strategic planning, and the nature of the Soviet threat can be debated at great length. One thing is certain: that although any Canadian government would have shared U.S. and West German concerns about the replacement of Soviet SS-4 and SS-5 missiles with more accurate SS-20s, a Canadian government which had a year and a half before called for the suffocation of the nuclear arms race should have at least raised some concerns about NATO's plans to install cruise and Pershing II missiles. The older Soviet missiles, in place since the 1960s, already posed a mortal threat to the cities of Western Europe. No new threat to population was posed by more accurate Soviet missiles. The upgrading of those missiles did not, therefore, necessarily require the deployment of even more sophisticated and, in the case of the cruise, undetectable and hence unverifiable, missiles by NATO. Canada could and should have questioned this plan.

Nuclear War Gaming and the Redefined NORAD

In light of the renunciation of a nuclear role for Canadian forces in Europe, Canada should long ago have ceased to participate in nuclear strategy war gaming. Yet Canadian forces and Canadian equipment continue to take part in nuclear strategy war planning and exercises: for instance, in July 1982, Canadian forces took part in U.S. Air Force Strategic Air Command nuclear attack exercises and planning. Canada also continues to play its sycophantic role at NORAD Headquarters in Colorado Springs. Indeed, in March 1981, Prime Minister Trudeau renewed the NORAD agreement with no questions asked and no hesitation. This agreement locks Canada into U.S. strategic and military assessments, planning, operations and nuclear command and now, with its name changed from "air" to "aerospace" defence, clearly threatens to lock this country into U.S. militarization of outer space. It was, after all, only the definition of NORAD as an "air" defence agreement that gave Trudeau and Canada a technical loophole out of participation in the ill-fated U.S. anti-ballistic missile (ABM) plans in 1969.[6]

Nuclear-Armed Warships in Canadian Ports

Despite Canada's claims of a near nuclear-weapons-free status the Liberal government has not only tolerated but welcomed warships with a nuclear capability on visits to Canadian ports, not caring whether or not they carried nuclear arms. In his response to criticism of the visit of U.S. nuclear warships to Vancouver during United Nations Disarmament Week in 1981, Defence Minister Gilles Lamontagne enthused: "Whether or not they have nuclear weapons, they are always welcome... we do not necessarily invite friends to come to our home; they drop in when they feel like it, and we are always glad to have them."[7]

With Seattle only a few hours sailing time away there was no need for such a visit by a 71,000-ton nuclear aircraft carrier and its escort vessels.

The visit was an intentional display of nuclear might, not only tolerated by the Liberal government but enthusiastically received. This compares poorly with, say, New Zealand's decision, while still remaining a member of ANZUS (its defence pact with Australia and the U.S.), to ban the visits of nuclear warships in 1973.

The New Round of Nuclear Weaponry

Another setback for hopes of a Canadian commitment to disarmament came with the prime minister's refusal to register any interest in, let alone opposition to, plans to deploy the neutron bomb in Europe. He admitted that he was not aware of the opposing vote in the Dutch Parliament and added: "... if European governments want to have the neutron bomb ... that is a matter for them to decide rather than for Canadians."[8]

The most serious setbacks, however, have come from Canada's active participation in the development, building and testing of new nuclear weapons and their delivery vehicles. The Canadian government, while preaching an end to such development, building and testing, has itself been participating in those activities and using public funds to do so. Litton Systems (Canada) Ltd. in Toronto has received $26 million in start-up grants and $20 million in loans to develop and build the guidance system for the cruise missile. And in the summer of 1982 it was learned that officials from the Department of Industry, Trade and Commerce were meeting with representatives from the Boeing aircraft company in Winnipeg in an effort to secure a Canadian contract for production of components for the MX missile system. These are but two examples (some others are found in Chapter 5).

The manufacture of nuclear weapons components is little different from the manufacture of the weapons themselves, although the former secretary of state for external affairs could not see this, as was revealed in his reply to the following question:

Miss Jewett: ... we say we will not create nuclear weapons but we will, however, create components for nuclear weapons systems and, furthermore, give grants to industries doing so.

Mr. MacGuigan: We may well do so, because it is not against any principle of ours. I cannot tell you since it is not my responsibility whether we are in fact doing that, but it may well be that we are. I can say that it would not offend any of our principles that we were doing so.[9]

Then, on 10 March 1982 a story datelined Washington by two Southam News journalists revealed that Canada was negotiating secretly with the

United States to test various U.S. weapons on Canadian soil, including unarmed cruise missiles. The secret negotiations had begun in October 1980 and were "probably the first occasion in peacetime that such an extensive agreement on defence weapons had been considered," according to a Canadian official in Washington.[10]

News of the cruise missile test plans was a devastating blow to what remained of any hope in either the spirit or substance of the strategy of suffocation. By testing the cruise missile and assisting in its development, Canada would take part in a major escalation of the nuclear arms race. According to a U.S. air force official, Canada would be the test site because Canada's north offered "more realistic flight profiles" with terrain and climate similar to conditions near Soviet silo sites.[11] Because the cruise missile, particularly with the new "stealth" technology, is undetectable by radar or satellite, verifiable nuclear arms reductions agreements will simply not be possible.

Canada's participation in such a deadly escalation of the nuclear arms race not only contradicts the strategy of suffocation and Canada's earlier practice of nuclear restraint, it also contradicts the overwhelming and consistent public sentiment in this country that Canada should seek nuclear disarmament.[12]

This development, more than any other policy or action, belies the rhetoric of the prime minister, the lip service to nuclear arms control by the secretary of state of external affairs, and the meagre efforts of the ambassador for disarmament. This news, more than anything else, caused six members of the House of Commons Standing Committee on External Affairs and National Defence to break away from the rest of the committee (who supported cruise testing) to write their own Minority Report in April 1982 (see Chapter 11).[13]

A Role for Canada

Canada can play an important and useful role in ending the nuclear arms spiral and its threat to humanity. Past practices and independent decisions and even unilateral moves by Canada on nuclear weapons policy pave the way for this country to take similar initiatives in these days of the escalating nuclear arms race. At home, Canada can build on its own decision to renounce nuclear weapons by establishing a nuclear-weapons-free zone on its territory and coastline and in its airspace. On the global scene, Canada can propose, suggest and demand nuclear arms control and disarmament actions at the councils of the UN, NATO and NORAD, and in Washington (and even Moscow) where Canada, more than many other nations, wields potentially important political and technological influence. Canada could draft treaties and agreements, proposed in the strategy of suffocation, on fissionable materials, a nuclear test ban and military spending. Canada could undertake major security, defence, arms control and disarmament research and analysis for its own policy needs and for greater international benefit. Canada could establish a model public education program on the arms race. The Canadian government could undertake industrial conversion studies and efforts to reduce its own financial support for nuclear weapons production and military support spending.

This activist approach to nuclear arms control and disarmament would not threaten Canadian security. It would, in fact, only enhance that security, for it is the escalation of the nuclear arms race and the possible deployment of unverifiable nuclear weapons that pose the real threat to security.

Moreover, this approach would not endanger Canada's friends and allies. The government claims, for example, that Canada will test cruise missiles as part of its NATO obligations. NATO has not asked Canada to test these weapons. The United States Air Force has asked Canada to test weapons that will be part of the American intercontinental strike force. NATO would not be harmed or Canada's allies threatened if Canada said "no" to the cruise missile tests. Nor would Canada's allies be threatened if this country actively promoted a comprehensive test ban. They, too, can only ultimately benefit from the control and reduction of the arsenal of nuclear holocaust.

The Liberal Failure

Why have the Liberals failed so miserably to put into practice the occasional utterances of Pierre Trudeau or give substance to their declared support for nuclear arms control and disarmament?

There is a three-part answer to this question. Trudeau's and Canada's failure to keep the strategy of suffocation alive can be explained partly by the prime minister's own vagaries and contradictions in defence and foreign policy matters. Another part of the explanation can be found in the like confusion in Liberal Party behaviour and policies on such issues. And a third part lies in Canada's continuing status as a satellite of the U.S. and a client of Washington's foreign and defence policies.

Pierre Trudeau has a muddy record on international relations in general and defence issues in particular. The Trudeau who cut Canadian forces in Europe in 1969 now advocates major increases in the Canadian defence budget to meet supposed NATO commitments. The Trudeau who, in

1963, denounced Liberal Party policy to accept U.S. nuclear warheads in Canada is now the leader of a government that plans to test far more lethal and destabilizing weapons on Canadian soil.

Having advocated reduced military spending, international agreements to limit weapons development, and a leadership role for Canada in pursuit of nuclear disarmament at UNSSOD I, Trudeau told a news conference in Saskatoon on 19 March 1982: "We must show the Soviet Union that we can meet them gun for gun."[14] Apart from being anachronistic, the phrase reveals Trudeau's unfailing inconsistency. The *Globe and Mail*, commenting on the "gun for gun" statement and the prime minister's subsequent lecture to the U.S. administration to pursue arms limitation negotiations, delivered at Notre Dame University less than two months later, said: "His nuclear doctrine, like his political one, is flexible response."[15]

The Liberal Party has a long record of confusing and contradictory responses to international affairs. Ministers contradict themselves in such well-known cases as Canada's policy towards El Salvador, or the imposition of martial law in Poland. And ministers, including the prime minister, reverse their own statements and opinions to suit the audience of the day.

Ministers have not been able to agree on the nature of the nuclear freeze or on whether or not Canada supports a nuclear freeze. Ministers have not been able to agree on the reasons for testing the cruise missile. Ministers and their parliamentary secretaries have not been able to agree on Canadian security needs, the nature of the Soviet threat, or the level of support for disarmament efforts.

And finally, there is Canada's continuing status as a foreign policy and defence satellite of the United States. This has more to do with Liberal unwillingness to embark upon independent Canadian information-gathering, research and analysis of defence-related questions, whether they involve nuclear or "conventional" responses, than any premeditated imperialist behaviour by the United States.

Professor Rod Byers of York University's Institute of Strategic Studies has complained about the government's and Canada's lack of analytical ability in defence-related matters. At the April meeting of the Disarmament and Arms Control Consultative Group, Professor Byers called for a "Canadian perspective on deterrence. What is the appropriate Canadian mix for arms control and preparedness?" he asked.[16] These calls from a well-placed questioner highlight the fact that there is no independent Canadian analysis of important international issues and that the government relies far too heavily on American information and assessment.

Not since the 1971 White Paper on Defence has there been any examination, let alone any serious analysis, of security needs or defence requirements, and there has never been any examination of the disarmament dimensions of security and defence by the government. Meanwhile Canada is spending and planning to spend billions of dollars on military aircraft and ships, and cabinet ministers continue to engage in strategic, military and foreign policy decision-making in an analytical vacuum.

As Ernie Regehr points out in Chapter 5, the government, in fact, has based its rationale for several profound decisions, including support for the NATO nuclear rearming of Europe and permission for U.S. cruise missile testing in Canada, on Canada's commitment to the concept of deterrence as practised by the United States and the NATO alliance. Yet the use of the concept of deterrence to justify a spiralling nuclear arms race is open to serious question. Plans for the neutron weapon, the MX, cruise and Pershing missiles, and vastly increased arms spending go far beyond the real needs of deterrence.

But it is not only in such strategic questions as deterrence that Canada has surrendered its independent judgment to the United States. Liberal governments have heavily tied Canadian jobs, industry and government spending to U.S. defence production industries. Canada now plans to spend $5 billion on U.S.-manufactured F-18A aircraft and plans to produce $1.3 billion worth of armoured vehicles for the U.S. Marine Corps, to give only two examples.

Canada has accepted, virtually without protest, a satellite relationship with the United States both economically and militarily. The cruise missile test plans provide the latest, most frightening evidence.

And so the nuclear arms race continues unabated, with Canada a willing partner. The strategy of suffocation becomes the strategy of nuclear weapons components production, cruise missile testing and sycophantic support for Ronald Reagan's nuclear war-fighting scenarios. If, in the words of the prime minister, "to kill hope in the possibility of disarmament is, in a very real sense, to risk killing life itself," then hope in Canada and life in general are in grave peril.

Notes

[1]   A copy of this letter was sent to all MPs and Senators on 29 June 1982.
[2]   See former External Affairs Minister Mark MacGuigan's opening statement at the Conference on Security and Co-operation in Europe, Madrid, 12 November 1980.
[3]   William Epstein, quoted with permission from private conversation, August 1982.
[4]   "I may be disappointing the honourable member, but I did not advocate a freeze in the sense which I believe it is understood by the honourable member. I did

advocate the policy of suffocation, which is a freeze...." Canada, House of Commons, *Debates*, 14 June 1982, p. 18416, External Affairs Minister Mark MacGuigan in response to a question from Pauline Jewett.

5   Canada, House of Commons, *Debates*, 18 March 1982, External Affairs Minister Mark MacGuigan in response to a question from Pauline Jewett; 29 April 1982, MacGuigan in speech on NDP motion.

6   John W. Warnock, *Partner to Behemoth* (Toronto: New Press, 1970), p. 207.

7   Canada, House of Commons, *Debates*, 2 November 1981, pp. 12387-88.

8   Ibid, 6 February 1981, p. 6969. This statement about the neutron bomb is reminiscent of the prime minister's approach to new weapons development a dozen years earlier. When asked for Canada's response to the U.S. Anti-Ballistic Missile plans, Pierre Trudeau told a CBC television audience on 23 April 1969 that the ABM "is no more our problem than it is the French, British, Chinese or the Hottentots — it is not a problem particular to Canada." Warnock, *Partner to Behemoth*, p. 218.

9   Canada, House of Commons, Standing Committee on External Affairs and National Defence, *Minutes of Proceedings and Evidence*, 1st Session, 32nd Parliament, 25 February 1982, p. 65: 51.

10   Don Sellar and John R. Walker, "U.S. Eyes Canada for Missile Tests," *Ottawa Citizen*, 10 March 1982, p. 1.

11   Ibid.

12   *Gallup Poll Results*, Gallup Polls, Toronto, 4 September 1982. Sixty-eight per cent of those polled said they would vote in favour of total nuclear disarmament in any United Nations referendum. On 17 January 1983, Gallup made public a poll showing 52 per cent of Canadians were opposed to the testing of the cruise missile in Canada, and only 37 per cent supported the government's plan.

13   The Minority Report on Security and Disarmament was prepared and signed by the three NDP members on the Standing Committee (Jewett, Ogle and Sargeant), two of the eleven Conservatives (McLean and Roche) and one of the sixteen Liberals (McRae).

14   Reported in the *Globe and Mail*, 20 March 1982, p. 1.

15   *Globe and Mail*, 20 May 1982, p. 6, commenting on Prime Minister Trudeau's speech at Notre Dame University, South Bend, Indiana, 16 May 1982.

16   Professor R. Byers. Quoted from the author's notes from a meeting of the Consultative Group on Disarmament and Arms Control Affairs, Ottawa, 1 April 1982.

11

Security and Disarmament: A Minority Report

Pauline Jewett, Walter McLean, Paul McRae, Bob Ogle, Douglas Roche and Terry Sargeant

During the first three months of 1982 the House of Commons Standing Committee on External Affairs and National Defence (SCEAND) held public hearings on issues related to security and disarmament. The committee invited Canadians from government, universities, business, labour and the peace movement to present their views to assist the committee in preparing recommendations to the government regarding Canadian participation in the then upcoming United Nations Special Session on Disarmament.

During the committee's deliberations a story was leaked to the press in Washington that Canada had agreed to permit testing of the cruise missile on Canadian territory. Government officials at the time confirmed that the cabinet had agreed "in principle" to the testing, but that the details of a final agreement had not been worked out (later, the government declared the agreement in principle to cover only the idea of testing weapons in Canadian territory in general and that the testing of the cruise remains an open question to be settled in a separate sub-agreement).

The cruise missile controversy exacerbated the fundamental differences within the committee, all of which finally led six members of the committee, representing all three political parties, to issue this report in April 1982.

E.R. & S.R.

We, the undersigned Members of the House of Commons Standing Committee on External Affairs and National Defence, members of all three political parties, dissent from the Standing Committee's Report on Security and Disarmament tabled in the House of Commons in April 1982.

Although there are aspects of the Committee's Report we agree with, we find grave deficiencies both in its analysis of the effects of the nuclear arms race and in its proposals for action by the Canadian government. The latter fall far short of the realistic, strong initiatives Canada could take to halt the headlong race to oblivion.

We, the minority, find a kinship with the growing number of Members of the United States Congress (now totalling 188) who have signed a House-Senate Joint Resolution sponsored by Senator Mark Hatfield, Republican, and Senator Edward Kennedy, Democrat, calling on the U.S. and USSR "to achieve a mutual and verifiable freeze on the testing, production and further deployment of nuclear warheads, missiles, and other delivery systems." This freeze, the Resolution states, should be "followed by reductions in nuclear warheads."

In the Canadian Committee on Security and Disarmament, the majority rejected the concept of a nuclear arms freeze, rejected the idea of there being even a pause that might allow negotiations to catch up with nuclear arms developments.

The debate over a freeze reveals the different ways reality is perceived today. Sincere people are divided on the meaning of security and the way to achieve a just peace.

Here is the way the signers of this statement view the world scene, followed by our proposals for Canadian action, proposals that were rejected by the Committee majority.

The World Scene

Military expenditures now exceed $550 billion per year, an amount that is more than the annual income of the two billion people in the world's poorest countries. At least 50 million people worldwide are directly or indirectly engaged in military activities, including those in armed forces, para-military forces, scientists and engineers in research and development for military purposes, and workers directly engaged in the production of weapons.

Over the past two decades, the world trade in conventional arms has quadrupled. At least 30 governments are in the business of peddling arms, a $35 billion enterprise concentrated in Third World countries, which are themselves dominated by military governments. Even the poorest countries are now the beneficiaries of the military research and development drive which has produced spectacular instruments of war: high explosives and incendiary agents that produce chemical fireballs, cannon-launched guided projectiles, cluster bombs that detonate into many steel pellets, fighter aircraft that travel at three times the speed of sound, and missiles that seek out a target hundreds of miles away. Killpower is depersonalized, destruction is indiscriminate, the distinction between combatant and civiiian meaningless.

All of this horror pales beside nuclear weapons, capable of destroying whole nations and possibly all life on earth. Five nations (U.S., USSR, U.K., France and China) possess incredible numbers of these weapons for delivery by land-based missiles, aircraft, or submarines. India, Israel and South Africa are now regarded as nuclear-weapons-capable. Pakistan is on the nuclear threshold; right behind are Iraq, Argentina, Brazil, Taiwan, South Korea and Libya. Atomic devices are spreading to volatile areas of the world where tensions are high and safeguards low. It is only a question of time before terrorists obtain a nuclear device. Although there are now 7,770 nuclear warheads in strategic missiles, 6,340 nuclear warheads in strategic submarines, 2,790 nuclear weapons in strategic bombers, and another 37,000 tactical nuclear weapons, the development and deployment of still more firepower never ceases.

Because the Soviet Union has a significant advantage in intermediate-range missiles currently aimed at Western Europe, NATO feels it necessary to deploy new single-warhead missiles in European sites. But the overall strategic advantage in long-range deliverable nuclear warheads rests with the U.S. and its allies. The U.S. has approximately 9,000 strategic nuclear warheads and the Soviet Union has 7,000. One Poseidon submarine, carrying 16 missiles, each with 10 warheads, and each warhead with over three times the explosive force of the Hiroshima bomb, is capable of destroying 160 targets, more targets than there are [major] cities in the Soviet Union.

There is, in short, rough parity today between the superpowers. Nonetheless, the dynamics of the nuclear arms race ensure that development of a new weapons system by one power will, in a relatively brief period, be followed by a comparable achievement by the other. The needs of deterrence having long since been met, technology is employed to perfect weapons to guarantee a successful pre-emptive strike. The next stage is laser weapons, positioned in outer space.

Anyone not yet convinced of the horrors awaiting mankind in a nuclear exchange should contemplate the warning issued by the 1981 Congress of International Physicians for the Prevention of Nuclear War. "Even a single one-megaton nuclear bomb explosion (80 times more powerful than that dropped on Hiroshima) over an urban area would cause death and injury to people on a scale unprecedented in the history of mankind and would present any remaining medical services with insoluble problems." People not immediately burned to death, blown apart or asphyxiated in shelters would find themselves in a nightmare world, populated by the dying, dead and insane. Food, crops and land would be contaminated, water undrinkable. The survivors would envy the dead. In an all-out attack, who would survive, as radiation sweeps across the oceans and into the atmosphere, depleting the ozone layer, and releasing lethal ultraviolet rays? The collapse of the ecosystem would leave a global wasteland.

Four years ago, when arms expenditures were about half of current figures, the first UN Special Session on Disarmament concluded with these words: "Mankind is confronted with a choice: we must halt the arms race and proceed to disarmament or face annihilation." When the second Special Session on Disarmament opens on June 7, little will have been accomplished in the interval. No agreement on a complete test ban of nuclear weapons. No ratification of the strategic arms limitation talks (SALT II). No establishment of new nuclear-weapon free zones. No convention on banning chemical weapons. No reduction of armed forces and conventional weapons. No reduction of military budgets. No cut in the international arms trade.

Instead, governments, ignoring their own words, pursue the arms race. Part of the reason for this is that governments continue to view security in narrow terms. As armaments accumulate competitively, countries become more intensely concerned about military security. Security becomes more elusive. The difficulty of resolving the underlying political issues increases. The growing insecurity generates a demand for more armaments. Thus, the arms race spirals upward ceaselessly.

Proposals for Canadian Action

Security today demands more than the acquisition of arms. One of the paradoxes of the modern world is that, although defence is necessary, the arms race itself is a threat to security. It is no longer enough to keep the peace; peace must be vigorously waged.

In a world so divided and dangerous, the primary object of Canadian foreign policy must be the building of conditions for peace.

Thus, at the UN Special Session, Canada should again press for the adoption of a "Strategy of Suffocation" to stop the arms race, including these four elements:

• a comprehensive test ban to impede the further development of nuclear explosive devices;
• an agreement to stop the flight-testing of all new strategic delivery vehicles;
• an agreement to prohibit all production of fissionable material for weapon purposes;
• an agreement to limit and then progressively reduce military spending on new strategic nuclear weapons systems.

These ideas are still valid; they must be pushed harder to make a political impact. Although Canada now has an Ambassador for Disarmament, the issue is still given a very low priority and a budget of only $150,000. Yet Canada's defence budget of $5.9 billion will be increased by 19 per cent this year.

To give weight to this strategy, the undersigned recommend these steps:

1. Nuclear Freeze

Canada should put its full strength into the campaign now gathering strength in many parts of the world: a global freeze on the testing, production and deployment of nuclear weapons and their delivery vehicles.

Such a freeze would forestall the further development of first strike or counter-force capability by one or both of the superpowers. A freeze is relatively easy to verify and could provide a crucial first step to substantial reductions of nuclear stockpiles. We do not accept the argument that a freeze would be impractical because there is an imbalance in tactical nuclear forces in Europe. What is the real effect of imbalance when both sides already possess the weaponry to destroy each other several times over? It is not unilateral disarmament that is being asked for. Rather, a practical policy is to promote mutual, balanced and verifiable disarmament by first of all freezing further growth. The Special Session should establish an international inspection organization to monitor disarmament and to establish immediately a workable and effective control system to detect violations of agreements.

2. No Cruise Testing

The Canadian government should deny the United States permission to test the new Cruise Missile system in Canada.

The advocates of this step hold that we have an obligation to our NATO partners to join in the strengthening of the Western defence system. We maintain, however, that Canada also has an obligation to humanity not to take an additional step — beyond where we are today — in improving the technological capacity for nuclear war. By allowing tests of new nuclear weapons delivery vehicles, such as the Cruise Missile, which is patently attack-oriented, Canada risks its credibility as a voice for peace.

The Cruise Missile will only stimulate the Soviets to develop one of their own. The world will then become an even more dangerous place than it is today. Although the missile to be tested in Canada will be unarmed, the symbolic value of the testing is enormous. By denying the tests, we are protesting against the arms race. By allowing the tests, we aid the arms race. Who will take Canada's words at the UN seriously if our acts are the opposite?

3. Pledge Against First Use

Canada should press all nations to pledge never to be the first to use nuclear weapons.

Such a stated policy would make it clear to all nations that their territories and peoples are safe from nuclear attack unless they use their own nuclear weapons first. This is one initiative that could be taken with a great increase in global security.

4. Canadian Disarmament Efforts

Canada should pledge that it will devote one-tenth of 1 per cent ($7 million) of its defence budget to disarmament efforts.

This was proposed by the Secretary-General of the United Nations at the first Special Session as a valuable step for nations to take in correcting the present huge imbalance in priorities. We recommend that Canada use such money to strengthen disarmament education, information and research activities. We particularly recommend the establishment by the Department of External Affairs of six Chairs on Disarmament at Canadian universities.

Among other disarmament efforts, Canada should consider such instruments as a UN-sponsored world referendum on multilateral, balanced disarmament. Such a referendum would be conducted by national governments with a ballot agreed upon in the United Nations General Assembly and with UN observers present for all national votes. We specifically note that the global referendum must also be conducted in the Soviet Union and Warsaw Pact countries. Although not intended to be binding, a strong mandate for disarmament can be expected to emerge, which would be a powerful force for progress by the negotiating parties.

Canadian public opinion is moving in this direction. Already there are now 27 Canadian municipalities, representing two-and-a-half million Canadians, that will hold local referenda on general disarmament. It is clear that people are increasingly demanding a voice on disarmament as an issue that involves their survival.

We believe the question before Canada — and all mankind — is clear. What is more important: adding to the danger of the arms race or building future security by comprehensive disarmament measures? We have made our choice. We condemn the continued arms race.

Pauline Jewett, MP
New Westminster-Coquitlam

Bob Ogle, MP
Saskatoon East

Walter McLean, MP
Waterloo

Doug Roche, MP
Edmonton South

Paul McRae, MP
Thunder Bay-Atikokan

Terry Sargeant, MP
Selkirk-Interlake

PART IV

Canadian Proposals for Peace

12

The Canadian Peace Movement
Ernie Regehr and Simon Rosenblum

Only the deaf cannot hear the clamour raising all over the world against the arms race. . . . Our publics today are reminding political leaders that what is at stake is the crucial matter of the life and death of mankind.

Pierre Trudeau
1982 UN Special Session on Disarmament

Only twice since World War II have there been sustained periods of broadly-based public concern about nuclear weapons in Canada. One such period, reflected in Prime Minister Trudeau's statement to the United Nations in June 1982, is now, and the other occurred just over two decades ago. At the end of the 1950s and in the early 1960s, Canadian opposition to the acquisition of nuclear weapons for Canadian forces (see Chapter 5) coincided with international protests against atmospheric testing of nuclear weapons. In 1959 two groups emerged to focus growing public concern about these two issues. The Combined Universities Campaign for Nuclear Disarmament (CUCND) circulated a petition opposing the placement of tactical, air-to-air nuclear missiles at Canadian bases, and the Canadian Committee for the Control of Radiation Hazards (CCRH) was formed to call for the immediate cessation of nuclear testing and for efforts to examine and control the dangers of radiation.

The two issues soon merged: the CCRH circulated a petitition opposing the acquisition of nuclear weapons for Canadian forces, and in 1960 James M. Minifie explored alternative Canadian security policies in his popular and influential book, *Peacemaker or Powdermonkey*. By 1962 the CCRH had become the Canadian Campaign for Nuclear Disarmament (CCND), organizing a series of marches and demonstrations to focus public atten-

---

This brief account relies substantially on a paper by Gary Moffat, "A History of the Peace Movement in Canada," for historical detail.

tion on the two prominent issues of the day — nuclear weapons testing and nuclear weapons for Canadian forces.

During the same period, one of the most persistent and effective of Canadian peace organizations was formed — the Voice of Women (VOW). Established in July 1960, following a Toronto newspaper columnist's remark that the women of the world acting together could alleviate the Soviet-American nuclear confrontation, the VOW approved a charter committing it to the promotion of international understanding, to oppose war and to work for the removal of its causes, and to provide the means for women to exercise more fully their public responsibilities.

Among the members of the early VOW was Marion Pearson, wife of Lester B. Pearson. When her husband reversed his opposition to nuclear weapons to advocate Canadian acquisition of U.S. warheads (see Chapter 9), Marion Pearson left the VOW along with a number of other prominent women. The organization continued to flourish, however, and the Mothers' Day Vigil became an annual event within a wide range of activities that included the opposition to both nuclear weapons in Canada and Soviet and American testing of nuclear arms.

Canadian religious communities, including members of the historic peace churches (e.g., Quakers and Mennonites) as well as the mainline churches, entered into the debates as well. The Society of Friends (Quakers) established a peace centre on Grindstone Island in Lake Rideau. The centre, now under the management of the Grindstone Island Cooperative, has operated without interruption since the early 1960s as a peace research, education and action centre.

Also active during this period was the Canadian Peace Congress (CPC). Formed in 1947, the CPC has had close links to the Communist Party in Canada (earlier the Labour Progressive Party in Canada) and currently remains affiliated to the World Peace Council, which in turn is identified with a prevailing sympathy with the policies of the Soviet Union.

Following the 1963 Liberal election victory and the subsequent confirmation of Lester Pearson's promise to acquire tactical nuclear weapons for Canadian forces, the peace movement weakened quickly. The CCND continued to call for a wider test-ban agreement, nuclear-weapons-free zones and opposition to military alliances, but by 1965 most of its chapters were inactive. The war in Vietnam reactivated student concern through the Student Union for Peace Action (a descendant of CUCND), while the VOW expanded its areas of concern to include the Vietnam War and the relationship between nuclear power and nuclear weapons.

While the issues of peace and disarmament were not prominent on the national political agenda during the 1960s, within the New Democratic

Party these issues were debated from time to time. The matter of Canadian membership in NATO, which has persisted as a controversial issue within the NDP, was debated and in 1969 the party passed a substantial resolution on international affairs and national defence, calling on more active Canadian involvement in the search for international peace and security and a more independent position from that of the United States.

During the hiatus of the 1970s, when few peace organizations remained active, the Voice of Women and the Canadian Peace Congress were the main exceptions. During the latter part of the decade, Canadian churches began to address issues of peace and war more directly through the formation of Project Ploughshares and increased internal education. And at the end of the decade, when detente was clearly in decline and the United States and the Soviet Union were, it was once again clear, accelerating their rearmament programs, many of the people who had been active in the early 1960s re-emerged to provide once again the leadership for a revived Canadian peace movement.

Now, in the early 1980s, Canadians have once again taken to the streets, union halls, church basements and community centres in the attempt to influence Canadian policy on nuclear weapons. The heart of that policy, of course, is Canadian support for nuclear "modernization" in Europe (namely the deployment of cruise and Pershing II missiles there), and plans for U.S. testing of the air-launched cruise missiles in Canada.

Groups like the Voice of Women and the Canadian Peace Congress remain active, but a number of new organizations, representing a broad cross-section of Canadians, have entered the movement and demonstrate the broad range of issues and tactics which the contemporary peace movement has adopted. In addition to the churches, perhaps most striking has been the entry of a wide range of professional groups into the Canadian peace movement. Physicians for Social Responsibility were first off the mark, focusing particularly on the medical effects of nuclear war, but soon followed by groups of lawyers, artists, veterans, scientists, educators and businessmen "for peace." In each case the professional skills of the groups are drawn upon to focus upon particular aspects of the problem of the nuclear arms race.

Two relatively new groups that have taken a leading role have been Operation Dismantle and Project Ploughshares. The main program of the former, a national campaign to promote an international referendum on disarmament, is described in Chapter 13. Project Ploughshares, sponsored by the Canadian Council of Churches, includes in its program a wide range of non-nuclear issues as well as being active in the promotion of Canada as a nuclear-weapons-free zone. The Project now has offices in Waterloo,

Ontario, Ottawa and Vancouver, and local affiliates in more than twenty locations. (A list of national peace groups is included at the end of the book.) While its growth has been impressive, the Canadian peace movement nevertheless suffers from a lack of central coordination and some differences on strategies, now as in the 1960s. (However, it can be argued that there is strength in the variety of approaches.)

While External Affairs Minister Allan MacEachen insisted in 1982 that demonstrations and other expressions of public concern would not influence Canadian policy on cruise and Pershing missiles, public opinion polls now show that 52 per cent of Canadians oppose cruise missile testing in Canada and a growing number of members of Parliament now also call for changes in Canadian policy. The "Minority Report" (see Chapter 11) was issued as a dissenting report by three members of the NDP, two Conservatives and one Liberal after the majority of members of the House of Commons Standing Committee on External Affairs and National Defence refused to oppose cruise testing in their report on security and disarmament. The entire caucus of the NDP supports the "Minority Report" and there are indications in 1983 that back-bench support for the minority position is also growing within the other two parties.

The NDP's policies are the most closely aligned with the policies advocated by the mainstream of the peace movement. These include withdrawal from military alliances, support for a verifiable bilateral nuclear weapons freeze, the pledge of no-first-use of nuclear weapons, the establishment of Canada as a nuclear-weapons-free zone, and public funding for peace research and education.

Most peace organizations have also declared support for the strategy of suffocation elaborated by Prime Minister Trudeau at the United Nations in 1978. This strategy calls for a comprehensive test ban on nuclear devices, a ban on the flight-testing of new strategic delivery vehicles, a prohibition on the production of fissionable materials for weapons purposes, and limitations and progressive reductions in military spending on new strategic nuclear weapons systems. While the proposals are widely supported, the main quarrel with the government is its failure actively to pursue these policies and, particularly, its own direct violation of the proposed ban on flight-testing.

If there is a core concern that motivates the Canadian peace movement it must surely be that the extraordinary destructive power of modern weapons has rendered war an inefficient and unacceptable means of settling human disputes and of restraining the unjust. If there once was a time when war was an effective instrument of national diplomacy, that time has now passed. Even if wars are fought regionally and on a limited scale, the threat of escalation grows as the major powers increasingly view their interests to be at stake in such wars. Even if those wars are confined to a particular locale, the destructive capacity of even conventional weapons has made war obsolete.

A key plank in the platform of the Canadian peace movement is the demand that the government of Canada devote substantially more funds to the search for alternatives to war as the final arbiter of human conflict. Successive governments, in Canada and around the world, have devoted high levels of public funds to the perfection of violence and war as instruments or extensions of diplomacy. Similar funds must now be made available for the pursuit of alternatives. Former Prime Minister Lester Pearson once said that "we prepare for war like precocious giants and we prepare for peace like retarded pygmies."

For that reason the peace movement has pressed the government to support what has come to be known as the Waldheim proposal. This proposal, tabled at the first UN Special Session on Disarmament by former UN Secretary-General Kurt Waldheim, called on governments to devote one-tenth of one per cent of their defence budgets to peace research and education. In Canada this would currently mean about $7 million, compared with a budget of less than $500,000 available to the ambassador for disarmament for these purposes.

Another point of clear consensus within the Canadian peace movement is the understanding that if Canada is to be allowed to fully explore alternatives to the present war system, it is going to have to undergo some international realignment. Independent Canadian initiatives require a more independent Canadian foreign policy — and on this continent that means greater independence from the policies and influence of the United States.

The search for a measure of independence is not the unique idea of the peace movement. In fact, it has been a prominent feature of official Canadian policy at particular intervals since World War II. Postwar Canadian foreign policy can be characterized in two policy streams — the first is the search for special status within the American empire (on the assumption that there are no realistic alternatives for Canada so it might as well try to get the best possible deal within the American empire), the second is the search for the "third way" (on the assumption that the cultivation of non-U.S. economic and political allies would lessen Canadian vulnerability to the ups and downs or, in Trudeau's image of the Canadian mouse in bed with the U.S. elephant, the twists and turns of our American neighbour).

The peace movement generally assumes that further detachment from

U.S. policy is essential for Canada if it wishes to contribute to international alternatives to the war system. Hence Canadian peace movement activity tends to focus on those points at which Canadian foreign and defence policies are most directly integrated into the policies of the United States.

At its best, the peace movement is, in the words of British disarmament leader E.P. Thompson, "a Third Negotiator," and must "monitor [the] propaganda falsehoods, and insert [its] own independent proposals." Within the framework of mutual and verifiable arms reduction, the Canadian peace movement calls for unilateral initiatives that will act as a catalyst. A leader of the Netherlands Interchurch Peace Council has made a very succinct case for such unilateral initiatives:

> This is not to be seen as an element of an approach towards complete unilateral disarmament, but as a first step, which is unilateral and independent, but fit to evoke a bilateral and multilateral process towards disarmament. A step, which should be drastic enough to be a clear expression of an alternative approach, but at the same time small enough to enable allies and others to respond to it on the military and political level.

And as the scientist Carl Sagan asks: "We have heard the rationales offered by the nuclear superpowers. But who speaks for the human species? Who speaks for earth?" In their sometimes faltering and divided ways, the peace movements of Canada and abroad have sought to press first the interests of the human species.

13

Towards a Global Referendum on Disarmament

T. James Stark and Peter Brown

In June and July 1982, the most publicized disarmament conference in history ended in total failure. The second United Nations Special Session on Disarmament, on which the hopes of millions of peace activists around the world had been pinned, made no progress with its mandate to produce a comprehensive program to end and reverse the arms race. In spite of the participation of thirteen heads of state and forty-four foreign ministers, national governments were unable or unwilling to rise to the task. Perhaps the best analysis of this failure came from UN General Assembly President Ismat Kittani, who described the final report of the session as "proof of the gap between what the people of the world want and need and what their governments are willing to do."

Failure of disarmament negotiations is, of course, nothing new. National governments have been talking to each other about preventing nuclear war and controlling, reducing or eliminating nuclear weapons almost since the first atomic bomb was used at Hiroshima. Except for a few very limited agreements which set controls on some peripheral aspects of the arms race, these attempts at negotiation have failed to remove or reduce the threat of global annihilation by nuclear war. Meanwhile the arms race itself has accelerated to the point where even if the two superpowers each dismantled ten nuclear warheads per year, it would take approximately 2,500 years to reach the point where each country had only a "credible deterrent," i.e., the ability totally to destroy the other superpower only once.

Yet national governments fully understand the dangers of relying on deterrence to prevent nuclear war. In 1978, all nations unanimously agreed to the Final Document of the first UN Special Session on Disarmament, which included the following blunt statement: "Mankind is confronted with a choice: we must halt the arms race and proceed to disarmament or face annihilation."

All national governments not only realize the need for disarmament, they have also already agreed in principle on precisely what must be done to achieve disarmament in a gradual, balanced and verifiable way. The agreement, called "General Disarmament," was negotiated by the super-powers in 1959 and adopted unanimously by the United Nations General Assembly in 1961 as the long-term goal of all disarmament negotiations. Among the elements of the agreement's program are: complete elimination of all nuclear weapons in gradual, balanced steps; reductions (but not elimination) of conventional arms forces; establishment of a permanent UN peacekeeping force with personnel contributed by each country; disso-lution of military alliances on a multilateral basis; reductions in military spending; and the establishment of a UN-supervised international disarma-ment organization to monitor and verify the disarmament process.

There would be little point in discussing the threat of nuclear war and the failure of national governments to deal with this threat unless there were reasons to hope that awareness of the problem could produce a possible solution. At the root of the problem of the arms race is the central contradiction that although governments know precisely what has to be done and how to do it, they are unwilling to act. After thirty-eight years of failure by national governments to reverse or to halt or even slow down the nuclear arms race, it would be naive to believe that governments, acting on their own, will ever succeed in negotiating disarmament. The political will to do so is simply not there.

Yet any strategy for disarmament must involve national governments, since they alone have the ability to carry out a disarmament process. Given their lack of motivation, however, another source of political will needs to be found, one which would put strong pressure on all governments — particularly the two superpowers — to negotiate and carry out disarma-ment agreements.

Of course the political will to end the arms race does exist: it abides in the hearts and minds of ordinary people of all nations. For evidence of the mobilization beginning to emerge against the arms race, one need look no further than the massive public demonstrations that have been held first in Western Europe and later in Canada and the U.S.

Although demonstrations are useful and necessary, there are limitations on their effectiveness in bringing about disarmament. The first is that, by definition, demonstrations involve only a small and vocal minority of the population. Second, and more important (as the opponents of disarma-ment never fail to point out), public demonstrations can be freely con-ducted only in the minority of nations which allow public dissent. On the same day as a massive rally in New York (12 June 1982), the media reported the arrest of most of the members of the first and only independent peace movement in the Soviet Union.

Beginning in 1977, Operation Dismantle sought a technique to harness, focus and unleash that small but collectively significant amount of power held by individual people. What was needed was a way to look beyond demonstrations for a strategy which would mobilize public opinion for disarmament in a more organized, calm and thorough manner, to build pressure to the point where governments could no longer ignore it. We arrived at the concept of a world vote on disarmament.

Towards a Global Referendum

The first step in launching a global referendum on disarmament would be to have it proposed by one nation (Canada, one hopes) in the United Nations General Assembly. Second would be the formulation of a ballot wording agreeable to all nations. The third step would be for governments voluntarily to conduct national referenda, country by country, probably alongside national elections in order to cut costs. It might be necessary or advisable for UN observers to monitor all the national referenda. The cost of the entire world vote is estimated at $400 to $800 million, or 10¢ to 20¢ per voter. Even the higher figure is just half the cost of a single Trident submarine.

The vote in any country, including the pre-vote activities and debate, would educate and mobilize public opinion in that country to an unprecedented degree. We estimate that the disarmament referendum would produce a "yes" vote of 60 to 95 per cent in every country. Even critics of the project concede that these estimates are realistic.

The referendum is not intended to replace government-to-government negotiations on disarmament, but to encourage the negotiating process and to apply political pressure on the participating parties to produce concrete results. While the entire global vote might take five to ten years to complete, the desire of humanity for disarmament would become clear in the first couple of years, after the first ten or twenty referenda. Early in the process, disarmament would be established as the most important issue of the time, and a sense of momentum and inevitability would gradually accrue to the cause of disarmament.

Yet on disarmament and any other issue, many governments consistently ignore the opinions of their own citizens. Why should we believe that governments would pay any attention to a global voicing of opinion? Indeed, a world referendum has never been done before, making it difficult to predict how governments will react to a mandate from the entire human race. Former U.S. President Dwight D. Eisenhower once said that "some day, the demand [for disarmament] from hundreds of millions will, I hope, become so universal and insistent that no man, no government, can withstand it." It is arguable that the governments of nations will find that it is simply not possible to ignore a strong global mandate from people of literally every background. In other words, even though the worldwide referendum on disarmament will have to be billed as "advisory" or "non-binding," the billions of votes cast for disarmament could turn out to be binding in their political effect.

Aside from the merits of the world vote proposal as a practical strategy, there is also a compelling philosophical appropriateness for such an approach in its democratic nature. In his 1980 Speech from the Throne, Prime Minister Trudeau described the issue of disarmament as "no less than human survival on this planet." The people of earth, not just governments, have a right to be consulted on such a crucial issue. We assert the existence of a human right of all people to participate in the choice for a disarmed world. In our view, the world referendum on disarmament is the ideal, democratic vehicle by which this right can be exercised.

A World Vote is Achievable

Our six years of work on this strategy have convinced us that it is quite practical and achievable. We feel we have good reason to believe that, sooner or later, there will be such a world vote on balanced disarmament.

In 1979, three Operation Dismantle staff members spent three months at the United Nations meeting with ambassadors and representatives of fifty UN member nations. It was this experience which convinced us of the feasibility of a world referendum on disarmament. We discovered that:

- A proposal for the world vote would pass overwhelmingly in the UN General Assembly, partly because it would be politically very difficult for national governments to oppose a democratic approach (the referendum) to a goal (disarmament) which all nations have already agreed upon (many times over) in principle.
- The basis for a ballot wording acceptable to all nations exists in the already agreed-upon goal of general disarmament.
- At least twenty-five to forty nations would voluntarily conduct the disarmament referendum without delay and without the need for domestic political pressure — a sufficient number to create a strong international momentum which would draw more reluctant nations into the process.

- It is in the interests of Soviet bloc nations to support the world referendum proposal in the General Assembly and to allow the referendum to be conducted among their own populations. While they might not be terribly keen to participate, they realize the political consequences of refusing in light of their attempts to cultivate a pro-disarmament image.

- Third World governments would support the proposal primarily because of their desire to link disarmament and development: the funds needed ($20-$40 billion annually) for economic development in the poorer countries simply will not be available until the world stops spending $600 billion per year on the arms race (conventional and nuclear) and there is a basic shift in superpower priorities.

- There are no insurmountable financial, constitutional or administrative problems which would necessarily prevent any government from holding a disarmament referendum (any government can pass "enabling legislation" to give itself the power to hold a referendum).

Nor is our initiative without international supporters. Robert Muller, the distinguished head of the UN Economic and Social Council, described our proposal as "inevitable, historic, and extremely constructive." Alessandro Corradini, former Acting Director of the UN Centre for Disarmament, said that "we need, and need badly, that missing ingredient: the weight of public opinion" for disarmament. He went on to describe the world vote proposal as "a very bright idea."

The Results in Canada

In Canada, we have been fortunate enough to have some experience, on a limited scale, of what the world vote on disarmament will be like. At Operation Dismantle's request, and thanks to the determined efforts of Ottawa mayor Marion Dewar and hundreds of sympathetic organizations and individuals across the country, 118 municipalities in six provinces held referenda on balanced disarmament along with their municipal elections in the fall of 1982. The results are much as we would expect from the eventual world referendum: of almost one million votes cast in the referenda across Canada, results ranged from 65 to 95 per cent saying "yes" for disarmament, with an overall average of 76.5 per cent.

Even before the referenda were conducted, the fact that so many citizens would be voting on disarmament began to have some healthy political effects. In June 1982, the Federation of Canadian Municipalities called on the federal government to propose the world referendum on disarmament at the United Nations. In many of the municipalities holding local referenda, "yes" campaigns sprang up to organize pre-vote activities such as public meetings, rallies and door-to-door canvassing. Provincial politicians became involved as well: in Ontario, a majority of MPPs from all three parties signed a petition calling for a world vote; in Quebec, the National Assembly endorsed the world referendum unanimously. The government of the Northwest Territories has also endorsed the world referendum proposal. *Maclean's* magazine reported that "the real impact of the referendum has been to force Trudeau, once again, to take up arms control as a matter for his personal diplomacy" (28 June 1982).

Operation Dismantle has spent over six years and half a million dollars exploring the world referendum idea and building support for it. The results have been encouraging. In addition to the above-mentioned endorsements, 140 MPs from all three parties have expressed their support for a UN proposal by Canada for the world referendum. The NDP has made the world vote concept part of its official foreign policy. Over sixty-five organizations have endorsed the proposal, including the Canadian Council of Churches and the Canadian Labour Congress. The national executive committee of the robust American Nuclear Weapons Freeze Campaign has now endorsed the world referendum concept. A Gallup poll conducted in Toronto in April 1982 indicated that 84 per cent of those polled would favour a world vote on disarmament and that 77 per cent would vote "yes" if given the opportunity.

As a result of the municipal votes alone, we have a strong mandate from Canadians for action by the Canadian government. It is our fervent hope that the prime minister will act on this mandate by proposing the global referendum on disarmament at the United Nations.

14

An International Satellite Monitoring Agency

John C. Polanyi

This chapter describes a proposal for a type of peacekeeping force in space, the International Satellite Monitoring Agency (ISMA). The proposal has been the subject of an extensive and favourable study by an international group of government experts at the United Nations. The proposal is one that, in the author's view, should commend itself to Canada since politically and technologically this country is well qualified to contribute. It is regrettable that the Canadian government was not a party to the UN study of this proposal. However, there is still time for Canada to make an important contribution to the realization of ISMA. It would be a peculiar failure of imagination on our part, were we not to do so. Prime Minister Trudeau, in his address to the UN Special Session on Disarmament on 18 June 1982, committed Canada to renewed efforts to make outer space the preserve of peace, and also to increased research into the technology of arms control verification. The ISMA could assist in the achievement of both these goals.

"Open Skies" Surveillance

Ignorance of what happens in potentially hostile regions of the world fosters suspicion, and preparations are soon made for the "worst case." This over-reaction further heightens suspicion, and hence military preparations, on the opposing side. Recognizing that fear engendered by ignorance fuels the arms race, U.S. President Eisenhower suggested in 1955 the adoption of worldwide "Open Skies" surveillance by aircraft.

Though "Open Skies" failed to materialize, open access to *outer space* is in the process of achieving Eisenhower's goal. For two decades the U.S. and USSR have been surveying each other's territory, day and night, from an increasingly large and sophisticated array of satellites. Their right to use these "national technical means" for mutual inspection is enshrined in well-established treaties extending back a decade (for instance, SALT I). This is one of the (few and precious) changes favourable to the prospects of peace that have taken place in the past twenty years.

The Proposal for ISMA

The ISMA proposal was discussed in private forums (such as the Pugwash Conferences) as early as 1977, but was first formalized by France in a speech by President Valéry Giscard d'Estaing at the UN Special Session on Disarmament in May 1978. The UN thereafter adopted a resolution (113 votes to 0, with the U.S. and USSR abstaining) to have the proposal studied in time for the 1982 UN session. The study was conducted, and was released in August 1982 (UN Report A/AC 206/14). This 120-page report is, as intended, an "in-depth study." It deals with the technical, legal and financial implications of the establishment of an ISMA. The thirteen government experts who made the study were unanimous in their approval of the ISMA concept, and in their verdict that it was "both possible and feasible."

The proposal calls for a step-by-step approach on the part of an unspecified consortium of nations linked to the UN to supplement the present bilateral U.S.-USSR space surveillance with a multilateral surveillance system. The objectives would be to provide credible *verification* of arms control agreements (which could be simply agreements to demilitarize a buffer zone), and also to provide reassurance in some tense region of the world that forces are not being readied for attack.

The rationale for spreading the responsibility for arms control verification and reassurance activities is that a broader group of nations can operate in areas and in questions where the superpowers clearly have a stake, but in which other nations are less directly implicated. Recognition of the validity of this concept has led to the procedures for selecting participants in UN peacekeeping forces; the superpowers are never participants and, so far as is possible, the active participants are selected from disinterested parties. The consortium that operates or advises ISMA should be broad enough that it can place the task of photo interpretation and the responsibility for arriving at a verdict in the hands of a balanced or (better still) impartial group, given the nature of the specific monitoring task. The IAEA (the International Atomic Energy Authority in Vienna) has largely succeeded in this, so a precedent exists.

It should be noted that ISMA is not envisaged as having a free licence to collect information and publicize it (for example information that could be of advantage to political and economic competitors of the nations being monitored); the agency would in general respond to specific requests for information and would limit itself to these tasks. The agency's activities are, therefore, predicated upon the idea that there are troubled areas in the world where the antagonists wish to avoid settling their differences by war, or can be induced by their allies to experiment with this sane and civilized option. Given the increasing awareness of the horrors of modern warfare, and the global dangers which stem from regional conflicts, this appears to be a reasonable supposition.

If ISMA is to be operating before the end of this decade it must rent time on the cameras that the superpowers already have in space. These cameras can be shared. Under the LANDSAT program of the U.S. they are, in fact, already shared for low-resolution surveillance. The resolution of 1-3 metres (i.e., ability to see objects of this size) required for ISMA represents, today, medium resolution. It will require a groundswell of opinion (fore-shadowed in the UN vote cited above) and cogent arguments to persuade one or both of the superpowers that there is a real gain for the prospects of world peace in permitting access by a suitable consortium to the medium-resolution cameras at times when these are stationed above selected regions of the globe. ISMA would then receive the raw data (directly from the electronic "camera" by radio telemetry) and process it into pictures which its own experts could analyse. In the unlikely event that the superpowers are united in withholding all cooperation, ISMA could make use of the medium-resolution cameras of other nations (France for example), as these facilities become available in the coming few years. The cost to ISMA would run into several hundred million dollars per annum for this type of activity.

ISMA would aim to have its own cameras in the sky within a decade. The cost for "hardware" spread over the consortium of nations would, in this case, amount to a total of about a billion dollars distributed over a number of years. No nation would need to spend more than 1 per cent of its annual defence budget in order to bring this scheme to fruition.

In absolute if not relative terms, these costs seem daunting, but we should recall that where the aim is to reduce pollution or conserve re-sources the expenditure of sums of this order of magnitude over similar periods of time is a commonplace. Twentieth-century warfare — if we wish to consider it in these terms — represents the most hazardous source of pollution, and most barbaric squandering of resources. If it escalates into a nuclear war it represents a crime against future generations.

Canada and ISMA

Canada has been involved in every UN peacekeeping force since the first. Canada has an annual space-technology commitment of approximately $100 million. Canada voted in favour of the UN study of ISMA, and has frequently spoken at the UN about the crucial role of verification in negotiating arms control and thereby "suffocating the arms race." Despite this, Canada was not represented on the thirteen-nation UN group of governmental experts making a detailed study of this proposal, nor so far as the public is aware, are Canadian experts studying this proposal independently of the UN Group. It is time that we became actively involved in the ISMA debate. The Canadian public has shown pride and interest in Canada's involvement in peacekeeping, and also in space technology. We have an opportunity now to focus this public support in a striking new way. Not only is this politically sensible, but it helps discharge our profound obligation to the maintenance of peace, which should take precedence over many lesser problems — but so seldom does.

15

Canada as a Nuclear-Weapons-Free Zone

Ernie Regehr

After nearly four decades in which East-West relations have been dominated by nuclear terrorism (i.e., the threat and counter-threat of nuclear
mass murder), there should remain few illusions that the denuclearization
of the national security systems of the major powers and their alliances is a
simple matter. Nuclear-weapon states obviously will resist appeals to
reduce nuclear weapons as long as they continue to see benefits in the
retention and "improvement" of present arsenals. Or, to put it another
way, the arms race and arms control are substantially a matter of incentives
— and at present the military, political and diplomatic benefits that are
assumed to flow from growing nuclear arsenals produce incentives to
escalate.

But the situation is changing. When President Ronald Reagan sends his
vice-president, George Bush, to the West German election campaign (as he
did in January 1983) to read an open letter to Western Europe declaring
America's unfaltering willingness to pursue arms reductions, then one can
be sure the incentives are shifting. Indeed, major elements of the present
public campaigns for nuclear disarmament have been to create domestic
and international political incentives to reduce arms and to point out that,
besides the perceived benefits of nuclear weapons, there are also substantial costs.

Some of the costs have already been discussed in this book. Chief among
these, of course, is the threat of global holocaust. While fear of nuclear
annihilation will not itself remove a single weapon, the growing perception,
one should really say knowledge, that nuclear weapons are harbingers of
catastrophe rather than of security is making an important impact upon
the political environment in which decision-makers seek approval and
funding for nuclear weapons programs. Similarly, there is growing awareness that the heavy militarization of national security, including nuclear
weapons, inevitably creates economic insecurity and ultimately contrib-

utes to national insecurity. Ultimately, the peace movements in Europe and North America have set out to create a political environment in which the incentives to negotiate arms reductions become greater than the incentives to stall negotiations in favour of the deployment of new and destabilizing weapons systems.

Besides being responsive to domestic political conditions, nuclear-weapon states must also contend with the international environment in which nuclear weapons systems are deployed and operational. And, as we have noted in Chapter 5, nuclear weapons are in effect huge international systems that rely for their effectiveness on the political, military and industrial cooperation of their allies.

In addition, nuclear-weapon states rely upon the cooperation of neighbouring and friendly states for rights of passage through their territory — an example known to Canadians being U.S. Trident nuclear submarines having to pass through Canadian waters off Vancouver Island when returning to their base at Bangor, Washington. Allies of nuclear-weapon states provide additional support through the production of component parts (see Chapter 5), the provision of port and refuelling facilities, and through cooperation in testing elements of nuclear weapons systems.

By hosting within their jurisdiction certain of these elements of nuclear weapons infrastructure, the allies of nuclear-weapon states facilitate more extensive nuclear weapons systems than would otherwise be possible and lend political/diplomatic legitimacy to nuclear weapons arsenals. The converse of this situation, of course, is that these same allies also have the means to withdraw this support for nuclear weapons. Even though they participate at various levels of the production, testing and operation of nuclear weapons systems, middle powers such as Canada (which are important allies of nuclear-weapon states but are not themselves in the nuclear club) are not major players in nuclear weapons arms control agreements. Nevertheless, by virtue of their peripheral role in building and maintaining these systems, these middle powers have the potential for influencing substantially the international environment within which nuclear weapons systems are either escalated or controlled.

One such approach is gradually to expand the world's nuclear-weapons-free territory — a kind of global liberation movement to liberate progressively territory from the grip of nuclear weapons. And the specific vehicle, which is now internationally recognized and has in fact been a part of debate in the United Nations almost from its beginning, for this nuclear liberation movement is the establishment of nuclear-weapons-free zones (NWFZs). Canada has given general support to the idea of NWFZs, and in the United Nations the idea has broad support as a "confidence-building measure" that would help to create an international climate in which more comprehensive arms limitation could be undertaken. While nuclear-weapon states have supported NWFZ proposals for some regions, in other areas they strongly oppose the idea — their opposition essentially confirming the fact that NWFZs are indeed a means by which non-nuclear-weapon states can place constraints upon the nuclear-weapon states and their systems.

The concept is a simple one. A 1975 UN expert's study of NWFZs describes some of the essential conditions of such zones:

- The zone must be and remain effectively free of all nuclear weapons.
- Member states of the zone (a zone can also be a single state) must not exercise control over nuclear weapons outside the zone.
- There must be effective means of verifying compliance with the conditions of the nuclear-free zone.
- Memeber states of the zone must enter into agreements with nuclear-weapon states providing guarantees by the latter not to use or threaten to use nuclear weapons against members of the zone.
- Member states of the zone should prohibit the use of their territories for the transit of nuclear weapons (although the question of the rights of innocent passage through territorial seas has not been satisfactorily resolved).

Within general guidelines, the characteristics of any particular NWFZ will depend upon the agreements reached by participating states.

The point of any state entering into a NWFZ agreement is not particularly an attempt to seek immunity from nuclear war. Once war breaks out, all bets are off and any country, whether in a NWFZ or not, will be vulnerable to direct attack — the relevant circumstance being whether or not the nuclear combatants will consider it to their advantage to attack or withhold attack. Treaties count for very little in war. But treaties do count for something in the behaviour of states in a pre-war world, and that is the point of any NWFZ — to influence behaviour during peacetime. The provision of guarantees by nuclear-weapon states not to use or "threaten to use" nuclear weapons against a NWFZ state is particularly important in that it provides effective immunity for the NWFZ from nuclear intimidation. Any clear threat against a NWFZ by a nuclear power would be an abbrogation of treaty responsibilities and would signal to the rest of the world major aggressive intent and would almost be tantamount to declaring war.

NWFZ proposals are active in an impressive number of regions of the world.

A Nordic nuclear-free zone has been the subject of discussion since 1969. All Scandinavian countries (Finland, Sweden, Norway, Denmark and Iceland) have taken independent decisions not to acquire nuclear weapons and not to permit stationing of nuclear weapons by other states on their soil in peacetime. They have also all signed the Nuclear Non-proliferation Treaty (NPT) renouncing the acquisition of nuclear weapons. But there is no agreement on whether or not the region should formally declare itself a NWFZ and seek security guarantees from nuclear-weapon states. Another point of disagreement is whether or not the Baltic Sea should be included in such a zone. In November 1982, however, the Swedish foreign minister said he would again be raising the topic of a Nordic NWFZ with his Nordic counterparts in the near future.

In 1981 a proposal for a Balkan nuclear-weapons-free zone, which would mean that it would include members of opposing military alliances, was made and endorsed by Bulgaria, Romania, Yugoslavia and Greece. Prime Minister Andreas Papandreou has become a particular proponent of the idea and in November 1982 told reporters that "it appears that the idea of setting up a nuclear-free zone in the Balkans has found response in the other Balkan countries. In the light of this encouraging development, within 12 to 18 months the dream of a nuclear-free zone could become a reality in the peninsula."

Other discussions have included proposals for NWFZs in the Middle East, South Asia, the South Pacific and Africa, and proposals for "zones of peace" (an extension of the NWFZ idea to include the elimination of foreign military bases) in the Mediterranean and the Indian Ocean.

In Latin America the Treaty of Tlatelolco came into force in 1968 to create the world's first formal NWFZ. It is signed by most of the major states within the region and in a protocol to the treaty the nuclear-weapon states acknowledge the region to be nuclear weapon free. Cuba and Guyana and several newly independent states in the Caribbean have not signed the treaty (Cuba says it is awaiting American withdrawal from its military base at Guantanamo). Argentina has signed but not ratified the treaty, and Brazil and Chile, though also having signed it, have not permitted it to enter into force in their countries. The refusal to recognize the treaty in the three countries most likely to become nuclear-weapon states has weakened the treaty substantially, but even in those countries it provides a focus of political activities for groups and individuals that oppose national nuclear weapons programs.

The proposal to make Canada a NWFZ has not been discussed at an official level, even though Canada is in the process of ridding itself of nuclear weapons themselves. But as also noted, there remain a number of additional ways in which Canada supports U.S. nuclear weapons systems and any Canadian NWFZ would have to take these into account.

The main proposal for a Canadian NWFZ has come from Project Ploughshares, a church-related Canadian peace organization, and identifies the following four conditions of such a zone:

- No nuclear weapons on Canadian soil;
- No transit for nuclear weapons through Canadian territory;
- No production in Canada of components for nuclear weapons systems of other states;
- No support systems (including testing) for nuclear weapons, whether based in Canada or operated by Canadians outside Canada.

An additional aspect of actually establishing Canada as a nuclear-weapons-free zone would be the negotiation of agreements with nuclear-weapon states to guarantee the NWFZ status of Canada and to refrain from using or "threatening" to use nuclear weapons against Canada.

The proposal has received widespread support in Canada and has been endorsed by groups as diverse as the New Democratic Party, the United Church of Canada, and the National Farmers Union. A variety of other groups, congregations and other organizations, as well as individuals, have also endorsed the idea.

The idea of Canada as a nuclear-weapons-free zone is proposed as a general framework for Canadian policy towards nuclear weapons. To change the policy framework from that of simple alliance loyalty (including uncritical acceptance of alliance nuclear weapons policies) to a Canadian-defined approach to the issue of nuclear weapons, the basic stance towards NATO and NORAD would shift from uncritical support to critical evaluation of alliance nuclear weapons policy in relation to Canadian policy. Such a critical stance of course need not be in conflict with alliance membership. Various European members of NATO — the Netherlands and Belgium for example — have frequently been at odds with certain alliance policies. And while the alliance leadership is anxious to characterize this as a threat to alliance unity, the dissidents are much more likely to characterize their dissent as evidence of strength and as essential to long-term unity. The Netherlands, for example, has not accepted that loyalty to NATO requires automatic acceptance of cruise missiles on its soil. There being disagreement within the country, the government has for the time being reserved decision on the matter.

Similarly, the assumption of the proposal to make Canada a nuclear-weapons-free zone is that there should be independent Canadian evaluation and decision-making regarding alliance nuclear weapons policy. An appeal to alliance loyalty is not deemed a sufficient basis for Canadian policy. The proposal then calls for a specific Canadian policy to reject nuclear weapons for Canada, to reject Canadian participation in alliance nuclear weapons, and to support the reduction and eventual elimination of NATO's reliance upon nuclear weapons.

For Canadian policy to conform with the four basic conditions of a Canadian NWFZ would require some significant, but hardly radical, changes in the actual activities of the Canadian armed forces — the radical changes would occur primarily in Canadian attitudes towards and support of the nuclear weapons policies of the alliances of which Canada is a part and which it claims to influence.

The first condition, that of prohibiting nuclear weapons on Canadian soil, is in the process of being implemented. Canada would also, in compliance with NWFZ status, find it necessary to pledge that this prohibition would also apply in times of crisis and that under no circumstances would the nuclear weapons of another power be permitted storage, stationing or, according to the second condition, transit through Canadian territory. On the latter point, current agreements under NORAD would permit, with approval of Ottawa, nuclear-weapon aircraft to use Canadian airspace and other facilities during an emergency.

The third condition, requiring a prohibition on Canadian production of components for nuclear weapons systems, would, obviously, have a direct economic impact on Canadian industry. But even here the impact would not be radical. While production for nuclear weapons, such as Litton Systems' involvement in the cruise, has received major public attention, as a proportion of total Canadian defence exports such direct involvement in nuclear weapons systems is relatively minor. The Canadian government's statistics make no distinction between nuclear and conventional military commodities; however, it is unlikely that more than 10 per cent of current military exports are directly related to nuclear weapons systems. And, given that Canadian industry involvement in nuclear weapon components production is heavily reliant upon government subsidies, a shift of those subsidies to non-military production would represent an essential and significant element in the search for alternative production.

Prohibiting Canadian involvement in support of nuclear weapons infrastructure, in accordance with the fourth condition, would also be more symbolic than material. Some specific and significant policy requirements flow from the provision (such as refusals to test U.S. and other NATO weapons, an end to most anti-submarine warfare activities, and changes in some communication links such as the Loran C network), but it is the symbolic importance of these changes that would inevitably bring forth a response, particularly from the United States.

The American response most feared, of course, is that of economic retaliation. With two-thirds of Canadian exports going to the United States, those fears are not altogether unfounded. And an area in which Canada is particularly vulnerable is that of defence trade. Canada now sells in excess of $1 billion worth of military commodities to the United States each year. This is allowed into the United States under terms of the Defence Production Sharing Arrangements which remove most trade barriers, and as the volume grows it attracts the attention of members of the U.S. Congress with an eye to repatriating some of the business to the United States for the benefit of their constituents. With a view to longer-term continental defence cooperation, on the other hand, succeeding U.S. administrations have generally come to the defence of Canada to forestall congressional defence trade protectionist measures — the most recent example being a 1982 intervention by U.S. Defense Secretary Weinberger to prevent a move in the Senate which would have restricted the import of defence commodities with certain specialty metals in them. What frightens Ottawa is that if, by refusing to test the cruise missile, for example, Canada signalled a shift towards non-cooperation in defence matters, U.S. administration officials would be less likely to intervene on behalf of Canadian industry seeking continued special access to the U.S. defence market.

The most likely and most immediate economic retaliation by the United States, in other words, would probably be to restrict the access of the Canadian defence industry to the U.S. market. That this would be a major blow to Canadian aerospace and electronics industries is undeniable. About 80 per cent of their military production goes to the U.S. market, and perhaps 30 per cent of their total production is defence related.

But while it is reasonable to assume that the United States would reach for this lever to retaliate to Canadian policy misdeeds, it is worth noting that dependence is usually something of a two-way street and the present example is no exception. Under the DPSA, the Canada-U.S. defence trade is maintained in rough balance, which means that if Canada exports $1 billion worth of defence commodities to the United States, it imports an equal amount. In fact, Canadian defence imports from the United States are currently exceeding exports. Ultimately, the United States knows that to interfere with Canadian exports to the U.S. would also be to interfere with imports from the U.S. Without special Canadian access to the U.S. market, it is likely that Canada's major defence procurement decisions, most recently involving the import of long-range patrol aircraft and fighter aircraft from the United States, would have been different (perhaps leaning more to domestic production in the case of patrol aircraft and to Europe in the case of fighter aircraft).

Furthermore, a curtailment of access to the U.S. defence market would not be a total disaster for Canada. Defence exports to the U.S. represent less than 2 per cent of total exports, and the last time that Canadian access to the U.S. defence market was sharply curtailed (in the early 1970s due to U.S. balance of payments problems and the end of the Vietnam War) it turned out to have a beneficial impact on the industry most affected: the aerospace industry. In the decade that followed, the Canadian government invested substantial funds in the civilian aircraft industry, including development and research funding for short take-off and landing aircraft, with the result that the industry's dependence on defence orders went down from about 75 per cent to about 25 per cent — a good example of industrial conversion from military to civilian production. The present arms boom, combined with recession in civilian markets, means that there is now a shift in the industry back towards heavier reliance on defence orders.

In the past, Canada has found that the development of trade with Europe has not been unrelated to Canada's military and political commitment to Europe. Here it is worth noting that only about 10 per cent of total Canadian exports go to Europe, and that lumber and resource products figure largely in this total. The opportunities for retaliation are constrained by Europe's own need for Canadian resources and its desire to maintain and increase exports to Canada. Nor must a military-political commitment to Europe be expressed in nuclear terms. Indeed, the greater European interest is in a more effective conventional deterrent in order to reduce reliance on the nuclear deterrent — giving Canada a variety of options or means of demonstrating loyalty to NATO besides through nuclear weapons testing and production.

A frequently-asked question is whether a Canadian NWFZ would automatically mean Canadian withdrawal from NORAD and NATO. The answer suggested by Canadian political tradition might very well be, alliances if necessary, but not necessarily alliances. Clearly, there is nothing intrinsic to a strict non-nuclear role for Canada that would preclude membership in military alliances. NORAD, which has to date primarily been a surveillance and early warning network, does not require by its nature Canadian involvement with nuclear weapons. Similarly, NATO's expressed need for an adequate conventional defence force does also not require that all members participate in nuclear roles.

However, the question of whether or not a nuclear weapons role is intrinsic to membership in NATO and NORAD, is not the same question as whether or not the alliance leadership, the United States, will tolerate a strict non-nuclear role, as defined by the NWFZ proposal, for its neighbour and bilateral ally. Pressure on Canada to perform certain roles in the provision of infrastructure for U.S. nuclear weapons systems does not come by virtue of Canada's being a member of NATO or NORAD, but comes by virtue of Canada's proximity to the United States and this country's economic interdependence with the U.S.

The United States, as noted in previous chapters, views its own defence to be indivisible from the defence of the continent. It views nuclear weapons to be essential to the defence of the continent and, while it has seriously never urged Canada to acquire its own nuclear weapons, it does expect that Canada will cooperate if and when the United States decides that such cooperation is important for the effective operation of those weapons.

The question facing Canada is not whether or not to be in an alliance or whether or not to be an ally of the United States — the former is optional, the latter, the vast majority of Canadians would agree, is desirable. The question is whether or not support for the further buildup and maintenance of its ally's nuclear arsenal is the best contribution that Canada can make to international peace and security. In the light of changes in nature and intent of that arsenal, as discussed in Chapter 1, the proponents of Canada as a NWFZ conclude that the time has come for Canada, as a friend and ally of the United States, to seek to chart a different course. Just as Canada's initial overtures regarding the recognition of mainland China were not fully appreciated, it should not be surprising that a bold initiative against the further nuclearization of national security might also not be fully appreciated. Ultimately, however, it is a course of action that will serve the interests of our friends as well as our own.

Further Reading

Here is a short list of key contributions to the growing literature on the nuclear arms race.

Barnet, Richard. *Real Security*. New York: Simon and Schuster, 1981. The best guide to the crisis in American foreign policy, along with Barnet's thoughtful alternatives.

Burns, Lt.-Gen. E.L.M. *Defence in the Nuclear Age: An Introduction for Canadians*. Toronto: Clarke, Irwin, 1976. A discussion of Canadian defence policy in the context of membership in a nuclear alliance.

Calder, Nigel. *Nuclear Nightmares*. Harmondsworth, Middlesex: Penguin Books, 1981. A superb introduction to both the technology and the politics of the arms race.

Kaldor, Mary, and Smith, Dan, eds. *Disarming Europe*. London: Merlin, 1982. Edited by England's foremost disarmament scholars, this collection includes the essential analysis which guides the European disarmament movement.

Kennedy, Edward M., and Hatfield, Mark O. *Freeze!* New York: Bantam, 1982. A short but well-argued case for a superpower nuclear freeze, by the sponsors of the freeze in the U.S. Senate.

Lifton, Robert J., and Falk, Richard. *Indefensible Weapons*. New York: Basic Books, 1982. Presents and debunks the underlying premises — both psychological and political — of superpower nuclear strategies.

Scheer, Robert. *With Enough Shovels: Reagan, Bush and Nuclear War*. New York: Random House, 1982. Portrays the men who are behind the drift towards nuclear war.

Schell, Jonathan. *The Fate of the Earth*. Toronto: Random House, 1982. A popular and penetrating humanistic critique of the nuclear arms race and its threat to life on the planet.

Thompson, E.P., and Smith, Dan, eds. *Protest and Survive*. Harmondsworth, Middlesex: Penguin Books, 1980. The classic document that signified the emergence of the European disarmament movement.

Wohlstetter, Albert, et al. *Swords From Ploughshares.* Chicago: University of Chicago Press, 1979. Demystifies the "atoms for peace" myth and demonstrates the links between nuclear power and nuclear weapons.

World Council of Churches. *Before It's Too Late: The Challenge of Nuclear Disarmament.* Geneva: The World Council of Churches, 1983. The report and proceedings of the "Hearing on Nuclear Weapons and Disarmament" organized by the World Council of Churches in Amsterdam, November 1981.

Canadian Peace Organizations

A complete "Directory of Canadian Peace Organizations with International Concerns" is available from:

> Lynne Martin
> Peace Unearth
> c/o The Mennonite Central Committee
> 1483 Pembina Hwy.
> Winnipeg, Manitoba
> R3T 2C7

This directory provides detailed descriptions of programs, publications and membership information for about 200 Canadian groups. The following groups are national peace organizations with programs related to Canadian nuclear weapons policies. Several groups limiting their operations to Quebec are also included.

Association Québécoise des Organismes de Coopération Internationale (AQOCI)
1115, boul. Gouin est, suite 200
Montréal, Québec H2C 1B3
(514) 382-4560

Canadian Catholic Organization for Development and Peace
3028 Danforth Ave.
Toronto, Ontario M4C 1N2
(416) 698-7770

Canadian Friends Service Committee (Quakers)
60 Lowther Ave.
Toronto, Ontario M5R 1C7
(416) 920-5213

Canadian Peace Congress
671 Danforth Ave., Rm. 301
Toronto, Ontario M4J 1L3
(416) 469-3422
(Affiliated with World Peace Council in Helsinki)

Canadian Peace Research and Education Association (CPREA)
25 Dundana Ave.
Dundas, Ontario L9H 4E5
(416) 628-2356
(Learned Society of Canada; affiliated with the Social Science Federation
of Canada and the International Peace Association)

Christian Movement for Peace (CMP)
427 Bloor St. West
Toronto, Ontario M5S 1X7
(416) 921-2360
(after hours) 925-7915

Coalition Québécoise pour le Désarmement
c/o Yellow Door Cafe
3625, rue Aylmer
Montréal, Québec H2X 2C3

Conseil Québécois de la Paix
8225, boul. St. Laurent
Montréal, Québec H2P 2M1
(514) 382-7670

Cruise Missile Conversion Project (CMCP)
730 Bathurst St.
Toronto, Ontario M5S 2R4
(416) 532-6720

Greenpeace Foundation
Head Office:
    2623 West 4th Ave.
    Vancouver, B.C. V6K 1P8
    (604) 736-0321
Eastern Branch and mailing address:
    427 Bloor St. West
    Toronto, Ontario M5S 1X7
    (416) 922-3011

Institute of Peace and Conflict Studies (IPACS)
Conrad Grebel College
Waterloo, Ontario N2L 3G6
(519) 885-0220
(Affiliated with University of Waterloo. Seeks to promote peace research and education via university degree program and administers University of Waterloo Peace Studies program.)

Operation Dismantle
64 Melrose Ave.
Ottawa, Ontario K1Y 1T9
(613) 722-6001
Mailing address:
   Box 3887, Station C
   Ottawa, Ontario K1Y 4M5
(Seeks to launch a global referendum on disarmament through the United Nations.)

Organisation Catholique Canadienne pour le Développement et la Paix
2111, rue Centre
Montréal, Québec H3K 1J5
(514) 932-5136

Peace Research Institute — Dundas (PRID)
25 Dundana Ave.
Dundas, Ontario L9H 4E5
(416) 628-2356
(Publishes *Peace Research Abstracts Journal* and *Peace Research Reviews*.)

Peace Tax Fund Committee
(Religious Society of Friends, Victoria)
1831 Fern St.
Victoria, B.C. V8R 4K4
(604) 386-0186
(Works towards the establishment of a federally-recognized Peace Tax Fund, to which taxpayers who conscientiously object to supporting arms and the military could direct the military portion of their taxes for peaceful uses.)

Peoples Assembly on Canadian Foreign Policy
109 Wilton St.
Toronto, Ontario M5A 4A3
(416) 368-3270
        732-6417

Physicians for Social Responsibility, Inc., Canada (PSR) "The Canadian
  Medical Coalition for the Prevention of Nuclear War"
Canadian National Office and Ontario chapter:
360 Bloor St. West, Suite 406
Toronto, Ontario M5S 1X1
(416) 922-7335

Project Ploughshares
Central office: c/o Institute of Peace and Conflict Studies
                     Conrad Grebel College
                     Waterloo, Ontario N2L 3G6
                     (519) 885-0220
Ottawa office: 321 Chapel St.
                     Ottawa, Ontario K1N 7Z2
                     (613) 236-4547
Vancouver office: 104 - 1955 West 4th Ave.
                     Vancouver, B.C. V6J 1M7
                     (604) 733-0141
(Project Ploughshares is affiliated with the Canadian Council of Churches.
Contact one of above offices for information on local Ploughshares groups
across Canada. *Ploughshares Monitor* and Ploughshares *Newsreport* are
published four to six times per year and are sent to all Ploughshares
Associates.)

Science for Peace
c/o Physics Department
University of Toronto
Toronto, Ontario M5S 1A7
(416) 978-2971
(after hours) 485-0990

United Nations Association in Canada (UNAC)
National office: 63 Sparks St., Suite 808
                     Ottawa, Ontario K1P 5A6
                     (613) 232-5751

Voice of Women (VOW)
National office: 175 Carlton St.
                     Toronto, Ontario M5A 2K3
                     (416) 922-2997
                     (after hours) 486-8750

Women's International League for Peace and Freedom (WILPF)
Vancouver office: 1768 West 11th Avenue
                    Vancouver, B.C. V6J 2C3
                    (604) 733-9018
                    (home phone)
Ottawa office: 18 - 3rd Avenue
                    Ottawa, Ontario K1S 2J6
                    (613) 236-2976

World Federalists of Canada (WFC)
Head office: 46 Elgin St., Suite 32
                    Ottawa, Ontario K1P 5K6
                    (613) 232-0647
                    (home phone) 592-4935

Index

11, 13, 14-16, 17-20, 24, 34-36, 37,
39, 40; intermediate-range, 10, 116;
Lacrosse missile, 108; Lance missile,
116; land-based, 13, 14-16, 17-20,
24, 34, 37, 39, 40; Mark-12 warhead,
35, 37; Minuteman force, 36, 38, 44;
multiple warhead, 34; Polaris missile
and submarine, 39, 67; Poseidon
missile and submarine, 39, 67, 218;
precision-guided, 37; short-range,
10; single warhead, 34; space-based,
116; SS missiles, 23, 35, 40, 85-86,
208-9; strategic, 11, 12, 14, 34-36,
41, 46, 50, 60, 218; submarine-based,
13, 16, 20, 37-38, 39, 44, 45-46, 56,
60, 94, 218; tactical, 11, 21, 28, 218;
Yankee-class submarine, 45. *See also*
Cruise missile; MX missile; Pershing
missile; Trident missile; Trident
nuclear submarine
Nuclear-weapons-free zone, 134,
242-44; Balkan, 88, 244; Canadian,
202, 203, 226, 227, 244-49; Nordic,
203, 244
Nuclear-weapon states, 10, 11, 130,
131, 135, 218, 241-42

Ontario Hydro, 127, 151, 154, 163
OPEC oil embargo, 133
"Open Skies" surveillance, 237, 238
Operation Dismantle, 227, 233, 234,
235, 236
Outer space, militarization of, 116-17,
209; monitoring of, 237-40

Pakistan, CANDU sales to, 127-28,
133, 134-35; and Nuclear Non-
Proliferation Treaty, 131; and
nuclear parity with India, 135;
nuclear-weapons capability of, 130,
218
Papandreou, Andreas, 88, 244
Park Chung Hee, General, 138
Pasti, Nini, 86
Pax Christi, 85

Peace movement, Canadian, 225-30;
European, 85, 88-96; influence of,
95, 241-42; North American, 93-94;
problems of, 93-95
Pearson, Lester, and Canadian
uranium exports, 106, 152; opposes
Canadian nuclear force, 109, 110; on
peace initiatives, 229; presses for
collective security arrangements,
101; reverses policy on non-nuclear
role for Canada, 109, 200-1, 226
Pearson, Marion, 226
Pelletier, Gérard, 201
Perry, William, 37
Pershing missile, first-strike capability,
23, 44; launch-on-warning capabil-
ity, 17-18; in NATO arsenal, 85, 86,
87, 96, 208-9, 227
Persian Gulf, 26, 49
Physicians for Social Responsibility,
227
Pipes, Richard, 41-42
Plutonium, Canadian production and
trade of, 123, 125, 126, 129, 132,
162-68; reprocessing of, 128, 132,
135, 136-37, 159-60; unaccounted
for, 140
Poland, 89
Pope, Maurice, 102
Popular Movement for the Liberation
of Angola, 52
Potter, Philip, 195
Presidential Directive 59, 18, 46, 49, 50
Primrose Lake Air Weapons Range,
118
Project Ploughshares, 227-28
Proliferation. *See* Nuclear
proliferation
Pugwash Conferences, 238

Qaddafi, Colonel, 134
Quakers. *See* Society of Friends

Rabbit Lake mine, 106